THE SOCIAL WORK PRACTICUM

SECOND EDITION

THE SOCIAL WORK PRACTICUM

A Guide and Workbook for Students

Charles R. Horejsi

University of Montana

Cynthia L. Garthwait

University of Montana

Allyn and Bacon
Boston • London • Toronto • Sydney • Tokyo • Singapore

Series Editor: Patricia Quinlin
Editor-in-Chief, Social Sciences: Karen Hanson
Series Editorial Assistant: Alyssa Pratt
Marketing Manager: Jacqueline Aaron
Production Editor: Christopher H. Rawlings
Editorial-Production Service: Omegatype Typography, Inc.
Composition and Prepress Buyer: Linda Cox
Manufacturing Buyer: Suzanne Lareau
Cover Administrator: Kristina Mose-Libon
Electronic Composition: Omegatype Typography, Inc.

Between the time Website information is gathered and then published, it is not unusual
for some sites to have closed. Also, the transcription of URLs can result in unintended
typographical errors. The publisher would appreciate notification where these occur so
that they may be corrected in subsequent editions. Thank you.

ISBN: 0-205-34018-0

Printed in the United States of America
10 9 8 7 6 5 4 3 2   06 05 04 03 02 01

Credits appear on page 251, which constitutes an extension of the copyright page.

*To the social work practicum instructors and field supervisors who give
so generously of their time to the education and mentoring of future social workers*

*To our families,
Gloria, Katherine, Martin, and Angela
Gary, Nathan, and Benjamin*

CONTENTS

FOREWORD

If you are like most social work students, beginning your practicum, internship, or field placement is an exhilarating yet challenging experience. It is exhilarating because this is the payoff of the years taken to obtain a social work education. You can now begin to work with people to change troublesome aspects of their lives and assist agencies and communities to eliminate or reduce factors that contribute to the problems people experience. It is an awesome responsibility to be trusted to work with people who have serious social issues in their lives, but, after all, that is probably why you chose to enter social work in the first place. At this point, you are likely to feel it is time to stop talking about social work and to start doing it. That is exhilarating!

What, then, makes learning from a practicum such a challenge? Several factors complicate learning to do social work. First, learning to apply knowledge is perhaps the most complex form of learning. In your classroom-based social work courses you have, no doubt, already learned many of the facts and theories that can inform your practice activities. And, maybe you have engaged in case discussions or practiced applying this knowledge in role play situations, but now you will be called on to apply that knowledge using your own unique personality and skills with real clients who are genuinely at risk if you don't do your work well. Whether you are engaged in an interview, group session, or committee meeting, you will be more or less on your own and required to make on-the-spot judgments and decisions. That can be a little scary.

Second, the practicum experience is further complicated by the fact that it takes place in a human services agency that will have its own requirements about how its staff (including students) should perform various roles and functions. You and your field instructor must select those potential practice activities that meet the goals and needs of the agency and yet also meet the learning requirements of the school. A difficult part of your job will be to combine these requirements that may not always match.

Third, you will be expected to play a much more active role in your learning than is typically expected in classroom learning situations. Your field instructor, although an experienced social work practitioner, may not be fully knowledgeable about all of the classroom content you have learned and are expected to apply. Although your field instructor will be an active participant in your learning, you will be the primary person responsible for shaping your experience.

Last, acquiring basic knowledge about human behavior, social policies and programs, social work intervention strategies, and so on is certainly prerequisite to successful practice, but it is not sufficient. You will need to seek out guidance regarding how to apply this knowledge in your practice from your field instructor, other agency personnel, and your faculty members, and by searching the social work literature. In short, the resources you will need to support your learning are not neatly packaged.

Compared to the abundant literature regarding the basic knowledge about social work and its clients, you will find there is relatively scant literature to help you understand what to do in social work practice—and even less to help you learn how to do it. This is where *The Social Work Practicum: A Guide and Workbook for Students* comes in. Charles Horejsi and Cynthia Garthwait have provided you with a valuable resource. It is written in a way that you (and your field instructor) can maximize your learning from the practicum. Take advantage of this helpful resource and you should develop needed practice competencies. On each topic, Horejsi and Garthwait give you useful background information, offer guidance and pose questions to help sort out issues, break complex tasks into understandable lists and checksheets to facilitate in-depth discussion and decision making, and point you to other literature that can assist you in understanding the topic more fully.

Because much of the primary responsibility for learning from your practicum rests with you, it is important to have a good overview of what this book has to offer. You may have some assignments from *The Social Work Practicum* for a seminar associated with the practicum, but it is unlikely that your need for the resources the book offers will follow a set pattern. You should be prepared to use it flexibly. My recommendation is to work through the first six chapters before beginning your practicum or very early in your placement. At the same time, you should become familiar with the Goals for Learning sections of Chapters 7 through 17 so that you can draw on that material as learning opportunities arise during the weeks of your practicum. Finally, as you get toward the end of your placement, it will be time for some in-depth introspection about your future as a social worker. Chapter 18, "Merging Self and Profession," and, new to this edition, Chapter 19, "Looking Ahead, Leadership, and Social Justice," should help you think through some of the issues that will lie ahead.

By making use of the helpful materials presented in *The Social Work Practicum*, the exhilaration from your practicum experience should be increased and the challenging aspects should become less difficult. In the end you will be a more competent and fulfilled social worker.

Bradford W. Sheafor, Ph.D.
Colorado State University

PREFACE

Our careers in social work span thirty-one and forty-one years. During those many years we have repeatedly served either as agency-based practicum instructors (field supervisors), faculty liaisons to practicum agencies, leaders of practicum seminars, or coordinators of university practicum programs. We have directly taught, assisted, and guided over 300 students during their social work practicum. Most were in baccalaureate programs; some were in graduate-level master of social work programs.

For the majority of these students, the practicum was the most useful and challenging learning experience during their formal social work education. Our observations have been confirmed by numerous surveys of student opinion.

We have been privileged to share in the students' excitement as they developed and polished their skills, expanded their knowledge base, and grew in self-confidence. We have also experienced pain and frustration as we watched some students flounder and become angry and disillusioned—either because their practicum setting failed to provide sufficient learning opportunities or because they could not make good use of the opportunities that did exist.

During our work with students we have also observed considerable variation in their ability to integrate concepts and theory drawn from the social work classroom with their experiences with real clients in a real agency. Some did it with apparent ease, but for others it was a genuine struggle.

For years we have experimented with various approaches to enhance the practicum experience and facilitate the integration of classroom and field learning. We were most successful when we added considerable structure and specific assignments to the process of practicum teaching and to our practicum seminars. We have required practicum students to search out and reflect on answers to specific questions about their agency's approach to practice, the community context of practice, relevant social policy, professional ethics in their agency, and numerous other topics. We have been pleased with the results.

This book grew out of those experiences and the search for a better way. It offers students, practicum instructors, and the leaders of practicum seminars a structure and a set of learning activities that facilitate learning in the practicum. At the same time, it allows for and encourages creativity and experimentation in learning. The student who makes use of the Background Information, Guidance and Direction, and Workbook Activity sections in this book will make significant progress toward developing the competencies required of beginning social workers.

AN OVERVIEW OF THE CHAPTERS

Chapter 1 serves to introduce the book and explain how it is to be used. In addition, it includes two workbook activities that focus on the prerequisites to and the process of learning. Chapters 2, 3, 4, and 5 are designed to assist the student in clarifying expectations and formulating a written plan for learning during the practicum. By reading these chapters and completing the workbook assignments, the student will identify many of the desired learning outcomes and activities that can be written into the school's practicum learning contract or learning agreement. Chapters 4 and 5 will be especially helpful in getting the practicum off to a good start and clarifying the relationship between the student and his or her practicum instructor (field supervisor). Chapter 6 focuses on a topic of growing importance in the practicum—personal safety.

Chapters 7 through 16 focus on broad areas of practice competency. Most schools ask their practicum students to formulate learning goals and objectives in relation to these areas. Chapter 17 offers the reader information and a perspective on the evaluation of student performance in the practicum. Chapter 18 addresses the issues and concerns related to developing self-awareness and the choice of social work as a career. Finally, Chapter 19 asks the students to look beyond graduation and consider several personal concerns, while also encouraging them to develop their leadership skills and commit themselves to the pursuit of social justice.

CSWE ACCREDITATION CONSIDERATIONS

The Council on Social Work Education's (CSWE) Commission on Accreditation requires programs of social work education to include certain content in their curricula. Some of those content areas are listed below in the column on the left. Chapters in this book that address these areas, at least to some degree, are listed to the right of each.

Values and Ethics	Chapters 14, 15, 18
Diversity	Chapter 12
Social Welfare Policy and Services	Chapter 11
Social and Economic Justice	Chapters 14, 15, 19
Human Behavior and the Social Environment	Chapters 7, 8, 9, 10
Populations at Risk	Chapter 12
Social Work Practice	Chapters 13, 16
Practice Research	Chapters 8, 10, 16

ACKNOWLEDGMENTS

Many individuals helped us to shape our ideas and offered encouragement as we worked on the manuscript. Although we cannot acknowledge all of them by name, we want to recognize and thank the dozens of students who helped us, even though they were not aware of what they were doing at the time. Their questions, criticisms, and practical suggestions have helped us to better understand the social work practicum from the student's point of view.

A special thanks to friends and colleagues who offered encouragement, suggestions, and assistance: Mary Birch, Frank Clark, Bob Deaton, Janet Finn, Maxine Jacobson, Ryan Tolleson-Knee, Peter Leech, Mark Lusk, Sue Polich, Jim Rolando, Tom Roy, Iris Heavy Runner, Brad Sheafor, David Schantz, and John Spores.

We want to acknowledge the helpful guidance received from Karen Hanson and other Allyn and Bacon staff. In addition, we would like to acknowledge the following reviewers for the first edition: Janice Andrews, University of St. Thomas; Greta M. Hawthorne, University of North Carolina at Pembroke; and Jane A. Kretzschmar, University of Texas at Austin. Finally, we would like to thank the reviewer of the second edition, David Spruill, Louisiana State University.

THE SOCIAL WORK PRACTICUM

1

THE PURPOSE OF A PRACTICUM

Welcome to the social work practicum. You are to be congratulated for reaching this stage in your professional education and for being selected and approved for a practicum. The practicum offers a unique opportunity to apply what you have learned in the classroom, to expand your knowledge, and to develop your skills.

We want to also welcome you to this guide and workbook. It is designed to provide direction and assistance during your exciting practicum journey.

BACKGROUND INFORMATION

A *practicum* is a type of course or a mode of study emphasizing the practical application of theory or conceptual knowledge. Most types of professional education—whether in medicine, nursing, law, speech therapy, or social work—employ some form of practicum, internship, or preceptorship to help the student learn how to apply knowledge and general principles to specific and very real situations, problems, and concerns.

Many social workers, agency supervisors, and social work educators use the terms *practicum, field work, field instruction, field education, field practicum,* and *internship* somewhat interchangeably. In this book we will use the term *practicum.*

The Council on Social Work Education's (CSWE) Commission on Accreditation (1994) states that:

> The field practicum is an integral component of the curriculum in social work education. It engages the student in supervised social work practice and provides opportunities to apply classroom learning in the field setting. (Items B6.13 and M6.14)

Jenkins and Sheafor (1981) explain that:

> Field instruction is an experiential form of teaching and learning in which the social work student is helped to: (1) consciously bring selected knowledge to the practice situation; (2) develop competence in performing practice skills; (3) learn to practice within the framework of social work values and ethics; (4) develop a professional commitment to social work practice; (5) evolve a practice style consistent with personal strengths and capacities; and (6) develop the ability to work effectively within a social agency. (3)

The social work practicum typically occurs within a social agency or a social welfare-related organization where the student works under the direction and supervision of an experienced professional employed by that agency. That organizational context or setting may be termed a *practicum agency, field agency, practicum setting,* or a *field placement.* In this book we will use the term *practicum agency.*

Students of social work at both the BSW and MSW levels usually describe their practicum as the single most useful, significant, and powerful learning experience of their formal social work education. It is during their practicum that the concepts, principles, and theories discussed in the classroom come to life. During the practicum students work with real clients and have the opportunity to try out the skills and techniques they previously rehearsed in role plays and simulations. It is also during the practicum that students make considerable progress in developing self-awareness and come to a better understanding of their particular strengths and limitations and the influence of their personal values, attitudes, and prior life experiences on their social work practice. The practicum can and should be a time of conceptual integration and a time when the student, as a unique person, merges with the values and fundamental principles of his or her chosen profession.

For many students, the practicum is an outstanding experience, but for others, the practicum falls short of expectations. Based on our experiences in the areas of practicum supervision and practicum coordination, we believe that the quality of every practicum experience can be enhanced if students are provided with guidance in identifying and making use of learning opportunities. Providing a structure that helps them to examine and analyze their setting in ways that build on prior classroom learning is of critical importance. We also believe that some of the most meaningful learning occurs as a result of having to deal with frustrations and unexpected events during the practicum.

HOW TO USE THIS BOOK

This book is designed to provide the student with guidance and structure during the social work practicum. If used in a thoughtful manner throughout the practicum, it will help the student make the best of whatever his or her practicum setting has to offer. Needless to say, this will not happen without effort. It requires a real commitment by the student and a willingness to invest time in the learning process. This book can be used in at least four ways:

1. As a teaching and learning tool in a practicum-related seminar or capstone course that is under the direction of college or university faculty. Such seminars may be termed *field seminars, practicum tutorials,* and *integrative practice seminars.*
2. As a self-study guide for the student during his or her practicum.
3. As a study guide for a group of practicum students who are all working within the same agency or organizational setting.
4. As a guide or teaching tool during supervisory meetings between the student(s) and the agency-based practicum supervisor or practicum instructor.

The practicum is a unique learning opportunity. As you begin your journey through the practicum experience, we ask you to always remember that:

When we are truly ready to learn, all people and all experiences become our teachers.

HOW THE CHAPTERS ARE STRUCTURED

Although the chapters are numbered in the conventional manner, this is not to suggest that the student is to move through the book sequentially, one chapter after another. Rather, it is expected that the student will be gathering information to complete the workbook activities in several of the chapters at the same time. Moreover, it is expected that he or she will move back and forth between sections and will also revisit the same section several times as he or she gains experience in the practicum and begins to look at various questions and issues from a new perspective.

Each chapter begins with a section titled Goals for Learning. It lists possible goals or desired outcomes related to the knowledge, values, and skills that the student can expect to learn and develop during the practicum.

The next major section, Background Information, presents selected concepts and principles related to the topic addressed by the chapter. The box titled Food For Thought will usually contain several relevant quotations. The concepts and definitions presented in these two sections are not a substitute for a textbook or assigned readings, but rather should act as a review of key ideas that set the stage for what follows, stimulate creative thinking, and raise important questions.

In each of the sections labeled Guidance and Direction, the reader is offered general suggestions, guidance, and advice, and sometimes a few specific do's and don'ts intended to encourage and facilitate learning in relation to the chapter's objectives and its particular focus.

In most of the chapters, several pages have been cast into a workbook format and titled A Workbook Activity. The student is asked to seek answers to each of the questions and record the answers or related comments in the spaces provided. Several of the questions in each chapter are written in ways intended to encourage critical thinking. If the student performs these tasks conscientiously, he or she will establish a detailed record of practicum learning.

A section titled Suggested Learning Activities lists several specific tasks and activities that might provide still other opportunities and experiences for learning to the student.

The sections labeled Additional Suggestions and Hints include a few additional ideas, words of encouragement, and specific cautions that may be important to the student and the practicum experience.

Each chapter ends with a Selected Bibliography that lists several books or articles related to the topics addressed in the chapter. The sources listed should be fairly easy for the social work student to locate in a college or agency library. Frequent reference will be made to the *Encyclopedia of Social Work* and to commonly used social work textbooks. Because the book *Techniques and Guidelines for Social Work Practice* by Sheafor, Horejsi, and Horejsi (2000) is frequently used in social work practicum seminars, the list will usually include a reference to specific sections in that book.

PRACTICUM-RELATED STRENGTHS: A WORKBOOK ACTIVITY

We wish to introduce you to the workbook format used in this book. This first workbook activity focuses your attention on the knowledge, skills, and experiences that you may bring to the practicum.

It is important for you to clearly identify your strengths and build on them. Below is a list of strengths that are important to a successful practicum experience. Depending on the nature of the setting, some will be of more importance and relevance than others. This list can also be used to assess the appropriateness of a match between a student and a particular practicum setting.

Place a check mark by all items that apply to you. There are no right or wrong answers. However, there are good answers. A good answer is one that is honest and accurate.

Important Strengths for a Successful Practicum

Attitudes and Values

_____ Friendly and comfortable in personal and professional relationships

_____ Empathethic, caring, and concerned for clients or consumers served by the practicum agency

_____ Personal values, beliefs, and perspectives that are compatible with the agency's mission, goals, and philosophy

_____ Personal values, beliefs, and perspectives that are compatible with the National Association of Social Workers (NASW) *Code of Ethics*

_____ Committed to achieving social justice

Abilities and Skills

_____ Writing ability (selecting and organizing content, drafting reports, preparing letters, and keeping professional records)

_____ Verbal ability (explaining, describing, and informing)

_____ Ability to listen (understand what others are saying and respectfully consider their views, perspectives, and opinions)

_____ Ability to quickly process information, understand new concepts, and learn new skills

_____ Ability to read rapidly, grasp ideas quickly, and pull meaning and information from the written word

_____ Ability to organize and plan work to be done and effectively manage and utilize available time

_____ Ability to meet deadlines and work under pressure

_____ Ability to follow through on planned actions and complete tasks and assignments

_____ Ability to make thoughtful and ethical decisions under stressful conditions

_____ Assertiveness and self-confidence in professional relationships and group discussion

_____ Ability to solve problems creatively and effectively

_____ A special ability or gift for being able to build relationships with the agency's clients or consumers (e.g., ability to work with children, adolescents, or elderly; ability to work with hostile, nonvoluntary clients)

_____ Thoughtful, organized, confident, and comfortable when conducting interviews

_____ Thoughtful, organized, confident, and comfortable when working with groups of clients or professionals

_____ Ability to identify a need and formulate a course of action to address that need

Knowledge, Capacity, and Experience

_____ High level of self-awareness (an understanding of how one's own values, beliefs, attitudes, family background, life style, appearance, and life experiences might be perceived by others)

_____ Familiarity with communication methods and equipment used in the practicum agency (word processor, e-mail, computer software)

_____ Prior successful experience in adapting to change, new situations, and new work environments

_____ Prior successful employment or volunteer experience with services or programs similar to those provided by the practicum agency

_____ Prior successful employment or volunteer experience in working with types of consumers or clients served by the practicum agency

_____ Working knowledge of the state and federal laws, rules, regulations, and policies relevant to the practicum agency

_____ Familiarity with community context of the practicum agency (the community's values, history, problems, leadership, politics, resources, etc.)

_____ Knowledge of the assessment and planning tools, methods, and techniques used by the practicum agency

_____ Knowledge of the intervention methods and techniques used by the practicum agency

_____ Knowledge of the research and evaluation tools, methods, and techniques used by the practicum agency

_____ Understanding of the process of planned change

_____ Understanding of the generalist perspective in social work practice and other practice perspectives, theories, and models relevant to the practicum setting

_____ Understanding of the major theories describing human and family development

_____ Understanding of groups, organizations, and communities

Motivation and Desire to Learn

_____ Eagerness to learn and openness to new learning experiences

_____ Self-discipline and motivation to do what needs to be done, even when you may not feel like doing it

_____ Willingness to take on new responsibilities for and perform tasks and activities within your range of abilities

_____ Professional interests and career goals that are compatible with the practicum agency's purpose, programs, and methods

_____ Adequate time and energy to devote to the practicum

_____ A sense of "calling" to the social work profession

_____ Excitement about helping people improve the quality of their lives

1. What are the most significant strengths that you bring to the practicum experience?

   _____

   _____

   _____

2. What can you do to build learning experiences on or around your special strengths?

   _____

   _____

   _____

   _____

   _____

   _____

3. In what areas do you hope to develop additional competence and skill during the practicum?

   _____

   _____

_____

_____

_____

_____

4. What are the most significant limitations that you bring to the practicum experience?

_____

_____

_____

5. What practicum-related learning experiences will help you to address or overcome your limitations?

_____

_____

_____

_____

_____

_____

Additional notes and comments:

_____

_____

_____

_____

_____

_____

HOW DO WE LEARN? A WORKBOOK ACTIVITY

The social work practicum is an opportunity to learn. Your experience will be enhanced if you are aware of how you learn. This workbook activity focuses on the learning process.

Learning is a type of change. Sometimes change can be exciting and exhilarating. Sometimes change is difficult and frustrating. We would like all of our learning experiences to be enjoyable and fun, but real and significant learning can also be scary and painful.

Basically, we learn when we take risks—when we begin to think in a different way, when we view the familiar from a different angle, or when we try out new behavior. We must find the courage to take the risks necessary to learn. Only when we are willing to place ourselves in situations where old habits of thought and behavior are stretched and challenged do we begin to learn.

The social work practicum, if it is effective, should push and pull you in new directions. It will create some discomfort, but that is the price of learning. When the learning is about ourselves—our biases, prejudices and emotional hang-ups—the experience can be especially painful. However, this can free us from attitudes and behaviors that limit personal growth and effectiveness. Answer the following questions about your learning style and learning goals.

1. What teaching methods and learning experiences are most effective in helping you to acquire knowledge and develop social work practice skills?

   _____

   _____

   _____

   _____

   _____

   _____

2. As you begin your social work practicum, what are you most excited and enthusiastic about?

   _____

   _____

   _____

   _____

   _____

   _____

3. As you begin your social work practicum, what are your greatest fears or worries?

   _____

   _____

   _____

_____

_____

4. Given what you know about yourself and how you learn, what types of assistance, guidance, or structure would help you to lower your defenses and be more open to learning?

_____

_____

_____

_____

_____

_____

5. If you have a diagnosed learning disability, what accommodations will you request in your practicum agency?

_____

_____

_____

6. What additional questions and concerns do you have about the practicum arrangement?

_____

_____

_____

_____

_____

_____

7. Who can you consult for the answers and information you need?

_____

_____

_____

Additional notes and comments:

_____

_____

_____

_____

_____

SUGGESTED LEARNING ACTIVITIES

- Conduct a cursory examination of each chapter in this book. Note the topics addressed and how the content is organized.
- Pay special attention to the various Workbook Activities presented in the book and to the types of questions you will be asked as you work through this book during your practicum experience.

ADDITIONAL SUGGESTIONS AND HINTS

- Keep this book with you while at your practicum agency and strive to answer all of the workbook questions. We suggest you write in pencil because you may wish to modify answers as you gain experience and new insights.
- Do not record in this workbook any information that might identify an agency client or violate rules of confidentiality.

SELECTED BIBLIOGRAPHY

Barker, Robert. *The Social Work Dictionary.* 4th ed. Washington, DC: NASW Press, 1999.

Chiaferi, Rosemary, and Michael Griffin. *Developing Fieldwork Skills.* Pacific Grove, CA: Brooks/Cole, 1997.

Cochrane, Susan, and Marla Hanley. *Learning through Field.* Boston: Allyn and Bacon, 1999.

Commission on Accreditation. *Handbook of Accreditation Standards and Procedures.* 4th ed. Alexandria, VA: Council on Social Work Education, 1994.

Edwards, Richard L., ed. *Encyclopedia of Social Work.* 19th ed. Washington, DC: NASW Press, 1995. (See the article by Frumkin and Lloyd on social work education.)

Jenkins, Lowell, and Bradford Sheafor. "An Overview of Social Work Field Instruction." In *Quality Field Instruction in Social Work.* Ed. Bradford Sheafor and Lowell Jenkins. New York: Longman, 1981.

Rogers, Gayla, Donald Collins, Constance Barlow, and Richard Grinnell. *Guide to the Social Work Practicum.* Itasca, IL: F. E. Peacock, 2000.

Rothman, Juliet. *Stepping Out into the Field: A Field Work Manual for Social Work Students.* Boston: Allyn and Bacon, 2000.

Royse, David, Surjit Singh Dhooper, and Elizabeth Rompf. *Field Instruction.* 2nd ed. White Plains, NY: Longman, 1996.

Schneck, Dean, Bart Grossman, and Urania Glassman. *Field Education in Social Work.* Dubuque, IA: Kendall and Hunt, 1991.

Sheafor, Bradford, Charles Horejsi, and Gloria Horejsi. *Techniques and Guidelines for Social Work Practice.* 5th ed. Boston: Allyn and Bacon, 2000.

Urbanowski, Martha, and Margaret Dwyer. *Learning through Field Instruction.* Milwaukee, WI: Family Service America, 1988.

2

SCHOOL, AGENCY, AND STUDENT EXPECTATIONS

Goals for Learning

- To understand what you can and should expect of your school's practicum program and your practicum setting
- To understand what your school's program of social work education and your practicum agencies expect of you

A key to making the social work practicum a quality learning experience is the clarification of expectations. For example, what do you expect? What does the agency expect of you? What does your college or university expect of you and your practicum agency? Identifying and clarifying expectations will insure a smooth and positive practicum experience. Not doing so may lead to problems. The purpose of this chapter is to encourage and facilitate a clarification of practicum-related expectations.

BACKGROUND INFORMATION

Standards issued by the CSWE's Commission on Accreditation (1994) require a minimum of 400 social work practicum hours at the baccalaureate level (BSW) and a minimum of 900 at the masters (MSW) level. Some programs of social work education require additional hours.

Five parties are usually involved in the social work practicum experience:

1. The social work student
2. The agency-based practicum instructor (also called a *field supervisor* or *field instructor*)
3. The school's practicum coordinator (also called *director of field work*)
4. The faculty member who serves as the school's liaison to the practicum agency (often called the *faculty supervisor* or *school-based supervisor*)
5. The faculty member who conducts a practicum-related seminar designed to help the student integrate classroom and practicum learning

It is important to note that schools may use slightly different terms to describe the personnel associated with a practicum program. In this book we usually use the term *practicum instructor* when referring to the agency-based person who is responsible for the day-to-day supervision of a practicum student. This person is usually an agency employee. He or she may also be called a *field instructor, field supervisor,* or an *agency supervisor.*

The faculty member who is responsible for organizing and guiding the practicum program is here termed the *practicum coordinator,* although other common terms are *director of field work* and *field coordinator.*

Most schools assign a faculty member to function as a liaison to individual practicum agencies and organizations. In this book we refer to this individual as the *faculty supervisor.* Other commonly used terms are *faculty liaison* and *school-based supervisor.* These individuals maintain regular contact with an agency's practicum instructor and with the student(s) placed in that agency setting. They monitor the practicum and serve as trouble shooters when problems arise. These individuals are usually involved with the practicum instructor in the evaluation of the student's performance.

Programs of social work education typically utilize some type of *practicum seminar* to help students connect or integrate what they have learned in the classroom with their "real world" experiences in their practicum setting. These seminars are usually under the direction of a faculty member.

From time to time in this book, we will include more than one term when we refer to the various people involved in the student's practicum experience. This will remind the reader of alternative terminology.

The specific objectives associated with a practicum can be found in the school's practicum or fieldwork manual, in official descriptions of the social work curriculum, and in other documents issued by the program of social work education. All parties to the practicum are expected to adhere to the National Association of Social Workers (NASW) *Code of Ethics.* Below we have listed general expectations of all the parties who will be involved in your practicum. (Please note that the expectations described by your school's practicum program may differ somewhat from the general expectations listed here.)

The Practicum Coordinator Is Expected to:

- Assume responsibility for the overall management and coordination of the school's practicum program
- Conduct an initial screening of students applying for a practicum and assess their readiness for this experience
- Assign a faculty supervisor (faculty liaison) to work conjointly with the agency-based practicum instructor
- Provide suggested learning goals to aid the design of learning objectives and the selection of learning activities by the student and practicum instructor
- Provide guidelines, evaluation tools, and protocols for the evaluation of the student
- Provide needed training on the practicum program and practicum instruction to agency-based practicum instructors
- Be available to the student, the practicum instructor, and the faculty supervisor to facilitate a resolution to problems that may arise
- Assign an academic grade to the student's performance in the practicum
- Monitor and evaluate the quality of practicum experiences provided by the various agencies and organizations utilized as practicum settings

The Social Work Student in a Practicum Setting Is Expected to:

- Meet with the practicum instructor (field instructor) on a regular basis (at least weekly)
- Prepare for all meetings with the practicum instructor and alert the practicum instructor to topics that need to be discussed during the upcoming meeting

- Meet with the practicum instructor (field supervisor) and the faculty supervisor jointly at least twice during each academic term
- Meet with the school's faculty supervisor according to a schedule that is consistent with school policy and requirements
- Be in attendance at the agency on days and at times agreed on by the student and practicum instructor, and if unable to attend, notify the agency supervisor prior to or at the start of the work day
- Behave in a professional manner: take responsibility as an adult learner to understand and carry out assigned duties, meet all deadlines, and seek direction when needed
- Carry out agency-related assignments in a manner consistent with agency policy and procedures
- Prepare records and reports in accord with agency policy, procedures, and format
- Identify learning needs and, if required, prepare a learning agreement with specific learning outcomes and learning activities that are acceptable to the practicum instructor and the school's faculty supervisor
- Provide proof of professional malpractice insurance, if required by school or agency
- Bring to the attention of the faculty supervisor or practicum coordinator any practice or behavior within the agency that is clearly unethical
- Complete and submit all practicum monitoring and evaluation forms and reports required by the agency and school (e.g., time sheets, evaluations of student performance, student's evaluation of practicum experience)
- Discuss with the practicum instructor, faculty supervisor, or practicum coordinator any areas of significant disagreement, dissatisfaction, or confusion related to the practicum experience
- Devote the required number of hours to the practicum

The Practicum Instructor and Practicum Agency Are Expected to:

- Describe and explain what is expected of the student during his or her practicum within the agency
- Provide the student with a thorough orientation to the agency, its purpose, structure, policies, procedures, and ethical standards
- Provide regularly scheduled supervision to the practicum student (at least weekly supervisory conferences)
- Provide the practicum student with suitable office space, equipment, and support staff
- Include the student in regular staff meetings and staff training sessions
- Assign duties and responsibilities that are appropriate to the student's learning needs and that are increasingly difficult, demanding, and challenging
- Assign duties and responsibilities that help the student develop a broad range of social work knowledge and skills
- Work with the student in ways that recognize the practicum first and foremost as a learning experience and in ways that expand the student's opportunities to learn
- Monitor the student's work and progress and regularly provide feedback and constructive criticism
- Evaluate the student's performance in a fair, respectful, rigorous, and thorough manner
- Meet at least twice each academic term with the student and the faculty liaison to discuss the practicum and the student's progress
- Complete all evaluation forms and reports required by the school

- Model ethical practice and refrain from any inappropriate or unethical behavior toward the student (e.g., verbal abuse, sexual harassment, dual relationships)
- Reimburse the student for any out-of-pocket expenses incurred in agency-related work (i.e., travel costs)

The School's Faculty Supervisor Is Expected to:

- Assume responsibility for working out a plan that will provide the student with an array of appropriate and challenging learning opportunities during the practicum
- Monitor the student's practicum experience and assist in evaluating the student's performance
- Help the practicum instructor and other agency personnel learn about the school's expectations of students, the social work curriculum, and the school's goals for the practicum
- Assist the student in identifying his or her learning needs, formulating learning objectives, and preparing a written learning agreement
- Facilitate the student's learning by providing guidance and serving as a source of information
- Meet at least twice each academic term with the student and the practicum instructor to discuss the practicum and the student's progress
- Assist the student in integrating social work theory and the specific experiences of the practicum
- Assume responsibility for arranging and securing an interim and final evaluation of the student's performance in the practicum

The Practicum Seminar Will:

- Bring together students from various practicum settings to give them an opportunity to learn about different types of agency settings and to learn from each other's experiences
- Arrange or structure learning activities that will help the students integrate social work theory with practice (e.g., discussions, student presentations, outside speakers)

The Student's Special Responsibilities to Agency Clients

Given the fact that the practicum student is in the process of learning to become a social worker and generally lacks experience, he or she must be especially concerned about how this lack of skill and experience might affect the client and the quality of the services provided to the client. The student has a special obligation to provide his or her practicum instructor with a complete and accurate description of his or her work with clients, including what has already happened and what he or she plans to do. The student is expected to consult with his or her practicum instructor whenever faced with an unusual or especially complex decision or issue.

The clients served by a student social worker are to be made aware that they are being served or assisted by a student. Section 3.02(c) of the 1997 NASW *Code of Ethics* states that:

> Social workers who function as educators or field instructors for students should take reasonable steps to ensure that clients are routinely informed when services are being provided by students.

Food for Thought

Practice and teaching go hand in hand. One cannot teach what is not practiced; one cannot practice what cannot be taught.

◆◆◆

What one hears, one forgets.
What one sees, one remembers.
What one does, one understands.
—*Chinese Proverb*

◆◆◆

Are you ready to change your mind? If not, you are not ready to learn, for learning is the process of changing your mind. We can learn—change our mind—only when we can admit that we don't yet know it all.

◆◆◆

The only person who is truly educated is one who has learned how to learn and continues to learn throughout his or her life.

GUIDANCE AND DIRECTION

The practicum placements that are most beneficial are those in which there is a good match between the student's learning needs and the learning opportunities available within the practicum setting. In contrast, the source of most problems in the practicum is a mismatch between what the student needs to learn and what the setting has to offer. For this reason, the careful assessment of your abilities and needs prior to the selection of a practicum setting is of critical importance.

Three major factors will determine the overall quality of your social work practicum experience:

1. Your motivation to learn
2. Your capacity to learn
3. Your opportunity to learn

In order for those who will be assisting you during the practicum to be truly helpful, they need information about your motivation. What do you really want and expect from the practicum? What are you willing to do to obtain the learning experiences you seek? Be sure to communicate your hopes and expectations to your practicum instructor, faculty supervisor, and practicum coordinator. Be honest and open in describing your expectations and motivation.

Similarly, in order for others to help you make the practicum a good learning experience, they need to know about your capacity to learn. They need to know both your special strengths and limitations. They need to know about your strengths so they can build on them. They need to know your limitations so they can help you find ways to work around them. Do not withhold important information.

When your practicum instructor accurately understands your expectations, strengths, and limitations, he or she will be in a better position to select and arrange those learning opportunities, activities, and work assignments that will advance your learning.

We urge you to acknowledge and confront any special limitations that may affect your practicum learning. You can expect to have significant difficulties and challenges during the practicum if you:

- Have poor writing skills
- Have difficulty in managing time, meeting deadlines, organizing work, and staying on task
- Are unusually shy and lacking in assertiveness
- Are unusually aggressive, dominating, or opinionated
- Are unable or unwilling to conform with agency policy and procedure
- Are unable to maintain an appropriate separation between your personal life and your professional responsibilities

In order to learn, you must have high expectations of yourself and place demands on yourself. No one can learn for you; others can only help you learn. You will need to set up a plan designed to facilitate learning. Chapter 3 will help you identify learning goals and objectives and formulate such a plan.

CLARIFYING EXPECTATIONS: A WORKBOOK ACTIVITY

1. You will be spending hundreds of hours in your practicum setting. What do you expect from this investment of your time?

_____

_____

_____

_____

_____

2. List the key things you are expecting of your agency-based practicum instructor (field supervisor).

_____

_____

_____

_____

3. List the key things you are expecting of your faculty supervisor (faculty liaison).

_____

_____

_____

_____

4. List the key things you are expecting of the practicum coordinator.

_____

_____

_____

_____

5. List the key things you are expecting of the practicum seminar.

_____

_____

_____

_____

6. As with all learning opportunities, what you are willing to invest in the practicum determines what you will get out of it. List the key things you are expecting of yourself during the practicum.

_____

_____

_____

_____

_____

_____

7. In what specific areas, if any, are your expectations of the practicum at variance with what will be expected of you?

_____

_____

_____

_____

_____

_____

Additional notes and comments:

_____

_____

_____

_____

_____

_____

SUGGESTED LEARNING ACTIVITIES

- Most schools make use of a signed contract or written agreement to clarify what the school expects of the agency and what the agency expects of the school. Read this document. (A sample school–agency agreement can be found in Appendix A).
- Read your school's practicum manual. Pay special attention to descriptions of what is expected of the practicum student.
- Ask your practicum instructor if there is a job description for social work practicum students. If there is, read it carefully to determine what your agency expects of its students.
- Carefully examine the student evaluation form, guidelines, and specific criteria that will be used to evaluate your performance in the practicum. What do these documents tell you about what is expected of you? (See Chapter 17 for additional information on evaluation.)

ADDITIONAL SUGGESTIONS AND HINTS

- Talk to former students who have completed a practicum in your agency. Ask them for advice and guidance on what to expect. Ask about any special problems they experienced. Ask them to identify any special learning opportunities and experiences available in your practicum setting.
- Listen carefully to other students in your practicum seminar. Are their concerns similar to or different from yours? Do various agencies have similar expectations of practicum students? What are they doing in their practicum settings that might work for you?

SELECTED BIBLIOGRAPHY

Bogo, Marion, and Elaine Vayda. *The Practice of Field Instruction in Social Work.* Toronto: University of Toronto, 1987.

Commission on Accreditation. *Handbook of Accreditation Standards and Procedures.* 4th ed. Alexandria, VA: Council on Social Work Education, 1994.

National Association of Social Workers. *Code of Ethics.* Washington, DC: NASW Press, 1997.

Watts, Nancy. *Handbook of Clinical Teaching.* Edinburgh; UK: Churchill Livingstone, 1990.

3

PLANNING TO LEARN

Goals for Learning

- To become familiar with terms such as *learning goal, learning objective,* and *learning activity;* use these ideas to construct a plan for practicum learning
- To identify learning goals and objectives relevant to your social work practicum setting
- To identify learning activities relevant to your practicum setting
- To write a learning contract (or learning agreement) outlining your proposed practicum experience

Good learning experiences do occur by accident, but not very often. For them to happen on a regular basis they must be made to happen. Thus, a good social work practicum experience is usually one that has been carefully planned.

As you begin your practicum, it is important to list your desired outcomes for learning and then identify and arrange activities and experiences that will help you reach those goals. A well-conceived learning plan will result in a challenging, exciting, and worthwhile learning experience. If you do not develop a plan, you may waste an invaluable learning opportunity and fail to maximize your practicum experience.

In this chapter we provide basic information, guidance, and a workbook activity that can assist you to develop a plan for learning. This plan will be extremely useful, but it is also important to recognize that not everything will go as planned.

BACKGROUND INFORMATION

A plan for learning during the practicum is like a road map. It identifies destinations and possible routes for getting where you want to go. The development of this plan is important, but it is not a simple or easy task. However, it is always better to have a plan—even if it is a rather general one—than to have no plan at all.

A plan for learning will incorporate educational goals and anticipated outcomes from three sources: the school's curriculum, the practicum instructor, and the student. These goals will usually fall into three categories: values, knowledge, and skills.

A *value* is a strong preference that affects one's choices, decisions, and actions and that is rooted in one's deepest beliefs and commitments. Values determine what a person considers important, worthwhile, right, or wrong. Social work values (e.g., service, social justice, integrity) can be learned or "caught" from others, but it is doubtful that they can be taught by others in a systematic and deliberate way. Typically, our values are "picked up" from observing someone who is respected and admired. (See Chapter 13 for a listing of core social work values.)

Social work *knowledge* consists of terminology, facts, principles, concepts, and theories. Compared to values and skills, knowledge is easier to teach and learn. The classroom is well suited to the teaching and learning of social work knowledge.

Social work *skills* are the behaviors of practice. They are the techniques and procedures used by social workers to bring about desired change in the social functioning of clients or in social systems within which clients interact. For the most part, skills are learned by watching and imitating the behavior of skilled practitioners. One can learn about skills from a textbook, but one cannot acquire skills simply by reading about them.

It is possible to separate social work values, knowledge, and skills for purposes of discussion and analysis, but in the actual practice of social work, they are interwoven. For example, one's skill (action, behavior) is a reflection of one's knowledge and values. Likewise, the possession of social work knowledge and values is of little use unless they are expressed in action.

PREPARING A PLAN FOR LEARNING

Below we describe two approaches to the formulation and writing of a plan for practicum learning. Different schools may prefer one over the other or use some other alternatives. The first approach we call the *Goals, Activities, and Criteria Approach*. We prefer this approach because it is the easiest for students and agency personnel to implement and provides sufficient direction in most practicum settings. The second approach we call the *Learning Objectives Approach*. It has several advantages, but is more difficult to use because it requires a high degree of specificity in the description of future learning activities—which can be a challenge in many settings—and also greater precision in the use of words.

The Goals, Activities, and Criteria Approach

In this approach, the written plan lists separately:

1. Relevant goals
2. The specific activities or experiences that will help the student progress toward each of those learning goals
3. Criteria for determining whether the specified goals have been reached

A form for preparing a written learning plan using this approach can be found in Appendix B. This sample form, and the ideas behind it, can be modified to fit the requirements of a particular program of social work education. This form lists the school's general goals for the practicum in the left-hand column. The field instructor or student selects additional goals specific to the practicum setting and adds them to the form.

A *goal* is a rather broad and general statement of intended outcome. For example, a learning goal might be: "To become familiar with the history of a social agency." Another would be: "To develop the skills of interviewing." The following verbs often appear in goal statements:

to acquire	to comprehend	to learn
to analyze	to develop	to perceive
to appreciate	to discover	to synthesize
to become	to explore	to understand
to become familiar with	to know	to value

Once the goals have been specified, various learning activities are listed in the second column. A *learning activity* is some specific task, activity, or assignment that, when performed by the student, will help him or her advance toward a learning goal.

Finally, this sample form has a third column for statements that describe the *method and criteria for evaluating progress* toward the goal. Two common methods of documenting and evaluating progress are listing proposed dates for completing the task or assignment and stating that the work is to be reviewed and critiqued by the practicum instructor.

The Learning Objectives Approach

A second approach to preparing a plan for practicum learning involves the writing of numerous statements termed *learning objectives*. Although the terms *goal* and *objective* are often used interchangeably, they do not mean the same thing.

A *learning objective* is a statement of desired outcome written in a way that allows measurement. An objective is more precisely worded, specific, and concrete than is a goal. It stipulates what the learner will do, how and when. The following statement is a learning objective.

> To learn the policies of my agency by reading the agency manual two times prior to October 15 and to write at least twelve questions about agency policy to be asked of my supervisor before November 1.

A learning objective, in a single outcome statement, brings together a goal, a description of learning activities, and evaluation criteria.

The writing of an objective can be a challenging task. Such writing requires the use of behavioral language. A behavior is an activity that can be observed. Drawing on the above example, we recognize that it is not possible to observe "learning," but it is possible to observe the activity of "reading," the "writing" of twelve questions, and the "asking" of those questions. The use of completion dates and the counting of completed tasks and activities can often transform an unmeasurable goal into a measurable objective.

The words and phrases used in writing objectives are ones that describe specific actions and activities. For example:

to answer	to decide	to obtain
to arrange	to define	to participate in
to circulate	to demonstrate	to revise
to classify	to direct	to schedule
to collect	to discuss	to select
to compare	to explain	to summarize
to compile	to give examples	to supervise
to conduct	to list	to verify
to count	to locate	to write

When selecting and writing learning objectives, it is important to remain focused on outcomes that are truly important and relevant to the learning of social work practice. Although being able to measure progress is desirable, one must avoid becoming so preoccupied with trying to achieve measurability that the focus shifts to outcomes that are most easily measured rather than most important.

THE GENERALIST PERSPECTIVE AND THE PLAN FOR LEARNING

The curricula for BSW programs and the first year of MSW programs are built around the concept of generalist social work practice. Thus, the practicum experiences of many students are expected to reflect a generalist perspective.

The *generalist perspective* is a way of looking at and thinking about the process and activities of social work practice. It is a set of ideas and principles that guide the process of planned change. According to the *American Heritage Dictionary*, the word *generalist* refers to "a person with broad general knowledge and skills in several disciplines, fields or areas." Keeping that definition in mind, we can better understand that the terms *generalist social work practice* and *generalist social worker* refer to a social work practitioner who:

- Has a broad range of knowledge and skills
- Draws upon several theories and models
- Is able to conduct beginning level practice at the micro, mezzo, and macro levels
- Is capable of performing numerous social work roles
- Can move quite readily from one field of practice to another

The opposite of the generalist practice is one characterized by specialization, either by type of client served, by method used, by level of intervention, or by the role assumed by the social worker.

The client of a generalist social worker may be an individual, a couple, a family, a group, an organization, or a community. Thus, the generalist is prepared to work with various client systems. He or she may, for example:

- Work at the face-to-face, one-on-one level with a single person
- Work with a whole family or household
- Work with a group such as a treatment or support group
- Work with committees or task groups
- Work with an agency or a network of agencies
- Work with legislators and policy makers

The generalist is prepared to assume a variety of social work roles. These include, for example, the roles of advocate, case manager, counselor or therapist, group facilitator, broker of service, fund raiser, program planner, policy analyst, and researcher.

A generalist social worker will examine and consider a wide range of factors that may contribute to a client's problems in social functioning. These may include conflicts among values and beliefs, broken relationships, distortions of thinking, lack of knowledge and information, destructive individual and family behavior, alienation and loneliness, oppression, injustice and racism, poverty and the lack of basic resources, misuse of power by those in authority, and misguided or unworkable social programs and policies.

The generalist fits or adapts his or her approach to the needs and circumstances of the client and the local community, rather than expecting the client or others to conform to the preferred methods of the professional or the agency.

The generalist avoids selecting an intervention method or approach until after he or she and the client have worked together to complete a careful assessment of the client's concern or problem and have considered various ways in which the client's problem or concern can be defined, conceptualized, and approached. Finally, the generalist is prepared to draw on and utilize a wide range of intervention techniques and procedures, and is not bound to a single theory or model.

Food for Thought

If you don't know where you are going, you will end up somewhere else.

◆ ◆ ◆

To learn the skills of a profession, the student has to observe much and do much.

◆ ◆ ◆

The only way to really learn social work practice is through the practice of social work.

◆ ◆ ◆

If you want to learn a specific skill or technique—first observe someone doing it, then do it yourself, and finally teach it to someone else.

◆ ◆ ◆

Teachers open the doors.
Students must enter by themselves.
—*Chinese Proverb*

◆ ◆ ◆

The function of education is to teach one to think intensely and to think critically. Intelligence plus character—that is the goal of true education.
—*Martin Luther King, Jr.*

GUIDANCE AND DIRECTION

Develop a written plan that will guide your practicum experience. A truly helpful plan—one that will enhance your learning experience—will take time to prepare. As a first step in this planing process, find out what your school expects. Your school may call this plan a *Learning Contract* or a *Learning Agreement*. Most likely, your school has a preferred format for organizing the content of your plan.

A learning contract or agreement is negotiated between you, your practicum instructor, and your faculty supervisor. It outlines what you want and need to learn, and identifies the activities you will undertake in order to learn. Most learning agreements are working documents that are modified throughout the practicum as additional learning needs are identified and new learning opportunities arise.

Your plan should be ambitious. It should stretch and expand your knowledge and skills. It must also be realistic given your practicum setting, your abilities, and your prior experience.

Build into your plan a set of experiences that will help you to learn about the many facets of your agency's operations, such as its funding, how its policies are formed, and how it selects new staff. Include learning activities that will help you to understand the community context of social work practice. (See Chapters 8 and 9 for more information.)

Each of us has a unique approach to learning or a particular learning style. As you develop your plan, consider your preferred method of learning. For example, you may be inclined to jump into the middle of an activity or opportunity because you learn best by doing. Or you may learn best by first observing others and then later trying your hand at the activity. Perhaps you need to first understand the theory or rationale behind an activity before you feel ready to take action. No one learning style is best or most effective in all situations. Examine your prior learning experiences and identify the methods and approaches that work best for you. You may want to utilize a learning styles inventory or assessment instrument to better understand your preferred method of learning. (See, for example, Kolb 1981.)

Give your practicum instructor as much information as possible about how you learn. That information may help him or her select assignments and responsibilities as well as determine your readiness for certain experiences. However, even if you and your practicum instructor could fully understand your learning style, that does not mean you should wait around for "just the right opportunity to come along." Rather, we urge you to follow the ancient principle of *carpe diem,* which means "seize the day" or "seize the opportunity." Take full advantage of whatever opportunities exist, whenever they appear.

If you have a learning disability or a condition that may in some way limit your learning or performance, be sure to share this information with your practicum instructor and faculty supervisor. Such conditions need to be considered in developing a plan for practicum learning. If you suspect you may have a learning disability, immediately consult with a learning specialist who can assess the nature of the disability, recommend ways of compensating for the limitation, and guide you toward a program of remediation.

Include in your plan experiences and activities that will help you to integrate theory and practice. Classroom learning should come alive during the practicum. Strive to identify the beliefs, values, and theory behind your decisions and your selection of an intervention. Seek exposure to practice and programs based on various beliefs about how, when, and why people and social systems are able to change.

If your practicum is to reflect generalist social work practice, construct your plan so it will allow you to:

- Learn a variety of skills, techniques, and approaches to intervention
- Assume several different social work roles (case manager, counselor, broker, educator, advocate, community organizer)
- Learn the basics of practice at various levels of intervention (micro, mezzo, macro)
- Learn how to match client need with resources, tailoring intervention to the individual client
- Learn skills that can be generalized to another agency setting

Describe your desired outcomes for learning in ways that permit the monitoring and the measurement of progress (see Background Information). However, also recognize that many important outcomes such as developing a commitment to social work values, growing in self-awareness and self-confidence, and perfecting interviewing skills are inherently difficult to quantify and measure. Describe your desired outcomes as precisely as possible, but do not get hung up on measurability. It is better to describe outcomes in only general and imperfect ways than to not mention them at all.

Once you have completed your plan and it has been approved by your practicum instructor and faculty supervisor, follow it! Review it often. Modify it as needed, but resist the temptation to abandon a part of the plan simply because it calls for a learning opportunity that is difficult to arrange. Do everything possible to obtain the experiences you need to advance your learning.

As you formulate your learning plan, give careful thought to your personal plans for the next five years. For example, if you are a BSW student hoping to go on to graduate school, what can you do during the practicum to prepare yourself for graduate study or to increase your chances of being accepted into graduate school? If you expect to enter the job market immediately after graduation, what can you build into your plan that will prepare you for the job you seek?

Your plan will contain what you hope to learn, but during your practicum you may learn some things that are surprising or even discouraging. For example, you will probably discover that not all clients are motivated, that some are difficult to like and respect, and that some will not make use of needed and available services. You will probably learn that change can be slow, that social problems are more complex than you realized, that you must be skillful in the art of politics, and that not all professionals are competent and ethical. Your faculty supervisor can help you gain perspective on such matters, so be sure to share these experiences and observations with him or her.

Do not be surprised if much of what you actually learn during your practicum was not anticipated and could not have been written into your plan. Expect some surprises. Perhaps your agency's funding will be drastically cut, and you may end up working in a different unit or service area. Maybe your practicum instructor will take another job and you must adjust to a successor with a different supervisory style. Although such experiences will be stressful, they may prove to be valuable learning opportunities. They will certainly teach you to be flexible and open to new experiences.

PLANNING TO LEARN: A WORKBOOK ACTIVITY

Your answers to the questions below will help you to identify desired outcomes and to prepare a plan that can guide and enhance your practicum. Answer these questions with honesty and as much precision as possible.

1. Does your school or practicum agency require you to prepare a written learning agreement or plan for your practicum?

   _____

   If yes, what format is to be used? (Note: if you do not have a format, consider using the form provided in Appendix B.)

   _____

   _____

   _____

2. What experiences and activities in your practicum will help you to deepen your understanding of the social work profession, its purposes, and core values?

   _____

   _____

   _____

   _____

   _____

3. What experiences will help you learn more about social work as a career and about social work jobs, working conditions, and salary in order to decide if social work is a good career choice for you?

   _____

   _____

   _____

   _____

   _____

4. What experiences will help you learn more about your "true self" (i.e., your special strengths and gifts, your core values and beliefs, your basic attitudes toward people, your prejudices, your emotional hang-ups)?

   _____

   _____

   _____

   _____

   _____

5. What experiences will deepen your understanding of social and economic justice and the skills of working toward needed social change and social justice?

_____

_____

_____

_____

6. What experiences and activities will help you learn about the various roles in social work practice (e.g., broker, case manager, therapist, organizer, administrator, advocate, trainer)?

_____

_____

_____

_____

7. What experiences will help you learn more about the ethical and legal aspects of social work practice?

_____

_____

_____

_____

8. What experiences will deepen your understanding of the human and social problems and conditions addressed by your agency?

_____

_____

_____

_____

9. What experiences will help you learn the skills of generalist social work practice and about other social work practice perspectives, theories, and models utilized in your practicum agency?

_____

_____

_____

_____

10. What experiences will help you learn the techniques or methods of data gathering and assessment utilized in your agency?

_____

_____

_____

_____

11. What experiences will help you learn the skills of planning an intervention and involving the client in this process of change?

_____

_____

_____

_____

12. What experiences will help you deepen your understanding of human diversity and culturally sensitive social work practice?

_____

_____

_____

_____

13. What experiences will help you learn methods of applied research and ways of evaluating the effectiveness of social work practice?

_____

_____

_____

_____

14. What experiences will help you to better understand your agency, its purpose, history, organizational structure, funding sources, reputation in the community, how it is changing, and how it is planning for the future?

_____

_____

_____

_____

15. What experiences will help you learn about the agency context of practice and such areas as agency administration, budgeting procedures, personnel matters, public relations, and fund raising?

_____

_____

_____

_____

16. What experiences will help you to deepen your understanding of how specific social policies and social programs have evolved, their intended purposes, their strengths and limitations, and their impact on the clients or consumers served by the agency?

_____

_____

_____

_____

17. What experiences will help you to learn the skills needed to build working relationships with agency clients and consumers?

_____

_____

_____

_____

18. What experiences will deepen your understanding of individual behavior and learn skills of working with individuals?

_____

_____

_____

_____

19. What experiences will deepen your understanding of families and help you learn the skills needed to work with families and various types of family systems?

_____

_____

_____

_____

20. What experiences will help you deepen your understanding of and learn skills for working with small groups (e.g., therapy groups, social support groups, committees)?

_____

_____

_____

_____

21. What experiences will help you deepen your understanding of and learn skills for working with organizations?

_____

_____

_____

_____

22. What experiences will help you deepen your understanding of and learn skills for working with communities?

_____

_____

_____

_____

23. What experiences will help you learn important support skills such as time management, stress management, report writing, and computer skills?

_____

_____

_____

_____

24. What type of orientation or initial training do social workers in your agency receive soon after they are hired? Can you take advantage of training offered by your agency?

_____

_____

_____

_____

25. What personal issues, experiences, or biases might get in the way of your learning? How will you deal with them so they do not interfere with your practicum experience?

_____

_____

_____

_____

Additional notes and comments:

_____

_____

_____

_____

_____

_____

SUGGESTED LEARNING ACTIVITIES

- Consult your school's practicum manual (or field education manual) and various descriptions of the curriculum in search of specific learning goals and objectives for the practicum.
- Work with a group of other students to brainstorm a list of possible tasks, activities, and special projects that might be pursued within your practicum agency as a way of expanding learning opportunities and enhancing the practicum experience.
- If your practicum agency cannot provide a learning experience that you need, ask your practicum instructor to help you gain that experience by working a few hours each week in another agency.
- Read your school's practicum evaluation form or rating instrument to better understand what you are expected to learn during the practicum and how you are expected to demonstrate that you have acquired specific knowledge and skills and that you possess certain values and attitudes.
- If you have a specific career goal such as chemical dependency certification, school social work certification, social work licensing, or graduate school, identify the requirements for this goal and seek practicum experiences related to that goal.

ADDITIONAL SUGGESTIONS AND HINTS

- You will be asked to perform tasks and take on responsibilities for which you feel unprepared. That may give rise to anxiety, fear, and embarrassment, which are understandable and normal reactions. You must be willing to take on tasks and responsibilities even when you do not feel ready. If you were to wait until you feel confident and certain that you would not make mistakes, you might not afford yourself opportunities to learn something new.
- If you feel disappointed with your practicum experience, discuss this concern with your practicum instructor. Do not delay or avoid this discussion. Do not let your negative feelings build up inside. Be very specific in describing what you had expected from the practicum. If your discussions with your practicum instructor do not result in an improved practicum experience, consult with your faculty liaison or the school's coordinator of the practicum.
- In Sheafor, Horejsi, and Horejsi (2000), read the section on "Teaching and Training."

SELECTED BIBLIOGRAPHY

Austin, Michael, Diane Brannon, and Peter Pecora. *Managing Staff Development Programs in Human Service Agencies.* Chicago: Nelson-Hall, 1984.

Bertcher, Harvey. *Staff Development in Human Service Organizations.* Englewood Cliffs, NJ: Prentice-Hall, 1988.

Kolb, David. *Learning-Style Inventory.* Boston: McBer and Company Training Resources Group, 1981.

Sheafor, Bradford, Charles Horejsi, and Gloria Horejsi. *Techniques and Guidelines for Social Work Practice.* 5th ed. Boston: Allyn and Bacon, 2000.

4

GETTING STARTED

Goals for Learning

- To meet and become familiar with the professional staff and other personnel within your agency
- To become familiar with the various units, departments, and divisions within your agency
- To become familiar with the basic routines and procedures of your agency
- To determine who in your agency will be supervising the work of practicum students and how tasks and responsibilities will be assigned

Previous chapters have asked you to read about, think about, and gather information concerning what will be expected of you in the practicum and what you can expect of the practicum. We have underscored the importance of formulating learning goals and identifying activities that can facilitate your learning and help you reach those desired outcomes. This chapter focuses on questions and concerns common to the first days and weeks of the practicum.

Beginning a practicum is similar to starting a new job. It is a time of excitement and confusion. Because there are so many new people to meet and so much to learn, the first few weeks can feel overwhelming. Entering the life of an unfamiliar organization is something like entering an unfamiliar culture. You will be aware that you are encountering a new set of norms, rules, and customs but you will be unsure what they are. Be assured that within a matter of weeks you will be familiar with the setting and much more comfortable.

BACKGROUND INFORMATION

The quality of the practicum experience is tied closely to decisions made by the practicum instructor about the types of cases, activities, or projects he or she is willing to assign to the student. If the assignments provide genuine opportunities to learn, the practicum will be positive and effective. If, for some reason, the practicum instructor is reluctant to assign demanding and challenging activities and responsibilities to the student, the practicum experience may be a disappointment.

First experiences are pattern setting. If the first days and weeks of contacts with a new student are positive for the practicum instructor and other agency staff, the practicum instructor will likely conclude that the student can be trusted. If, on the other hand, these first contacts give the practicum instructor cause to doubt whether the student is capable and responsible, he or she may hesitate to assign meaningful work to the student.

In order to do his or her part in getting the practicum off to a good start, the student must anticipate how he or she might be perceived by the practicum instructor and agency staff and what they might be thinking and feeling about the student's presence in the agency. Among the practicum instructor's thoughts might be the following:

> I look forward to having a student. Practicum students usually have a lot of enthusiasm, and they tend to look at the work of this agency from a fresh perspective.

> I'm glad that we have a practicum student. We're understaffed and have too much work to do. Hopefully, the student can relieve some of our work pressure.

> I hope this student works out. I remember one student who did not do well in this agency because he was too insecure and immature.

> I wonder if I can find the time necessary to properly supervise this student. I have too much to do already. I hope the student catches on quickly, because I don't have time to baby-sit.

> Will I be able to trust this student to follow my instructions and agency policy and procedure? I worry about students overstepping the bounds of their assignments and responsibility. I dislike having to clean up a mess made by others.

> I assume the student knows the textbook theory and principles that apply in ideal situations. However, this agency is in the real world and we have yet to encounter an ideal situation. Many of our clients are just plain difficult and frustrating. I hope the student is prepared for a taste of harsh reality.

Some of the challenges encountered in a practicum are related to the need for the social work student to shift from the university's focus on education to the agency's focus on training. The faculty within a program of social work education emphasize the learning of general knowledge, theory, and broad principles that can be applied in many practice settings. By contrast, agency administrators and supervisors are concerned mostly with training that emphasizes the learning of policies, procedures, and skills specific to their agency. Education encourages discussion, debate, and the consideration of alternative ways of assessing and responding to a problem or situation. By contrast, training is designed to teach what the agency has established as the standard or "correct" responses to given situations. Since these responses reflect the agency's purpose, policy, and procedures, they are to be followed by the student rather then challenged and debated.

All organizations, including human services agencies, have a political dimension. For example, an agency's managers must make difficult and unpopular decisions, and thus must use their power and authority to accomplish the agency's goals. Some conflict and power struggles are inevitable in organizational life, and these will soon become apparent to the practicum student. Practicum students need to be alert to the pitfalls of aligning themselves with one side or another in these conflicts.

The term *office politics* refers to the undercurrent of power struggles created by factors such as conflict between various factions within an organization, personal ambition, manipulations and jockeying for greater power, and efforts to lobby on behalf of a certain position. The larger the organization, the more complex its internal politics. If a practicum student becomes caught up in these power struggles and conflicts, learning opportunities may be closed to the student and some agency staff may withdraw their support from the student.

Food for Thought

The social worker's primary responsibility is to promote the well-being of clients. In general, clients' interests are primary.

This general principal from the *Code* will affect decisions regarding what work and responsibilities a student is assigned during the practicum. Given that the good of the client is of highest priority, an agency-based practicum instructor must rank the educational needs of a practicum student as secondary to the client's well-being. A student should not be assigned an activity or a responsibility that places a client at risk of identifiable harm or that would constitute a real disservice to an agency client. (NASW 1997, Section 1.01)

◆◆◆

Like professions and other occupations, all organizations develop their own cultures, complete with taboos, folkways and mores. . . . These cultures reflect the history of the . . . organization, its internal structure and the way in which it deals with its external relationships. It may be influenced by the types of people the organization attracts [both clients and staff], its work processes, physical layouts, modes of communication, and the exercise of authority within the system. The culture in turn exerts its own influence [on staff and practicum students]. (Lauffer 1987, 140–141)

◆◆◆

. . . ongoing learning within organizations is inevitable. Workers *will* learn every day. They learn from co-workers, supervisors, subordinates, clients, clerical staff, and any one else with whom they have contact. The issue . . . is *What* do they learn, and is what they learn desirable for promoting effective and efficient client services? Sometimes it is, and sometimes it most definitely is not. . . . If an [agency] manager fails to provide for formal learning, other learning will take place to fill the void. But it could just be learning that should never be allowed to occur. (Weinbach 1994, 127–128)

As a general rule, the larger and more political an organization, the more active the office grapevine. Rumors, gossip, and speculations are common within organizations having many bureaucratic layers, and are especially frequent during times of uncertainty, conflict, and rapid change. Participating in agency gossip can be another major pitfall for the practicum student.

GUIDANCE AND DIRECTION

First impressions have a powerful impact on personal and professional relationships. It is vital that you make a favorable first impression on your practicum instructor (field supervisor) and the other staff members in your practicum agency. Make a deliberate effort to get the practicum off to a good start.

As suggested above, there are a number of reasons why an agency-based practicum instructor might be hesitant about assigning challenging responsibilities to a student. To make these assignments, the practicum instructor must trust the student and believe that he or she is capable of doing the work and is not likely to make significant mistakes. Very often, the practicum instructor makes this decision on the basis of patterns he or she sees in the student's ordinary behavior (i.e., on the basis of the "little things" he or she notices about the student). Thus, you should strive to display behaviors that can assure your practicum instructor that you can and will perform in a responsible manner. For example:

- Take all assignments seriously, no matter how trivial and unimportant they may seem.
- Demonstrate initiative and a willingness to take on responsibility and assignments.
- Inform your practicum instructor of your prior work and volunteer experiences to help him or her better understand your abilities.

- Keep your practicum instructor informed about what you are doing, why, and what you plan to do next.
- Immediately consult with your practicum instructor if you encounter an unusual or unanticipated problem or difficulty, especially one that has legal ramifications or one that might create a public relations problem for the agency.
- Be a good listener and be attentive to your practicum instructor and to other staff members during supervisory conferences and staff meetings.
- Demonstrate the ability to accept and use constructive criticism of your work, skills, and attitudes.
- Prepare all letters, reports, and client records with great care, according to the agency's prescribed format, and in a timely manner.
- Meet all deadlines. Be on time for all scheduled appointments and meetings. Remain on the job for all the hours you are expected to be in the practicum agency.
- If you must make a change in your work schedule or discover that you will not be able to keep an appointment, contact your supervisor immediately and work out an alternative plan.
- Be well prepared for all meetings with your practicum instructor and for agency staff meetings.
- Demonstrate that you have read agency manuals and other materials and are therefore familiar with your agency's mission, programs, policies, and procedures.
- Ask questions that reveal a desire to learn and to understand the work of the agency, its policies, and procedures, but avoid asking in a manner that appears to challenge or criticize agency policy and procedure.
- Do your best to understand a new assignment or responsibility the first time it is explained to you.
- Keep your desk and work space neat and organized.
- Pay attention to your personal grooming, and dress appropriately for the practicum.
- Do not engage in gossip or spread rumors concerning other agencies or professionals. Do not "bad mouth" other students, agency staff, clients, or other agencies in the community.
- Be extremely careful to protect your clients right to privacy and the confidentiality of agency records.
- Volunteer to take on tasks that are not attractive to regular agency staff.
- Make friendly overtures to others in the agency. Demonstrate a capacity to build relationships and get along with a variety of different people.

As you encounter office politics, make very thoughtful decisions concerning how you can respond in ways that will protect your practicum experience and avoid offending others. Although it is difficult to offer guidance on how to handle office politics because every situation is different, we will offer some general guidelines for you to consider:

- Use the first several weeks and months in the practicum to carefully observe the ways in which people maneuver and use their power and influence.
- Do not jump to conclusions concerning who is most valued and respected within the agency and who has the most power and influence. Power relationships are often more subtle and complex than they appear at first. Consequently, your first impressions may be erroneous.
- Be cognizant of and sensitive to the official lines of authority and to the power relationships inherent in the chain of command as described by the agency's organizational chart. Follow the chain of command. To disregard

those established power relationships will cause confusion and may put your practicum in jeopardy.

- Cultivate relationships with those in the agency who command the respect of most fellow professionals and the support staff and who are respected and valued by their administrative superiors. Longtime office staff are often very powerful in an organization.
- Do not align yourself with someone in the agency who has a reputation for being a "complainer," a "loose cannon," a "troublemaker," a "back stabber," or with someone who has little loyalty to the agency.

Deciding how to respond to office gossip and rumors is also difficult for a practicum student. In general, there are two types of office gossip and rumors: people gossip and professional banter. *People gossip* has to do with purely personal matters (e.g., who is dating whom, who is getting a divorce, who is deeply in debt). *Professional banter* focuses on matters related to the work of the agency (e.g., who is getting promoted, who is getting hired, what is being said by top administrators, what new policies are being discussed).

We offer some general guidance on dealing with the gossip and rumors you may hear in your practicum agency:

- Avoid becoming a party to people gossip. It is not relevant to your work as a practicum student. Engaging in gossip may cause others to view you as unprofessional and untrustworthy.
- In some situations, you may have no choice but to passively listen to someone engaging in people gossip. Say nothing that would further encourage their gossip. Never repeat what you have heard.
- Pay attention to professional banter because it may reveal important information about the informal structure of your agency, but do not assume that what you are hearing is necessarily true. Often this banter is inaccurate or only partially true. Do not base a decision on rumor. If it is an important matter, get accurate information before making a decision.

Every organization has many unwritten rules. It is likely that no one will think to tell you about them until after you have broken one. For example, you might be breaking a rule if you bring food or drink to a staff meeting, or you might be breaking a rule if a certain report is submitted late even though it is permissible to be a little late on other types of reports. The best way to learn about these informal rules and procedures is to observe the work of others in the agency and ask why things are done a certain way.

Remember that there is no such thing as a stupid question. Your practicum instructor expects you to ask many questions, especially in the beginning, but he or she also expects you to remember the answers that you are given. Thus, record the answers so you do not ask the same questions over and over. Your practicum instructor expects that you will make some mistakes, but he or she expects you to learn from each mistake and not make it a second time.

Also remember that your actions—your behavior—always speak louder and more clearly than do your words. In the professional world, you will be judged primarily on the basis of your performance. Judgments concerning what you are capable of doing will be based mostly on what you are now doing and have done previously.

BASIC INFORMATION ABOUT YOUR PRACTICUM: A WORKBOOK ACTIVITY

The following questions are designed to assist you in securing the information and orientation needed to get your practicum experience off to a good start. Some can be answered by your practicum instructor. Others will need to be answered by the practicum coordinator of your school.

1. Who are the agency employees who will supervise your work during the practicum?

   Name   Phone Number   E-Mail Address

   _____

   _____

   _____

2. Who is your school's practicum coordinator?

   Name   Phone Number   E-Mail Address

   _____

3. Who is the faculty member who will serve as liaison or primary contact to your practicum agency?

   Name   Phone Number   E-Mail Address

   _____

4. Who are you to contact if you encounter unusual or unexpected problems related to supervision, learning opportunities, or learning activities within your practicum?

   Name   Phone Number   E-Mail Address

   _____

   _____

5. What are the names and numbers of other practicum students in your agency?

   Name   Phone Number   E-Mail Address

   _____

   _____

   _____

   _____

   _____

   _____

   _____

6. How many hours each week are you to be at your practicum agency?

_____

7. How are you to document the number of hours you devote to your practicum? To whom is this documentation to be submitted? How often are you to report?

_____

_____

_____

8. On what days each week and at what times each day are you to be at your practicum agency?

_____

9. Are there certain regularly scheduled agency meetings that you are expected to always attend such as weekly staff meetings? If yes, when and where are they held?

_____

_____

_____

10. What are you to do if you are sick or for some other good reason cannot be at the practicum agency when scheduled and expected to be there? Who do you contact? Who will fill in for you when you are absent? How much notice are you required to give?

_____

_____

_____

_____

11. How are you expected to dress when at the agency? Is there a dress code? What types of clothing, jewelry, or attire are considered inappropriate?

_____

_____

_____

12. How do the regular staff members want to be addressed? Do they prefer to be called Ms., Mrs., Mr., or Dr.? Is it appropriate to use first names?

_____

_____

_____

13. What term is used to refer to the people who make use of your agency's programs and services (consumers, clients, members, patients, customers, recipi-

ents)? How are they to be addressed (Mr., Mrs., or Ms.)? Is the use of first names permitted?

_____

_____

_____

14. Do you need to obtain an agency staff identification card, name badge, or keys? If so, how is this to be done?

_____

_____

_____

15. Is there a special support staff person assigned to work with you? If yes, what is his or her name?

_____

16. Are you permitted to send out a letter from the agency without prior approval or a countersignature? If no, who must approve or countersign your letters and reports?

_____

17. Are there personal safety concerns that you need to understand and keep in mind while in this agency, neighborhood, and community? (See Chapter 6 on Personal Safety.)

_____

_____

_____

_____

18. Are you permitted to make personal phone calls or send personal e-mail while in your practicum agency? What rules apply?

_____

_____

_____

Additional notes and comments:

_____

_____

_____

_____

_____

_____

SUGGESTED LEARNING ACTIVITIES

- Locate and read agency manuals that describe agency policy and procedures.
- Request opportunities to be introduced to agency staff. Write down their names and job titles so you will learn their names quickly.

ADDITIONAL SUGGESTIONS AND HINTS

- Maintain an up-to-date appointment book in which you enter the times and dates of all staff meetings, appointments, and other obligations.
- Carry a notebook in which you can record important information and instructions.
- Take a walk around the agency building. Locate the restrooms and potentially critical features such as emergency exits, fire alarms, and fire extinguishers.

SELECTED BIBLIOGRAPHY

Lauffer, Armand. *Working in Social Work.* Newbury Park, CA: Sage, 1987.

National Association of Social Workers. *Code of Ethics.* Washington, DC: NASW Press, 1997.

Rothman, Juliet. *Stepping Out into the Field: A Field Work Manual for Social Work Students.* Boston: Allyn and Bacon, 2000.

Weinbach, Robert. *The Social Worker as Manager.* 2nd ed. Boston: Allyn and Bacon, 1994.

5

USING SUPERVISION

Goals for Learning

- To understand the nature and purpose of supervision
- To understand the types of supervision, including individual, group, and peer supervision
- To utilize supervision for practicum learning and professional growth
- To understand the levels of supervision provided within your practicum agency
- To identify styles of supervision

The quality of your practicum is closely tied to the nature and quality of the teacher–student relationship you develop with your practicum instructor. Learning from a skilled and caring supervisor can enrich a practicum experience and provide a positive model of staff interaction.

Every supervisor or practicum instructor, like every student and every client, has both strengths and limitations. You will need to identify your practicum instructor's strengths and plan your practicum to take advantage of them.

BACKGROUND INFORMATION

In order to understand practicum supervision and how to make good use of it, it is necessary to examine the purpose and functions of supervision within an organization. Although the word *supervision* has its roots in a Latin word that means "to look over" or "to watch over," modern supervisory practice places less emphasis on being an overseer of work and more emphasis on the supervisor being a skilled master of the work to be done, a leader, and a teacher.

There are few jobs more challenging than that of a supervisor in a human services agency. It is a job that takes more sensitivity, skill, common sense, commitment, good humor, and intelligence than almost any other kind of work. These supervisors are mediators between the line-level social workers and the higher-level agency administrators. They frequently represent the agency in its interactions with other agencies and the community. In addition, they are often faced with the challenging tasks of responding to the complaints of clients who are dissatisfied with the agency's programs or with the performance of a social worker or other staff member.

Although being a supervisor can be demanding, it can also be a satisfying job, especially for those who understand and appreciate the teaching aspect of supervision. Watching a new social worker or social work student learn and develop on the job can be a rewarding experience. That is one reason why many busy agency supervisors volunteer to serve as practicum instructors to social work students.

Kadushin (1992) identifies three components of agency-based supervisory practice: the administrative function, the supportive function, and the educational function. The *administrative function* includes such responsibilities as recruiting, selecting, and orienting new staff; assigning and coordinating work; monitoring and evaluating staff performance; facilitating communication up and down the organization; advocating for staff; serving as a buffer between staff and administration; representing the agency to the public; and encouraging needed change within the agency.

The *educational function* is concerned with providing informal training and arranging for needed in-service staff training. Basically, the supervisor is responsible for making sure the workers know their job and how to do it.

The *supportive function* has to do with sustaining staff morale, cultivating a sense of teamwork, building commitment to the agency's goals and mission, encouraging workers by providing support, and dealing with work-related problems of conflict and frustration. This aspect of supervision is extremely important in human services agencies where stress and burnout are common problems. The supervisor must strive to create a work environment that is conducive to the provision of quality services to clients, while also supporting staff who may at times feel demoralized and unappreciated.

An agency-based practicum instructor, even when not officially an agency supervisor, will be concerned with these three functions as they relate to practicum students. He or she will pay attention to whether or not the student is performing the work of the agency in an appropriate manner and in keeping with agency policy and procedure. He or she will be sensitive to the student's fears and insecurities, and to the fact that the student has personal responsibilities in addition to those related to the practicum. He or she will want to do everything possible to facilitate the student's learning but, in the final analysis, his or her primary obligation must be to the agency's clients or consumers and to the agency that serves those clients.

A practicum student may receive supervision in a number of ways. These include:

- *Individual supervision*—regularly scheduled, one-to-one meetings between the practicum instructor and the student (e.g., one hour per week)
- *Group supervision*—regularly scheduled meetings between the practicum instructor and a small group of students
- *Peer supervision*—regularly scheduled meetings attended by a small group of social workers who assume responsibility for providing guidance and suggestions to each other and to the agency's practicum students
- *Formal case presentations*—regularly scheduled meetings at which one or more social workers (including students) describe their work on a specific case and invite advice and guidance on how it should be handled
- *Ad hoc supervision*—brief and unscheduled meetings with a practicum instructor to discuss a specific question or issue

A social worker who assumes the role of practicum instructor or field supervisor has special ethical obligations. According to Section 3.01 of the NASW *Code of Ethics* (1997), social workers who provide supervision:

- Should have the necessary knowledge and skill to supervise . . . appropriately and should do so only within their areas of knowledge and competence

- Are responsible for setting clear, appropriate, and culturally sensitive boundaries
- Should not engage in any dual or multiple relationships with a supervisee in which there is a risk of exploitation of or potential harm to the supervisee
- Should evaluate the supervisee's performance in a manner that is fair and respectful

Certain behaviors or patterns may prompt the school's faculty supervisor or practicum coordinator to reevaluate the suitability and appropriateness of using a particular practicum instructor. For example:

- The practicum instructor is seldom available to the student or often does not keep scheduled appointments with the student.
- The practicum instructor shows little interest in teaching and helping the student learn social work knowledge and skills.
- The practicum instructor's behavior or practice is discovered to be unethical.

Supervisors have a variety of styles or preferred ways of doing their job, which will affect the student's experiences in the agency. No one style or approach is necessarily more right or better than others. Different styles are more or less effective depending on the nature of the work to be done and the level of training and experience of those being supervised. Consider the following examples of differences among supervisors:

- Some focus mostly on the tasks necessary to get the job done, while others focus on the interactions or processes required to get it done.
- Some prefer to make decisions alone, while others prefer to involve many people in making decisions.
- Some make decisions quickly, while others take much time to do so.
- Some strive to obtain and retain authority and power, while others easily share power and try to empower others.
- Some are reluctant to share information with others unless they have a need to know, while others are eager to share information.
- Some prefer routines and clear procedures, so they will not be caught unprepared, while others prefer to keep things flexible and fluid and function well on an ad hoc basis.
- Some want decisions and agreements in writing, while others are comfortable with verbal agreements.
- Some pay great attention to the details of the work, while others prefer to deal with only the "big picture," leaving details to others.
- Some closely monitor the work of others, assuming that things can and will go wrong, while others assume "everything is OK" unless someone says there is a problem.
- Some work at a fast pace, while others are more relaxed, "laid back," and work at a slower pace.
- Some pay little attention to the personal needs, concerns, and problems of colleagues and those they supervise, while others pay close attention to such matters.
- Some are quick to delegate work to others, while others are hesitant and cautious about making new work assignments.
- Some emphasize organizing, planning, and directing the work assigned to those they supervise, while others assume that they will know what to do and can figure out how to do the work.

Food for Thought

If practitioners are to treat their clients with the deepest possible integrity, they must have a place to go where they can carefully and honestly examine their own behavior. That place, ideally, is the supervisory relationship. (Kaiser 1997, 7)

◆ ◆ ◆

Supervisors are apt to forget the steps they followed to deepen their own insights into the content. Ideas that have become obvious to them in their current practice may not be simple or obvious to their staffs. . . . Unless supervisors work at it, they can forget how they had to construct, element by element, their understanding of a complex construct such as contracting. They believe they can hand over the years of learning and are surprised to discover that a student or staff member is having great difficulty constructing even a simple version of the idea. . . . [Because they] have discovered some of the shortcuts, and are aware of some of the pitfalls, supervisors can guide their staff members and make their journey more certain and quicker, but they cannot take the journey for them. (Shulman 1993, 159)

◆ ◆ ◆

There is an inescapable element of authority in supervision. The student is accountable for his work to the supervisor; ultimately the supervisor will have a considerable say in whether the student passes or fails; and the student may feel all too dependent upon his supervisor for acquiring the knowledge and skill necessary to pass. All of this is difficult enough for any student; for the student with unresolved problems about authority, it can seriously impede learning. . . . The supervisor will have to call on his practical knowledge in helping the student with this problem, but he must remember he is a teacher not a therapist. . . . It is reasonable to try to help the student to see that he is impeding his own learning, and to expect him to try to do something about it. Even though he dislikes authority, the student still has the right to expect that his supervisor will set those limits that may prevent him from destroying his chances of learning. (Peters 1979, 121)

◆ ◆ ◆

Supervisors have experienced an increase in liability actions. . . . Court cases against supervisors have found them liable for the actions of supervisees who ordinarily are directly under their supervision. . . .

In the case of social work student interns, vicarious liability can be extended beyond the field instructor to agency administration, school or university administration, field staff, or anyone else involved in the decision to place the student in the internship. However, the field instructor or supervisor has the central responsibility to know the student's caseload and activities well enough to anticipate and prevent problems. This knowledge requires intensive involvement and close communication with students, a problem in a busy, under-resourced agency. Therefore, social workers should not accept student interns if they lack the time and resources to supervise them correctly.
(Houston-Vega et al. 1997, 139–140)

GUIDANCE AND DIRECTION

Learning to use supervision is of central importance to the practicum student. Because social work is challenging and stressful, and also because your work directly affects clients' lives, you will need guidance, direction, support, and feedback from your practicum instructor.

Strive to use supervision in a purposeful and responsible manner. We recommend a regular supervisory meeting time each week, since this will help you avoid the difficulties of constantly having to arrange a suitable meeting time. Prepare for each meeting. Do not expect your practicum instructor to do all of the talking. Bring questions, observations, and requests for input and feedback to the meeting. Use this time to examine your performance and explore new ideas.

Your practicum instructor will have expectations of you and it will be important for you to understand these expectations. In general, you will be expected to exhibit:

- Dependability and follow-through on assigned work
- Attention to detail and proper procedures

- Initiative in work-related assignments
- A cooperative attitude toward the practicum instructor and other staff
- Willingness to learn from whatever tasks are assigned
- Openness to supervision, including asking for, and learning from, constructive criticism
- Willingness to seek help when needed

Expect your practicum instructor to ask some very pointed questions in order to learn about and monitor your work in the agency, help you analyze your performance, understand why an intervention was successful or not, and develop your critical thinking skills. Possible supervisory questions include the following:

- What specific problem, concern, or issue were you attempting to address?
- What were your goals and objectives?
- What were you trying to accomplish?
- What information did you gather?
- What meaning did you assign to this information?
- Why did you choose that specific intervention?
- What ethical and legal concerns affected your decision?
- Was the intervention successful?
- How do you know the intervention was or was not successful?
- What other interventions might have worked better?
- What did you learn from this experience?
- What would you do differently next time?
- What needs to be done next?

You may be anxious because your practicum instructor will be evaluating your performance. Indeed, that is his or her responsibility. He or she has been asked by your school to guide your learning and offer constructive criticism in order that you might learn about yourself and develop your knowledge and skills.

Your practicum instructor should evaluate your performance in an ongoing and continuous manner. You should receive feedback and constructive criticism during all phases of your practicum. If this is not happening, discuss the matter with your practicum instructor and ask for an ongoing critique of your performance.

Your practicum instructor is responsible for conducting a comprehensive evaluation of your learning and performance at the end of the academic term, and this will likely translate into a final grade in your practicum. You can expect that this evaluation will be based on:

- Direct observation of your work by your practicum instructor or other social workers in the agency
- Your verbal descriptions of what you are doing and learning
- Your written documentation, reports, and case notes
- Feedback received from clients regarding your work
- Observations and input from social workers in the community who have worked with you

As you begin your practicum and take on new responsibilities, you may be afraid of making a serious mistake or in some way hurting your clients. Such worries are to be expected. In fact, your practicum instructor will become concerned if you do not have these worries. Do not hesitate to express your fears. Your practicum instructor may be able to help you with these issues.

Supervision is an interactional process that parallels in many ways the social worker–client relationship and the helping process (Shulman, 1993). In order to help you describe your performance—what you did and why you did it—your practicum instructor will employ many of the helping skills and techniques that you and other social workers use in working with clients. However, supervision is not therapy. If the supervision you receive feels too much like therapy, consult with your faculty supervisor.

Practicum instructors use a variety of techniques to help students examine and process their experiences and deepen their learning. For example, your practicum instructor may use didactic instruction (lecture or presentation), role play and behavioral rehearsal, demonstration or modeling, and case consultation. Do not feel threatened or "put on the spot" by these teaching techniques. View them as valuable learning opportunities.

You will move through several stages during your practicum experience. We identify three stages: orientation, exploration and skill building, and beginning competency. Your practicum instructor will provide specific types of help at each stage.

When you begin your practicum, you are in what we call an *orientation stage*. At this stage, you may feel anxious, overwhelmed, unsure, and incompetent. It is your practicum instructor's job to provide orientation and training so that you know what the agency is all about and what is expected of you. He or she will offer guidance, provide encouragement, help you select learning activities that build skills, and help you develop confidence so you are willing to take on additional tasks and responsibilities.

After becoming familiar and comfortable with your practicum setting and what is expected, you enter the *exploration and skill building stage.* During this stage, you will gain knowledge, skills, and confidence as you participate in various interventions and projects and take on added responsibilities. You will feel less anxious than when you first began the practicum and although you will still make mistakes, you can analyze them and learn from them. Your practicum instructor will help you to build on prior experiences, become comfortable taking risks and working with more difficult and challenging situations. He or she will help you learn general principles of practice, as well as the theory underlying interventions. You will be able to function more independently at this stage.

As the end of the practicum approaches, you will enter the *beginning competency stage.* At this stage, you will have developed a variety of skills and acquired considerable knowledge about your agency, its clients, and its specific programs and approaches. You will have identified your strengths, your limitations, and your interests. Your practicum instructor will reinforce your successes, encourage you to refine your skills, and expect you to work with an even wider variety of clients and projects. You will be encouraged to examine how the work of the agency addresses community needs and fits into the social welfare system.

Some students begin the practicum with the hope that their practicum instructor will become a true mentor. When this happens, it is a great experience for a practicum student. However, this may not be feasible. When seeking a mentor, you may need to look to persons outside your practicum agency.

Conflicts may arise in the supervisory relationship. For example, you may feel that your practicum instructor does not devote enough time to you and your learning needs. Or you may feel that your practicum instructor is either too controlling or not structured enough. The two of you may have very different personalities. Perhaps you and your practicum instructor differ in terms of gender, race, ethnic background, or age and this somehow affects your relationship. Whatever the conflict, talk about it. Do not avoid the problem. You will be expected to find ways to deal with these issues. If the problem cannot be worked out with your practicum instructor, consult with your faculty supervisor.

We caution you on developing a dual relationship with your practicum instructor. He or she is to be a supervisor, not a friend or a counselor. If personal problems arise during your practicum, do not ask or expect your practicum instructor to provide counseling. If you need such services, arrange to receive them in another way.

The sexual harassment of a student by a practicum instructor is a very serious matter that should be immediately reported to the student's faculty supervisor or practicum coordinator. An allegation of sexual harassment is a messy and complex legal concern. Should this problem arise in your practicum, immediately seek consultation on how to proceed.

If you observe that your practicum instructor violates the NASW *Code of Ethics,* consult with your school's practicum coordinator or your faculty supervisor.

USING SUPERVISION FOR LEARNING: A WORKBOOK ACTIVITY

1. Is your practicum instructor also an agency supervisor of other social workers or agency staff?

_____

If yes, whom does he or she supervise?

_____

_____

_____

_____

2. Who supervises your practicum instructor?

_____

3. Has your practicum instructor previously supervised practicum students?

_____

If yes, about how many students?

_____

4. Has your practicum instructor received special training on the process of staff supervision?

_____

If yes, what was the nature of this training?

_____

_____

_____

_____

5. Has your practicum instructor attended training on practicum supervision and instruction provided by your school's practicum program?

_____

If yes, what was the nature of this training?

_____

_____

_____

_____

6. In what areas do you want and welcome feedback from your practicum instructor regarding your performance?

_____

_____

_____

_____

7. In what areas of performance are you overly sensitive or fearful about receiving feedback from your practicum instructor?

_____

_____

_____

_____

8. What might these feelings be telling you?

_____

_____

_____

_____

9. Do you withhold or hide certain information about your life experience or your performance in the practicum from your practicum instructor?

_____

If yes, why? What are you afraid of? Are these fears realistic? Might the withholding of this information become a barrier to further learning?

_____

_____

_____

_____

10. It has been said that people often avoid the experiences they need most in order to learn and grow personally. What practicum-related experiences are you avoiding?

_____

_____

_____

_____

11. What specific types of knowledge and skills can you learn from your practicum instructor? Is your practicum instructor known to possess some special knowledge and skills? Has your practicum instructor had uncommon practice experiences or special training?

_____

_____

_____

_____

12. What knowledge or skills do you seek that your practicum instructor is unable to teach you?

_____

_____

_____

_____

13. Who else besides your practicum instructor could meet your learning needs in those areas of knowledge and skill (e.g., other professionals in your agency, faculty, other students)?

_____

_____

_____

14. In what ways does your practicum instructor provide an atmosphere and environment conducive to learning? If this learning atmosphere is not what you desire, what can you do to change it?

_____

_____

_____

_____

15. What teaching techniques does your practicum instructor use (lecture, presentation, demonstration, case consultation, role playing, or direct observation)?

_____

_____

_____

_____

16. Has your practicum instructor pointed out any personal problems or biases which are affecting your work? If so, what are they?

_____

_____

_____

_____

17. How can you make sure these problems or biases do not negatively affect your work or your clients?

_____

_____

_____

_____

18. Which of the following specific types of activities and experiences help you learn most quickly and easily? Which work best for you?

_____ Discussing the pros and cons of your decisions and actions with your supervisor *before* you have met with your client.

_____ Discussing the pros and cons of possible decisions and actions with your supervisor *after* you have met with your client.

_____ Discussing how your actions and decisions fit with a particular conceptual framework, theory, model, or perspective.

_____ Using role play and simulations to rehearse the techniques, skills, or approaches you want to learn.

_____ Observing others performing the skill or technique you wish to learn.

_____ Brainstorming various ways in which a situation might be handled.

_____ Watching a video or listening to an audiotape of an experienced worker's session with a client.

_____ Reading and discussing an article related to the skills you wish to learn.

_____ Reviewing and discussing the case notes and the written record of others' work with their clients.

_____ Keeping a journal of your thoughts, feelings, and observations related to your performance.

19. How can you work with your practicum instructor in order to have as many of these learning experiences as possible?

_____

_____

_____

_____

Additional notes and comments:

_____

_____

_____

_____

_____

_____

_____

SUGGESTED LEARNING ACTIVITIES

- Attend any group or peer supervisory sessions offered in your agency in order to learn about the various modes of providing and receiving supervision.
- Present a case you are working on at a peer supervisory session, asking for input from other social workers besides your practicum instructor.
- If appropriate and feasible, work with a variety of social workers, supervisors, and managers in your agency so that you can observe differing supervisory styles.
- Ask your practicum instructor how your agency provides support to its employees, such as through an employee assistance program or continuing education.
- Read your university practicum manual so that you understand what is expected of both your faculty supervisor and your practicum instructor.

ADDITIONAL SUGGESTIONS AND HINTS

- In Sheafor, Horejsi, and Horejsi (2000), read the sections on "Using Agency Supervision" and "Developing Self Awareness."

SELECTED BIBLIOGRAPHY

Baird, Brian N. *The Internship, Practicum, and Field Placement Handbook: A Guide for the Helping Professions.* Upper Saddle River, NJ: Prentice-Hall, 1996.

Ellison, Martha L. "Critical Field Instructor Behaviors: Student and Field Instructor Views." *Arete, Journal of the College of Social Work at the University of South Carolina* 18.2 (Winter 1994): 12–21.

Houston-Vega, Mary Kay, Elane Nuehring, and Elisabeth Daguio. *Prudent Practice: A Guide for Managing Malpractice Risk.* Washington, DC: NASW Press, 1997.

Kadushin, Alfred. *Supervision in Social Work.* New York: Columbia University Press, 1992.

Kaiser, Tamara. *Supervisory Relationship: Exploring the Human Element.* Boston: Brooks/Cole, 1997.

National Association of Social Workers. *Code of Ethics.* Washington, DC: NASW Press, 1997.

Peters, Dorothy. *Staff and Student Supervision: A Task Centered Approach.* London: Allen and Unwin, 1979.

Sheafor, Bradford, Charles Horejsi, and Gloria Horejsi. *Techniques and Guidelines in Social Work Practice.* 5th ed. Boston: Allyn and Bacon, 2000.

Shulman, Lawrence. *Interactional Social Work Practice: Toward an Empirical Theory.* Itasca, IL: F. E. Peacock, 1991.

Shulman, Lawrence. *Interactional Supervision.* Washington, DC: NASW Press, 1993.

6

PERSONAL SAFETY

Goals for Learning

- To identify the sources and types of danger most often encountered in social work practice
- To become familiar with agency policies and procedures that can reduce risk and protect staff and clients
- To become familiar with precautions and preventive actions that can reduce the risk of being harmed
- To become familiar with steps and actions that can de-escalate an already dangerous situation and protect a social worker in such a situation

Although social workers see themselves as helpers and expect most clients to be cooperative, at times they find themselves in situations where they must deal with clients who are angry, volatile, and threatening. Accounts of violence toward social workers are increasing, due to client frustration with human service systems, increased levels of crime and violence in society, and antiauthority or antigovernment attitudes.

Exposure to job-related danger can lead to worker anxiety, low morale, burnout, family stress, and high staff turnover. Social work practicum students must be cognizant of the dangers they face. They will need to exercise certain precautions so as to reduce risks to their own safety. Moreover, they must know what steps to take when they encounter a dangerous situation. This chapter will address these concerns.

BACKGROUND INFORMATION

Broadly speaking, the potential sources of harm to a social worker include the following:

- Clients who are angry and feel mistreated by the agency and its staff
- Persons who are not clients, but who are acquainted with or related to clients and are aware that the clients feel mistreated by the agency and its staff
- Clients who present a special threat because of alcohol or drug use, a pattern of violent behavior, antiauthority attitudes, or unstable mental condition
- Persons with criminal intent and inclination who are to be found in neighborhoods near the agency or in areas where the social worker travels and works. These individuals are not clients, nor do they have a relationship with the workers' clients

- Biohazardous and toxic materials that may be encountered in hospitals and other health care facilities and during visits to clients in their homes

Certain practice settings present more risk to social workers than others. Such settings include child protective agencies, programs in prisons, forensic units of psychiatric hospitals, shelters for the homeless, and residential facilities for youth who are especially aggressive and impulsive. These settings are inherently dangerous because many of those served have tendencies toward the use of violence. However, any practice setting can be threatening, because client–worker interactions often involve emotionally charged situations and concerns. Even clients with no previous history of violence or high risk behaviors can, under certain circumstances, pose a threat to social workers.

Individuals with mental illnesses are not inherently more dangerous than persons who do not suffer from such impairments. However, a small percentage of those with certain symptoms are a potential threat. Included in this group are persons who hear voices commanding them to harm others, and those who hold bizarre, fanatical, or paranoid beliefs or delusions, and who as a result feel especially threatened by social workers.

Certain social work practices and interventions have a greater likelihood of placing the worker at risk. Such activities include the initial investigation of child abuse allegations, the involuntary removal of a child from a parent's home, providing protection to a victim of domestic violence, outreach to youth involved

---

Food for Thought

Daily interaction with those who are asked to reveal their private lives, discuss sensitive family matters, and even have their children removed from their custody, produces the potential for violence, running the gamut from verbal abuse to physical assault. Agencies which ignore worker safety issues, or accept them as a normal part of the job, imperil both their staff and the families they serve. Staff who ignore their own gut feeling about personal risk and fail to take defensive precautions are not dealing realistically with danger. (Farestad 1997, 2)

◆◆◆

Human services workers are at risk for a number of reasons. When serving clients with high levels of frustration, coupled with desperate needs, hopelessness, and an inability to cope with the problems in their lives, risk is ever present. A client's perception that you are unable or unwilling to help them could make you a target for a tremendous unleashing of anger, frustration, and violence. Home visits, child protective issues, and transporting clients are all powder-keg scenarios that need only a small spark to set off a chain reaction that could put your life or safety in imminent danger.

Even office visits can be high risk without a safety net, [that includes] . . . policies and procedures that address risk management, proper office layout, escape routes, and personal safety training.

One major potential obstacle in assessing danger is the strong commitment toward helping others. This desire may lead to overlooking or dismissing the danger signs and failing to recognize that some people do not want to be helped. . . . With no weapon, no power of arrest, no bulletproof vest, and generally no backup, . . . [social workers] go into battle armed with only a genuine concern for their fellow human beings and a mission. (Harman and Davis 1997, 15)

◆◆◆

Owing to the nature of their practicum placements, most students enter practicum agencies with limited background and skills to deal with difficult circumstances and have virtually no training in dealing with violence. . . . Without experience and training, students may be unable to manage or contain potentially dangerous situations with clients. . . . Although students may experience violence within their practicum sites, the occurrences may go unreported. Because students are evaluated on their performance in their field practicum, they may be unlikely to report their experiences for fear of receiving a negative grade. (Tully, Kroph, and Price 1993, 191–192)

◆◆◆

Violence is the language of the unheard.
                                                    —*Martin Luther King, Jr.*

in gangs, treatment of aggressive youth, intervention with drug- and alcohol-involved clients, the transporting of clients who do not wish to be moved, the behavioral management of persons with certain forms of brain injury or mental retardation, and the monitoring of clients in correctional settings.

In their work with clients who are potentially dangerous, social workers face the difficult challenge of remaining humane, open, and accepting of clients while also being alert to the possibility of attack. It is important not to expect every client to be a threat, but to recognize a client who might be.

Social workers who routinely or frequently face verbal abuse from clients may become complacent. They may come to view verbal threats as "part of the territory," mistakenly assuming that the clients are bluffing and consequently fail to take reasonable precautions. Some social workers mistakenly assume that because they have been trained in basic helping skills, they will be able to talk their way out of a dangerous situation. These overly confident workers tend to minimize the risk and erroneously conclude that they do not need special training in how to respond in truly dangerous situations.

Practicum students in hospitals or other health care settings should be alert to the existence of biological hazards and receive instruction on how to protect themselves against infectious diseases and how to avoid or properly handle biohazardous materials such as used tissues, clothing, bed sheets, or pillows that have been stained with body fluids. In some instances, students will need to wear a mask and gloves when interviewing a patient. In some cases this will be done to protect themselves from disease and in other cases to protect a vulnerable patient.

GUIDANCE AND DIRECTION

Most dangerous interpersonal situations are the result of tensions that have grown and intensified over time. It is vital to understand the phases of escalation, the person's needs and feelings during each phase, and what actions or interventions by the social worker might reduce the tension and level of risk. It is preferable to intervene as early as possible in order to prevent escalation and eventual loss of control by the angry person. Irwin (1997, 89) describes four stages of crisis management and suggests approaches to use at each stage to reduce the likelihood of violence. Consider these principles and employ these approaches should you feel threatened by the behavior of a client or another person.

Stage 1: Initial Tension and Frustration
At this stage, the individuals who may become violent are anxious and experiencing high levels of emotion, especially anger, but are still rational and in control of their behavior. They are not yet acting on their feelings, so they will respond best to an approach that helps them vent emotions, reflect on the situation, and devise a solution on their own. The worker's use of active listening will help these individuals express and examine their feelings and usually reduce the level of tension. The use of basic listening skills also helps the worker build rapport and assess the severity of the crisis and the danger it presents.

Stage 2: Verbal Attack
During this second stage, the individuals are feeling threatened and vulnerable. They become very defensive and go on the offensive with verbal attacks. Irrational thoughts and strong feelings begin to override their self-control. They may direct their anger toward the worker, using verbal abuse and intimidation. Verbal communication with them becomes more difficult and further escalation is likely.

Effective threat-reducing approaches by the worker include the display of calm body language, using a nonthreatening tone of voice, reflecting clients' feelings and behaviors, and setting limits on what behavior is allowable. The worker should calmly validate the feelings being expressed and provide clear guidelines, choices, and alternatives if possible.

Stage 3: Loss of Control

Individuals at this stage have lost control of their behavior. They have physically struck, or are very close to striking others. They pose a real danger. Workers need to immediately assess the level of danger and their ability to provide control; they should be preparing to escape, if necessary. Because most clients will fear their own loss of control, workers are more likely to gain control of the situation if they can empathize with the clients' fear about doing something they will regret. Workers must remain calm and continue to build rapport, while shifting focus to the threatening behavior. The out-of-control person must be controlled, either by the worker or by legal authorities.

Stage 4: Recovery after the Outburst

At this stage, the crisis has peaked and imminent danger has passed. Individuals struggle to regain their composure and, having fallen apart, need help in putting themselves back together. To help them recover, workers should allow them to further vent their anger, explain their feelings, and come to some closure regarding the incident. Allowing people to stabilize themselves decreases the risk of re-escalation. At this stage, people may gain insight, allow mutual problem solving with the worker, and plan ways to prevent another such incident in the future.

Dealing with the Potentially Violent Client

- Remember that past behavior is the best single predictor of future behavior. Before meeting with a client that you do not know and who may be dangerous, consult agency records or the local police in search of information that may help you assess the risk.
- Be very cautious when dealing with a person who is under the influence of alcohol or drugs, even when you know the person fairly well. A person under the influence of chemicals should be viewed as inherently unpredictable.
- Be cautious when around persons who may be involved in illegal activities and may, therefore, feel threatened by your presence or by what you have seen. They may be willing to harm you in order to protect themselves from discovery by police.
- Remove all potential weapons from your office when dealing with a potentially dangerous client, including scissors, staplers, paperweights, and other small but heavy objects.
- Leave your office door partly open during an interview with a potentially dangerous client.
- Notify others if you are planning to meet a potentially dangerous client in your office and arrange for a way to signal for help. Arrange your office so that you are closest to the door. Place a desk or other barrier between you and the dangerous client.
- Avoid meeting with clients when you are alone in the office. If you must have the meeting, turn lights on in other offices and lead clients to believe that others will be coming into the office.
- Remember that worker attitudes play a role in either controlling or provoking threatening behavior. Maintain a positive, nonjudgmental attitude toward clients.

- Recognize that both increased structure and decreased stimuli may help clients to remain calm and gain self control.
- Remember that clients use threats and violence when other forms of communication fail them, so utilize skills that facilitate communication and help clients to express themselves in words.
- Address the person by name. Do not argue with or criticize an angry person. Avoid doing anything that might be perceived as ridiculing or embarrassing the person.
- Trust your instincts. Assume that you have a built-in unconscious mechanism that can recognize danger more quickly than your rational thought processes. If you feel afraid, assume that you are in danger, even if you cannot clearly identify why you feel this way.
- Remember that an attack by a client is almost always the reaction of someone who is afraid and feeling threatened. Thus, strive to speak and act in ways that lessen the client's need to be afraid of you. Demonstrate empathy and that you understand the reason behind their anger and fear.
- Avoid standing above others. If possible and safe, take a sitting position. Standing is more authoritarian and threatening than sitting.
- Attacks by clients are most likely when they feel trapped or controlled, either psychologically or physically. To the extent possible, give clients options and choices. Your location in a room should be one that allows the client to escape without having to come close to you.
- Be alert to signs of an imminent attack such as rapid breathing, teeth grinding, dilated pupils, flaring nostrils, choppy speech, clenched fists, and bobbing and dipping movements of the body.
- Allow angry persons to vent their feelings. Most angry persons will begin to calm down after two or three minutes of venting or name calling. While this is going on, it is usually best to listen respectfully and allow them to express their feelings. However, some people are stimulated by their own words and grow even more angry because of what they are saying. If that occurs, the level of risk is increasing.
- Do not touch an angry person, especially if they may be under the influence of a drug. Do not move into their personal space. Remain at least four feet away from the person.
- An angry or dangerous person is more likely to attack someone who appears weak, insecure, and unsure. Therefore, present yourself as calm, composed, and self-confident, but not haughty.
- If an individual threatens you with a gun or other weapon, assure him or her that you intend no harm and slowly back away. Do not attempt to disarm the person. Leave that to the police, who have special training.

Handling the Dangers of a Home Visit

- Do not enter a situation that could be dangerous without first consulting with others and formulating a plan to reduce risk. Do not hesitate to seek the assistance of others, including other workers or the police.
- When visiting clients in their homes, keep your agency informed of your plans and itinerary and check in by phone on a prearranged schedule. When away from the office, carry a means of calling for help (e.g., cellular phone, push-button emergency signals, or radio).
- Assign two staff members for potentially dangerous home visits whenever possible.
- Do not enter a home or apartment building until you have taken a few minutes to determine its level of danger. Listen for sounds of violence or out-of-

control behavior. Consider whether other people are nearby and if they would respond to a call for help. Identify possible escape routes.

- Be aware that guns are most often kept in a bedroom and that a kitchen contains knives and other potential weapons. Leave immediately if a threatening person appears to be moving toward a weapon.
- Do not sit in an overstuffed chair or couch from which you cannot quickly get to your feet. Select a hard and movable chair. If necessary, it can be used as a shield.
- Keep your vehicle in good running order and full of gasoline so that you will not find yourself stranded in a dangerous or isolated area.
- If you are being followed, go immediately to a police or fire station or to a public place. Do not go to your home if you believe someone is following you or watching your movements.
- If you are likely to encounter dangerous situations while at work (or while walking to work), wear shoes and clothing that permit running. Avoid wearing long earrings or jewelry that could easily be grabbed and twisted to inflict pain and prevent your escape.

Handling an Intense Argument between Two or More People

- When two or more individuals are in a heated argument and you need to intervene, begin by gaining their attention. Anything short of physical force may be used. A shrill whistle, a loud clap, a loud voice, a silly request, (e.g., "I need a glass of water") or other attention-getting devices may be used for this purpose.
- Ask those in conflict to sit down. If they will not sit, remain standing also.
- Separate the disputants as necessary. Bring them back together only after they have quieted down and gained self-control.
- If possible, always intervene in a crisis situation with a partner.

Agency Procedure and the Dangerous Client

- The agency's record-keeping system should use color codes or other markings that identify individuals or households that have a history of violence.
- The agency should maintain a log of all threats of violence so staff can identify those individuals and situations that present a special risk.
- The agency should institute security measures within the agency. This might include the installation of a call-for-help button in each office space and establishing telephone code words that are requests for police assistance.
- The agency should develop policy and protocols on how staff are to respond to dangerous situations, such as bomb threats or hostage taking. These procedures should be rehearsed regularly.
- The agency should develop a protocol about when and how to use police assistance. The agency should have a written agreement with local law enforcement officials.
- The agency should file criminal charges against those who harm or threaten physical injury to either the worker or the worker's family.
- When a worker is harmed, the agency should respond with appropriate counseling and emotional support to lessen the effects on the worker and the worker's family.
- The agency should designate a specific office or room for meetings with potentially violent clients. This room should be one that is easily observed by others nearby.

- The agency should keep waiting rooms and offices clean and strive to create a pleasant and inviting physical environment. Rooms that are dirty, unpleasant, or unkempt convey disrespect to clients and tend to generate hostility.
- The agency should post in waiting rooms and in other prominent places a statement explaining that alcohol, drugs, and weapons are not allowed in the building and that threats and violence or the possession of a weapon will prompt an immediate call to the police.
- The agency should make sure that the exterior of the agency's building and its parking lot are well lighted.
- The agency should provide training on personal safety and related agency procedures to staff and students and repeat or update this training on a regular basis.

REDUCING THE RISK OF HARM: A WORKBOOK ACTIVITY

1. Have any employees in your practicum agency been threatened or harmed by clients or consumers? If yes, describe the circumstances that gave rise to the incident.

   _____

   _____

   _____

   _____

   _____

2. What precautions, if any, might have prevented the above incidents or reduced their seriousness?

   _____

   _____

   _____

   _____

   _____

3. Have any employees in your practicum agency been threatened or harmed while traveling to or from the agency or while near the agency? If yes, what precautions might have prevented the incident or reduced its seriousness?

   _____

   _____

   _____

   _____

4. What agency policies and procedures are designed to ensure personal safety and reduce risk to agency employees and clients?

   _____

   _____

   _____

   _____

   _____

5. What training is provided in your agency to help workers prevent and deal with threatening or violent clients or situations?

_____

_____

_____

_____

6. Do agency workers carry defensive devices such as mace or pepper spray? What are the pros and cons of doing so?

_____

_____

_____

_____

7. What do the experienced workers in your agency describe as the most dangerous situations you are likely to encounter during your practicum?

_____

_____

_____

8. What high-risk clients or situations are you likely to encounter in your practicum? How will you prepare yourself to deal with them?

_____

_____

_____

_____

9. Given the area served by your agency, what specific locations or neighborhoods are known to be especially dangerous?

_____

_____

_____

10. What services does your agency provide to workers who are threatened, injured, or traumatized by threats or violence (e.g., counseling, critical incident stress debriefing, or support groups)?

_____

_____

_____

11. Does your agency have an incident reporting system for documenting threats and violence toward workers?

12. Does your agency have a formal, written agreement with the police about when they are to be called?

13. Are there any clients or situations that frighten you? If so, how can you deal with your fears?

14. If your practicum is in a hospital or health care setting, what precautions are you to take in order to protect yourself and your vulnerable clients from infectious diseases or biohazards?

Additional notes and comments:

SUGGESTED LEARNING ACTIVITIES

- Invite a local police officer to offer guidance on how to reduce risk in and around your agency.
- Interview experienced social workers and get their advice on how to reduce personal risk.

ADDITIONAL SUGGESTIONS AND HINTS

- In Sheafor, Horejsi, and Horejsi (2000), read the section on "The Dangerous Client."

SELECTED BIBLIOGRAPHY

Farestad, Karen. "Worker Safety: Agencies Should Recognize the Issue." *Protecting Children* 13.1 (1997): 2.

Harman, Patricia, and Molly Davis. "Personal Safety for Human Service Professionals: A Law Enforcement Perspective." *Protecting Children* 13.1 (1997): 15–17.

Horejsi, Charles, Cindy Garthwait, and Jim Rolando. "A Survey of Threats and Violence Directed against Child Protection Workers in a Rural State." *Child Welfare* (March, 1994): 173–179.

Irwin, Diane. "Safety Training for Human Services Professionals." *Protecting Children* 13.1 (1997): 8–10.

Rey, Lucy. "What Social Workers Need to Know about Client Violence." *Families in Society* 77 (January, 1996): 33–39.

Sheafor, Bradford, Charles Horejsi, and Gloria Horejsi. *Techniques and Guidelines for Social Work Practice.* 5th ed. Boston: Allyn and Bacon, 2000.

Tully, Carol, Nancy Kropf, and Janet Price. "Is the Field a Hard Hat Area? A Study of Violence in Field Placements." *Journal of Social Work Education* 29.2 (Spring, 1993): 191–199.

7

COMMUNICATION

Goals for Learning

- To identify the communication methods utilized by your agency
- To become aware of skills and guidelines that can improve verbal and written communication
- To identify common sources and occasions of miscommunication and misunderstanding
- To identify barriers to effective communication

Communication is at the heart of social work practice. A social worker must be able to communicate with clients or consumers, other social workers, members of other professions (such as physicians, teachers, lawyers, and judges), agency supervisors and administrators, leaders and decision makers (such as elected officials), and with a cross section of the people who make up the community served by the agency. The social worker must be able to communicate in a one-on-one situation, within the context of a small group, and sometimes before a large audience. Moreover, the worker must be able to use several modes of communication effectively, including the written word, the spoken word, and nonverbal communication. A social worker must also be able to use a variety of communication tools effectively, including a telephone, a computer, and an e-mail system.

Students are often surprised at how much time social workers must devote to reading and writing. Written communication may take the form of a letter, memo, case record, the minutes of a committee meeting, a lengthy formal report, or a grant proposal. The extensive use of written communication in social work requires that the worker be able to write well and read rapidly.

A variety of problems can result from insufficient, inaccurate, or somehow distorted and misunderstood communication. Even during the practicum, many of the problems that frustrate the student are fundamentally problems in the communication between the student and the practicum instructor or between the student and the practicum coordinator. This chapter is designed to assist students in developing essential communication skills.

BACKGROUND INFORMATION

Communication can be defined as the process by which a person, group, or organization (the sender) transmits information (the message) to some other person, group, or organization (the receiver). The practicum student will be involved in two types of communication, interpersonal and organizational.

Interpersonal communication refers to communication that involves talking, listening, and responding in ways that place an emphasis on the personal dimensions of those involved. It usually takes place in a face-to-face exchange but may occur on the telephone or in highly personalized correspondence or e-mail. Providing direct services to clients requires frequent and fairly intense interpersonal communication.

The term *organizational communication* refers to the somewhat impersonal exchange of messages and information between the various levels, departments, and divisions of an organization, and also between the organization and various individuals and groups outside the organization. Because most social work practicum students have completed course work related to the skills of interpersonal communication utilized during the helping interview and basic counseling, this chapter will focus mostly on organizational communication.

As compared to other types of communication, the communication within an organization tends to be more formal and more often in written form. Moreover, the nature and flow of information within an organization is strongly influenced by lines of authority and the chain of command.

Downward communication consists of directions and instructions from those higher in the chain of command to subordinates at lower levels in the organization. The term *upward communication* refers to communication from a subordinate to those higher in the chain of command, such as when a supervisor sends a message to the agency's executive director. As a general rule, upward communication occurs less often than downward communication. This can be a source of problems within an organization. *Horizontal communication* refers to the exchange of messages among persons or units at the same level within the organization.

A wide variety of communication networks exists within human service agencies. Mainly, they differ in the degree to which they are centralized. In a highly centralized network, all messages must flow through some central office or person who can then control what information moves up or down. A decentralized network is characterized by an exchange of information between people and organizational levels without first passing through a particular channel or central point. As a general rule, centralized networks are faster and more accurate if the information has to do with relatively simple tasks. Decentralized networks are faster and more accurate if the communication is about complex tasks and unique activities. This type of communication network may also be more informal and feel more personal to those within an organization.

A common problem within organizations is *information overload*. This refers to frustration and miscommunication caused by an overwhelming volume of messages, instructions, and reports. A centralized communication network and highly bureaucratic organizations are especially vulnerable to information overload because so many messages must pass through all levels as they move up and down the organization.

Modern communication technology (e-mail, fax machines, cellular phones) has solved some problems caused by slow communication, but it has created others. It has probably added to the problem of information overload because it is now very easy to send a message and copies of it to many more people. E-mail encourages the use of written communication over face-to-face and phone communication, thus eliminating the opportunity to observe nonverbal communication in order to accurately interpret a message.

Professions and organizations develop a specialized language, or jargon, as a way to simplify communication. However, this has the effect of making many of their messages unintelligible to outsiders, including students and clients.

The goal of communication is for the receiver to accurately understand the message being sent by the sender. That sounds like a simple process, but as everyone knows, communication is complex and many factors can prevent or disrupt the process. Sheafor, Horejsi, and Horejsi (2000, 143) observe that communication problems develop whenever:

- We speak for others rather than let them speak for themselves.
- We let our prejudices and stereotypes affect what we hear and say.
- We do not take the time to listen to, and understand, what the other person is trying to say.
- We keep things to ourselves because we think others will disapprove of what we believe and feel.
- We make no attempt to communicate because we assume others already know, or should know, how we feel and what we think.
- We discourage or suppress communication by ordering, threatening, preaching, judging, blaming, or humoring.
- Negative feelings about ourselves (low self-esteem) cause us to conclude that we have nothing to say and that no one wants to listen to us.

These impediments to communication can occur at the organizational level as well as at the interpersonal level. Practicum students may erroneously assume that because they are trained to use interviewing and counseling skills, they will be able to easily communicate at the organizational level. However, organizational communication has its own set of unique challenges and requires as much practice and special skill as communication with clients.

The existence of trust between the sender and the receiver is a critical prerequisite to effective communication. To a large degree, it determines how the receiver will respond to the sender's message. There are three major barriers to the development of trust: insincerity (e.g., when managers ask for feedback from staff but do not value or listen to their opinions), time pressures (e.g., when the push to accomplish a task precludes a supervisor from hearing what the workers are saying), and defensiveness (e.g., when the manager's ego is threatened by an open discussion of agency operations).

A variety of factors can become barriers to effective communication. For example, in verbal communication the sender may speak too fast or too slow, or the receiver is distracted and does not listen. The sender may write or speak without first planning his or her message. The sender may use words that the receiver does not understand or words that mean different things to different people without clarifying how he or she defines the words.

Defensiveness and fear are major barriers to communication. When people are in an environment in which they feel safe, accepted, and supported, they concentrate more on the content and meaning of the message, rather than spending time protecting themselves or searching for the sender's hidden agenda. Behaviors that tend to lower defenses include messages that give facts without value judgments, are spontaneous and genuine, offer mutual trust and respect, and display a willingness to consider different points of view.

Physical or environmental factors can interfere with communication. Examples include background noise, too much distance between sender and receiver, physical crowding that interferes with privacy, rooms with poor acoustics, uncomfortable room temperatures, and uncomfortable chairs that make paying attention difficult.

The factors of dress, grooming, and image have a significant impact on communication—a fact well known to business people and public figures. Agencies may establish a dress code as a way of improving communication with certain people and groups in the community.

Food for Thought

Communication in normal social interaction is a means by which individuals express feelings and develop relationships. In organizational life, such communication is stripped of its emotional significance. Communication becomes one-way and top-down. Language becomes a matter of technical jargon, a secretive way of maintaining control and organizational channels. Meaning is transformed into the context of organizational understandings and not human communication.

Social workers, however, prize the importance of two-way communication and are trained in the use of active listening, perception checking, paraphrasing, and giving feedback. Social workers who value interpersonal communication skills, such as the ability to express feelings and emotions, attending, genuineness, respect, and mutuality, often become confused when those skills are ignored in organizational communication. In many cases, mutuality in communication is actually precluded and is seen as dysfunctional. One-way communication is expected by those at the very top of organizations.

Faced with these difficulties, social workers in organizational settings must separate authentic two-way communication when relating to clients and social work colleagues from functional, organizational modes of communication that are used in relating to the chain of command. (Brueggemann 1997, 298)

◆◆◆

There are several problems with paper. One is that there is so much of it around that most of us are . . . wasting lots of time dealing with it. . . . Another problem with paper is that from time to time you have to write on it. And whenever you do, you put a little bit of yourself down on the paper to be examined and judged by someone else. Solely on the basis of what you set down on paper, someone may decide whether you . . . have exercised your professional judgment wisely.

There is something fleeting about a judgment or opinion that is expressed orally; it is less available for scrutiny than is the written word and it will probably be less far reaching in its impact. But ideas can be transformed by writing. Once put down on paper, mere suggestions or daily routines become rules and policies. And one person's (perhaps ill-informed) opinion becomes the last word on the subject.

So . . . you cannot afford to be a poor writer. If the words you put down on paper are not clear to your reader, they can take on a life of their own that is contrary to your intent. Or they can die on the spot, when you want them to come alive and make the reader take action. (Kantz and Mercer 1991, 221)

◆◆◆

Concise writing is a reliable indicator of clear thinking. For example, if you cannot describe the project your are proposing in a single written page, you are probably still unsure and unclear about what you are proposing.

Many socio-psychological factors can become barriers to communication. Examples include the sender's or the receiver's moods, emotional state, level of stress, defensiveness, and lack of trust. One's expectations have a great deal to do with communication. In general, we hear what we hope to hear and pay most attention to positions and information with which we agree. We also have a difficult time accepting criticism or negative feedback.

Communication is also influenced by such factors as one's life experiences, culture and ethnicity, familiarity with the language being used, social class, religious beliefs, and education. The symbols we use in language do not have universal meanings—they are influenced by our background, experiences, and the cultural content of the exchanges between sender and receiver. (See Chapter 12 on cultural diversity for additional information on cross-cultural communication.)

GUIDANCE AND DIRECTION

Good communication skills, both verbal and written, are of central importance in social work practice. Do your best to learn communication skills now because you will need them throughout your career. Do not underestimate the difficulty of developing these skills and develop methods by which you can monitor the effectiveness of your communication.

Carefully observe the patterns and processes of communication in your agency. For example, when you attend a staff meeting or committee meeting, consider the following questions:

- Who initiates communication and who introduces new topics for discussion?
- Who are the active communicators? Who are the quiet ones?
- Who speaks to whom? Who interrupts whom? Who decides when discussion of a topic has ended? Is there a certain hierarchy that affects the direction of the messages?
- Are the meetings formal or informal? Are the meetings structured by an agenda and the use of *Robert's Rules of Order* or are they unstructured and freewheeling?
- What matters are appropriate for discussion? Are the topics related only to work or do people also share personal information and talk about their families and leisure-time activities?
- Which staff members work hard at listening and understanding others? Which ones seem quick to assume they know what others are trying to say without really listening?

In nearly every organization you will have the opportunity to observe effective and ineffective, functional and dysfunctional communication. Take note of which styles and methods work and which do not. Consider why communication may be especially difficult and flawed at times. Knowing some of the pitfalls of communication may keep you from making these same mistakes. Major pitfalls to communication include the following:

- People who are busy and hurried sometimes forget or neglect to communicate with those who are in need of a certain message or information.
- People take shortcuts in communication to save time.
- People make erroneous assumptions about how much other people know and don't know.
- Communication often must go through several levels within an agency, and the meaning or clarity of the message can change at each level.
- Personal communication styles vary, and people may not be able to adapt to or appreciate other styles.
- People do not see the need to share information, and those who need it may not receive it.
- The message itself is confusing or flawed in logic and content.
- People do not feel empowered or listened to, so they withdraw and avoid communication with others.

Sheafor, Horejsi, and Horejsi (2000, 136–137) offer the following suggestions as ways to improve your listening skills:

- Stop talking. You cannot listen when you are talking.
- Put the message sender at ease. Do what you can to lessen his or her anxiety. Remove distractions (e.g., close the door).
- Demonstrate, verbally and nonverbally, that you want to listen. Really pay attention.
- Be patient with the message sender. Do not interrupt.
- Ask questions if it will help you understand or help the sender to clarify his or her message.
- Control your emotions. Do not criticize or argue, for that will erect a barrier to further communication.

When sending a message, follow these rules:

- Use clear, simple language. Speak distinctly and not too fast.
- Pay attention to your body language, making sure it is congruent with your message. Maintain appropriate eye contact and utilize gestures.
- Do not overwhelm or overload the receiver with information. Break up a lengthy or complex message into several parts so it can be more easily followed and understood.
- Ask for comments, questions, or feedback so you will know whether you are being understood. (Sheafor, Horejsi, and Horejsi 2000, 136–137)

Practicum students are often surprised at the amount of documentation required in agency practice. You will learn to write memos, letters, case notes, assessments, treatment plans, reports, and perhaps public relations material and grant proposals. At various times your writing will be used to document important events or actions, provide information to the general public, persuade someone to take some action, provide a base for legal action, or report to a funding source. First and foremost, all such written materials must be clear, accurate, and as concise as possible. Follow these guidelines in your written communication:

- Be sure you understand who your audience is, what they need to know, and how they want the information presented.
- Organize your material before starting to write, and recognize that you may need to make several revisions.
- Use language that is professional, but do not overuse jargon.
- Avoid slang and language that could be seen as judgmental, derogatory, or that could be interpreted in more than one way.
- Use direct, clear language rather than tentative, insipid words.
- Anticipate the reader's questions and answer them.
- Adhere to the KISS principle (Keep It Short and Simple).
- Use the format required by your agency.
- Make copies of all written communication that is sent out of the office, including correspondence, reports, and grant proposals.

Agencies differ somewhat in their standards and expectations. Therefore, it is important to ask your practicum instructor for specific directions on how to prepare work-related written materials. Also, ask your practicum instructor for feedback regarding the quality of your writing. Doing so will demonstrate your openness to learning and willingness to receive constructive criticism. It will help you to better understand your strengths and limitations and help you avoid patterns of ineffective communication.

Because case record documentation is time-consuming, students often wonder how much detail is required. A good guideline to follow regarding documentation about clients is to include enough detail to "bring the client to life" for anyone reading it, while not overwhelming the reader with unnecessary and extraneous information. When writing about programs or client systems, remember to be clear, convincing, and attuned to the needs or motives of those who may be the readers.

Finally, learn to communicate via e-mail, voice mail, and fax. Pay attention to the advantages and disadvantages of each method, and know that they provide convenience and accessibility, but do not substitute for face-to-face communication. Do not use them as replacements for speaking directly with people if that would be more appropriate or effective.

DEVELOPING COMMUNICATION SKILLS: A WORKBOOK ACTIVITY

1. What are the major forms of written communication expected of social workers in your agency (e.g., assessments, treatment plans, reports, memos, letters, and grant proposals)?

   _____

   _____

   _____

2. Do social workers in your agency receive special training in the use of written communication (e.g., use of medical terminology, report writing, grant proposal writing, and correspondence)?

   _____

   Can you participate in such training?

   _____

   _____

   _____

   _____

3. Do social workers in your agency receive special training in the use of word processing, e-mail, voice mail, and faxes?

   _____

   If so, how is it offered? Can you participate in such training?

   _____

   _____

   _____

   _____

4. Does your agency have specific policies regarding written communication (e.g., deadlines for completion, suggested or required formats, and supervisory review of documentation)?

   _____

   If yes, list those of special relevance to your work assignments.

   _____

   _____

   _____

   _____

5. Do the above mentioned policies contribute to more effective organizational communication?

_____

Why or why not?

_____

_____

_____

_____

6. What do social workers in your agency identify as the most common types of communication problems within the agency?

_____

_____

_____

_____

7. What do they see as the causes of these communication problems?

_____

_____

_____

_____

8. What are the effects of these communication problems on agency operations?

_____

_____

_____

_____

9. Is communication between management and staff mostly one way and from the top down, or does it flow easily both ways?

_____

10. What types of communication styles, patterns, and problems have you noticed in the following meetings?

Case conferences _____

_____

_____

Meetings with agency administrators _____

_____

_____

Meetings with board members or funding sources _____

_____

_____

Meetings between you and your supervisor _____

_____

_____

11. How does your agency's chain of command affect communication patterns and the flow of information? (Refer to your agency's organizational chart.)

_____

_____

_____

_____

12. In your agency, how are the patterns and the effectiveness of communication affected by the following factors?

Titles and positions of message senders and receivers

_____

_____

_____

Level of professional experience of message senders and receivers

_____

_____

_____

Gender of message senders and receivers

_____

_____

_____

_____

Racial, cultural, or ethnic background of message senders and receivers

_____

_____

_____

_____

13. How might your cultural background, life experiences, gender, and special training enhance or limit your ability to communicate with agency clients or agency staff?

_____

_____

_____

_____

14. How do such factors as room size, comfort, chair and table arrangement, and acoustics affect communication during meetings?

_____

_____

_____

_____

_____

15. What steps can you take to enhance your writing skills?

_____

_____

_____

_____

16. What steps can you take to enhance your verbal communication skills?

_____

_____

_____

_____

Additional notes and comments:

_____

_____

_____

_____

_____

_____

SUGGESTED LEARNING ACTIVITIES

- Ask your practicum instructor to show you examples of both well-written and poorly written letters, memos, reports, and case records. Examine these materials and observe how the writing style, organization, and choice of words affects their quality.
- Rewrite a report you have written (3–5 pages in length), using only half the space. Pay attention to eliminating unnecessary words. Shorten your sentences. Eliminate all repetition of content.
- Seek opportunities to make a speech or presentation before either agency staff members or a community group.
- Schedule time with your practicum instructor to focus exclusively on the quality of your oral and written communication and identify specific steps you can take to improve your skills in communication.

ADDITIONAL SUGGESTIONS AND HINTS

- In Sheafor, Horejsi, and Horejsi (2000), read the sections on "Report Writing," "Letter Writing," "Effective Telephone Communication," and "Using Information Technology."

SELECTED BIBLIOGRAPHY

Brueggemann, William. *The Practice of Macro Social Work.* Chicago: Nelson-Hall, 1997.

Kantz, Mary Kay and Kathryn Mercer. "Writing Effectively: A Key Task for Managers." In *Skills for Effective Human Services Management.* Ed. Richard Edwards and John Yankey. Washington, DC: NASW Press, 1991.

Sheafor, Bradford, Charles Horejsi, and Gloria Horejsi. *Techniques and Guidelines for Social Work Practice.* 5th ed. Boston: Allyn and Bacon, 2000.

8

THE AGENCY CONTEXT OF PRACTICE

Goals for Learning

- To understand your agency's mission, goals, and objectives
- To understand your agency's organization and administrative structure
- To understand your agency's sources of funding and operating budget
- To understand how your agency's history, structure, and administrative procedures may affect its ability to provide effective services and programs
- To understand how your agency is perceived in the community
- To understand how your agency relates to and interacts with other agencies within the overall social welfare system
- To understand how your agency might be changed in order to improve services to its clients

The daily activities and decisions of a social worker are heavily influenced by the nature and purpose of the organization that employs the social worker. Throughout its history, social work has been an agency-based profession. A majority of social workers are employed by agencies, and they provide their services within an organizational context. Given this reality, a practicum student must strive to examine and understand his or her practicum agency's mission, goals, structure, funding sources, and level of effectiveness.

BACKGROUND INFORMATION

The word *agency* refers to an organization that is authorized or sanctioned to act in the place of others. An agency performs activities that some larger group or organization desires and is willing to fund. This larger entity might be a community, a church, or a governmental body.

Most social workers are employed by human services agencies that fall into two broad categories: private, nonprofit agencies and public agencies. Others are employed by private, for-profit organizations such as hospitals or drug treatment facilities. In addition, some social workers create private practice organizations.

Public agencies are created by a legislative body made up of elected officials (e.g., a state legislature, the U.S. Congress, or county commissioners). Such agencies are funded by tax dollars and possibly by fees charged for service. The purpose and goals of public agencies are described in legal codes and government regulations. Elected officials are ultimately responsible for the operation of public agencies.

Private nonprofit agencies (also called *voluntary agencies*) are created by a legal process known as incorporation, which has the effect of creating a legal entity known as a nonprofit corporation. This type of agency is governed by a board of directors that represents the interests of the community or the group that wants the agency to exist and supports its work. The basic responsibilities of a *board of directors* (or *board of trustees*) are to establish the agency's mission and direction, set policies for its operation, set and approve budgets, ensure adequate funds for the agency, maintain a communication link with the wider community, and hire and regularly evaluate the executive director.

The basic responsibilities of an agency's *executive director* are to implement policy set by the governing board, hire staff and regularly evaluate their performance, make programmatic decisions, and direct and monitor day-to-day operations.

Private, nonprofit agencies are funded by private contributions, by grants and contracts, and sometimes by fees charged for the services they provide. Some conduct their own fund-raising activities and some receive funds from the local United Way organization. Private agencies may receive tax dollars indirectly through contracts with public agencies.

Some private nonprofit agencies are called *sectarian agencies,* which means that they are affiliated with or operated by a religious organization (e.g., Jewish Community Services or Catholic Social Services). The term *membership agency* is used to describe an agency (e.g., YMCA) that derives some of its budget from membership fees and in which members set policy.

Both public and private agencies may establish *advisory boards* that provide advice and guidance to the executive director or to the board of directors. As suggested by the name, an advisory board does not have the authority to make final decisions or set policy. It simply serves in an advisory capacity.

In contrast to a public agency or a private, nonprofit agency, a *for-profit agency* is a business corporation that sells a set of services and is designed and operated to yield a profit for investors and stockholders. Increasingly, not-for-profit hospitals, treatment centers, and nursing homes are being purchased by large corporations and operated as for-profit organizations.

Many social workers are employed in *host settings* in which the organization's primary mission or purpose is something other than the delivery of social services. Examples include schools and hospitals where the primary missions are the provision of educational and medical services. In these host settings, the social worker must work with many other professionals (e.g., doctors, nurses, physical therapists, teachers, or school psychologists) and may be under the supervision of someone who has only a limited understanding of social work and possibly holds values somewhat different from those of a social worker.

A typical social agency is designed and structured to provide one or more *social programs*. A social program is an organized and planned activity designed to accomplish either:

- *Remediation of an existing problem* (i.e., address a problem such as child abuse, unemployment, or delinquency)
- *Enhancement of social functioning* (i.e., improve functioning when no significant problem exists, such as programs of marriage enrichment)
- *Prevention of a social problem* (i.e., prevent a problem from developing, such as the reducing teen pregnancy)

According to Morales and Sheafor (2001), there are three categories of social programs:

> *Social provisions* are the tangible resources given to persons in need, either as cash or as direct benefits, such as food, clothing or housing. . . . *Personal services* are intangible services that help people resolve issues in their social functioning [e.g., counseling, therapy, protective services, client advocacy, direct care of a handicapped person]. . . . *Social action programs* help change conditions that created difficulties in social functioning. (21–22)

In order to achieve its purposes, a social program may use one or more broad strategies:

- *Socialization*—assisting and encouraging people to understand, learn, and abide by the fundamental norms of society
- *Social integration*—encouraging and helping people to interact more effectively with other individuals and with the various social systems or resources they need in order to function effectively and cope with special problems
- *Social control*—monitoring and placing restrictions on those who exhibit behavior that is self-destructive or dangerous to others
- *Social change*—expanding the number and types of life-enhancing opportunities available to people, taking actions that will improve the environment in which people must function, and taking action necessary to reduce or eliminate negative and destructive forces in their social environment

The study of a social agency might begin by analyzing the following components and how they interact:

- *Agency goals* refer to an agency's mission, purpose, and reason for existence.
- *Agency structure* refers to the way the agency is organized in order to achieve its goals. Structure defines the division of labor within the agency and assigns various tasks and responsibilities to individuals with certain job titles and to specific units, departments, and divisions. Structure also defines patterns of authority, decision making, accountability, and the flow of communication.
- *Agency technology* refers to the various tools, methods, approaches, or conceptual models used by agency personnel to achieve agency goals. Examples include the use of behavior modification in a treatment center or the use of in-home interviews in family preservation programs.
- *Agency personnel* refers to the people who have been hired and assigned to do the work of the agency in order to achieve agency goals

A close examination of several human services agencies, their policies and procedures, and the models and theories that guide their decisions and activities will reveal considerable variation in their underlying attitudes and orientation toward their clients. Some may view their clients essentially as objects to be manipulated or processed, others tend to view clients as recipients of services, and still others view clients as partners, experts, and resources to the helping process. Such varying attitudes bring forth different behaviors from the professionals. For example:

> *Clients as objects:* Professionals are the experts and know what should be done; clients are expected and encouraged to do what the professionals decide is best for them.

Clients as recipients: Professionals possess and control the services needed by the clients; the clients are expected to use the services given to them in a cooperative and appreciative manner.

Clients as resources: Professionals presume that the clients are in the best position to know what they need and what will and will not work. They actively solicit the clients' ideas on the problems they face and on possible solutions. The clients' thoughts and decisions are respected.

An agency's budget describes anticipated income and expenses for a given period of time, usually one or two years. The common categories of expense include: salaries, employee benefits, payroll taxes, consultation fees, staff training, malpractice insurance, supplies and equipment, telephone, printing and copying, rent, property insurance, staff travel, and membership dues. Once a budget has been set or approved, the agency administrator has only limited authority to shift funds from one category to another.

It is important to understand that the donations, grants, and legislative allocations received by an agency typically have many "strings attached." In other words, the money is given or allocated to the agency for a specified purpose and cannot be spent for another purpose. In addition, the agency's acceptance of money from a certain source (e.g., United Way or a federal agency) may require that it adhere to certain rules, regulations, and accounting procedures that add administrative costs. When much of an agency's money is earmarked for very specific purposes, the agency has limited capacity to modify its programs and little flexibility in responding to emergencies or unanticipated expenses.

Most human services agencies are quite bureaucratic, especially public agencies. Bureaucracies are characterized by:

- A clear chain of command in communication and assigned authority
- An organizational structure consisting of a vertical hierarchy with numerous units (e.g., divisions and departments), each of which has a designated leader (e.g., an administrator or supervisor) who is responsible for that unit's operation and who has authority over those working in the unit
- A set of written rules, policies, and guidelines that outline the procedures to be followed in performing the work of the unit
- A division of labor where each employee has a specific job to perform. The nature of this job is outlined in a written job description. Everyone in the organization knows (or can find out) what the other employees are to be doing in their jobs.
- Supervision of each employee's work
- An emphasis on formal communication, written documentation, and record keeping
- A higher level of job security than that which exists in a business or in non-profit organizations

The term *authority* is used in a number of ways. In one sense, authority is the right to be obeyed, or the power to compel obedience, or both. For example, a judge has the legal authority to send a person to jail, and an agency administrator has the authority to order those working under him or her to proceed on a certain course of action. Another use of the word is implied when we refer to a person as *an authority* on a particular topic. This usage implies that the person is someone whose judgment deserves our attention and serious consideration. Both types of authority can be found within social agencies.

Some agencies have developed less bureaucratic structures in an effort to be more responsive to clients and to their ever-changing environment. They often

Food for Thought

We live in an era in which organizational life is characterized by shifting priorities, changing patterns in the allocation of resources, and competing demands. Human services managers are often called on to function in a milieu of reduced governmental appropriations for human services, heightened demands for those services, and higher expectations for accountability. It is sometimes suggested that the only constant in management today is change. Contemporary managers must contend almost daily with rapidly changing political, economic, and social conditions. (Edwards and Austin 1991, 5)

◆◆◆

As employees, we are accountable to our employers, but as professionals, we may feel ourselves more accountable to the norms and values of our chosen profession or to the clients on whose behalf we practice. As individuals, we have personal goals and needs that may or may not be adequately fulfilled through our occupational pursuits. The extent to which your work within the agency is satisfying and fulfilling will depend . . . on the congruity or fit between your interest and capacities and the demands and expectations of both the employer and the profession with which you identify. (Lauffer 1984, 22)

◆◆◆

Bureaucratic rules present a constant dilemma for professionals. When a division of labor exists [within an organization], each person provides only a part of the work for the agency. Procedures, or rules, must then be established to facilitate interaction among the workers and coordinate their activities. Those rules are inherently arbitrary and somewhat inflexible, making it difficult for professionals to respond to unique client needs, thus limiting their autonomy in delivering client services.

Bureaucratic standards also present difficulties for the professional. Standards are ordinarily based on a perception of the "typical client," but in reality, clients present great variability and require services that may not fit the profile that was followed when a social program was created. (Morales and Sheafor 1998, 129)

◆◆◆

Over time, organizations may stagnate, lose sight of their mission and goals, and begin to provide services that are unhelpful or even harmful to clients. This can occur because of inadequate resources, poor leadership, poor planning, inappropriate procedures or structures, or a combination of these factors. . . . We believe that professional social workers have an obligation to attempt to correct problems in their organizations for the benefit of both their clients and themselves. Just as agencies can lose a sense of mission and direction, so too can they regain it. The path to change begins with an understanding of the organization itself—its history, its underlying theoretical principles and assumptions, and the causes of its current problems. (Netting, Kettner, and McMurty 1998, 193)

◆◆◆

You cannot have quality services without quality staff. And you cannot attract and retain quality staff unless they are paid a competitive salary.

use feminist and empowerment principles, seek to involve their clients in the work of the agency, promote shared power and decision making at all levels, develop flexible guidelines and approaches, and strive to individualize and customize their interventions and services. As a general rule, these agencies are more flexible and provide a less stressful environment for the social workers employed by them.

All organizations, including businesses, universities, hospitals, and human services agencies, develop policies and procedures as ways of dealing with recurring situations, problems, and questions. These are written into a document usually called a *policy manual*. In a social agency, this document may be called the *manual* or *agency manual*. Basically, it is a compilation of statements intended to guide the day-to-day activities of social workers and other staff employed by the agency. The content of the manual will reflect the mission and goals of the agency and, usually, certain social policies (see discussion of social policies in Chapter 11).

The content of an agency's manual is shaped, directly and indirectly, by many external forces. They include:

- Federal laws, rules, and regulations
- State laws, rules, and regulations
- Court decisions and legal opinions
- Accrediting bodies (e.g., Joint Commission on the Accreditation of Health Care Organizations)
- Formal interagency agreements
- Purchase of service contracts
- Requirements established by local fund-raising organizations that support the agency (e.g., the United Way)
- Requirements of managed care organizations
- Contracts with employee unions

An agency manual must be constantly updated in response to changes in legislation, court orders that give new interpretations to existing laws, and to new governmental rules and regulations.

In addition to a manual of policy and procedure, most agencies have developed an *employee handbook.* It typically contains information on the organization's mission, purpose, and chain of command, but focuses mostly on personnel policies (i.e., performance evaluations, advancement and promotion, salary, benefits, and vacations) and on behaviors by employees that are considered inappropriate or unethical within the organization.

As the practicum student enters into the life and activities of an organization, he or she must be alert to the fact that all organizations have both a formal and an informal structure. The *formal* or *official structure* of an agency is described by organizational charts, policy manuals, and documents that explain the structure and function of various organizational units and the official chain of command. The term *informal structure* refers to various networks of employees and unofficial channels of communication based mostly on friendships and personal associations. This informal structure is sometimes cynically described by staff as "the way the agency really works." It becomes apparent only after working in the agency for an extended period of time.

GUIDANCE AND DIRECTION

Expect to learn a great deal from your practicum agency. It will be a laboratory in which you will develop professional social work skills, observe other social workers providing services, and learn how agencies are organized and structured to address social needs and problems. Although every agency is different, you will begin to understand how organizations are administered and managed, learn about the common problems of organizations, and learn how to work effectively with others within an organizational context.

Agencies are always changing. Notice how shifts or cuts in funding cause changes in the services that can be provided. Observe how public attitudes and political forces shape the ways in which your agency functions. Most likely your agency will go through some significant changes during your practicum. You may even observe the birth of a new agency, or perhaps the dismantling of one that has lost its support or outlived its usefulness. You will learn about the dynamic nature of a human services organization if you closely observe the functioning of your own agency and that of others in the community.

Learn about your agency's history, including the reasons why it was established, when it began, and how it has evolved over time. Find out if your agency began as a grassroots effort to address a social need or problem, and if so, whether it has changed its focus over the years of its existence.

Inquire about how your agency may have modified its original mission, changed its structure, and adapted to a changing community and political context. This will help you understand how agencies survive within an ever-changing environment and continually adjust and adapt their efforts to address the changing social problems and needs on which they focus.

Find out whether your agency was established as a response to state or federal legislation, and how that legislation has guided its development. If it began as a project of a religious organization, try to understand how specific values and religious beliefs may have influenced the agency's formation and operation.

Ask your practicum instructor about external forces that shape or limit your agency, such as funding priorities and sources, community attitudes, client feedback, regulatory bodies, political pressure, and research findings. Ask how much influence internal forces such as staff suggestions, changes in personnel, and staff morale have on the agency.

Read agency-related materials written by agency staff, including policies and procedures manuals, grant proposals, minutes of board meetings, financial reports, and public relations brochures. Each one will reveal a different facet of your agency, including its reason for being, the conceptual framework underpinning its programs, its accountability to funding sources, its problems, its effectiveness, its way of attracting financial supporters, and its method of attracting clients or consumers.

Notice how your agency's type (e.g., public or private, for-profit or nonprofit) affects its work. For instance, public agencies will tend to be quite attentive to the decisions of elected officials, sectarian agencies will reflect the values of the religious organizations that sponsor them, and for-profit organizations may at times focus on making a profit for their owners to the possible detriment of clients.

Observe how staff members are affected by the organizational structure of your agency. Social workers in bureaucratic settings often become frustrated because their agencies are overly structured, are unable to treat clients as individuals, and resist change. On the other hand, watch how some social workers seem able to provide high quality and personalized services to their clients, even within a system with many rules and regulations.

If your agency is less bureaucratic, watch to see if this structure has reduced staff frustration and results in an agency that is more responsive to clients. If possible, compare your agency's structure with that of another agency with a very different structure, observing how their structures affect both staff and clients.

Your agency will use one or more specific theories, models, or approaches in the design and provision of its services and programs. Determine what they are, and why they were chosen. Does your agency use a behavioral, psychodynamic, or family systems approach to counseling? Does your agency invest its resources in prevention, early intervention, or rehabilitation? Is the approach therapeutic or correctional? Review courses you have taken and books you have read to help you understand why that particular approach was chosen by your agency to address the problem or concern it has identified.

Become familiar with your agency's methods of evaluating its programs and services. Find out how your agency assesses its effectiveness, determines whether it is reaching its goals, measures client or community satisfaction, and decides whether or not it is making a difference. Your agency may use formal or informal methods of evaluation, process or outcome measures, and collect quantitative or qualitative data. Ask your practicum instructor whether he or she thinks these approaches or evaluation tools are valid and adequate. Ask what methods he or she would ideally recommend using to evaluate services provided enough time, money, and staff were available.

GETTING TO KNOW YOUR AGENCY: A WORKBOOK ACTIVITY

1. What is the complete, official, and legal name of the organization in which you are a practicum student?

_____

_____

2. What are the location, mailing address, and e-mail address of the organization's central office or headquarters?

_____

_____

_____

3. Does your agency have an official mission statement? If yes, what is its mission?

_____

_____

_____

_____

4. List your agency's major programs and services.

_____

_____

_____

_____

5. Who is your organization's chief executive officer (i.e., director, administrator, or executive director)?

_____

6. What person or official body has the authority to hire or fire your agency's director or chief executive officer?

_____

7. Is the directorship of your agency a political appointment (e.g., appointed by the mayor or governor)?

_____

If yes, who makes this appointment?

_____

8. Is your organization a public agency? A private agency? A nonprofit agency? A for-profit agency?

   _____

9. If your practicum agency is a public agency, is it a federal, state, county, or city agency?

   _____

10. If your agency is a public agency, what specific legislation or statute created the agency and/or assigned responsibilities to it? (Cite legal code.)

    _____

11. If your practicum is in a private, nonprofit agency, how many people serve on the board of directors? Do people want to serve on the agency's board or does the agency find it difficult to attract new board members?

    _____

    _____

    _____

12. If your practicum is in a private agency, how might the members of the board of directors be described in terms of such variables as their age, sex, ethnicity, race, socioeconomic class, occupation, and personal experiences with the agency's programs and services?

    _____

    _____

    _____

    _____

13. What percentage of the board of directors fall into the following categories:

    _____ % Human services professionals

    _____ % Business or community representatives

    _____ % Current or former agency clients or consumers

14. If your practicum is in a private sectarian agency, with what religious organization or denomination is it affiliated?

    _____

15. If your practicum agency is a membership organization, how does someone become a member?

_____

_____

_____

16. If it is a for-profit organization, who are its owners? For whom is it to make a profit (e.g., stockholders, another corporation, and a partnership)?

_____

_____

_____

17. Does your agency have an advisory board? If yes, what is its purpose?

_____

_____

_____

18. Do any current or former agency clients serve on the advisory board?

_____

_____

_____

19. When was your agency first created or established? Has the agency or organization undergone a major reorganization within the last ten years?

_____

If yes, why was it reorganized and perhaps renamed?

_____

_____

_____

_____

20. What geographic areas or communities are served by your agency (e.g., specific neighborhoods, a city, a county, and the whole state)?

_____

_____

_____

21. List the department(s), division(s), or unit(s) with which you will be associated during your practicum.

_____

_____

_____

22. What is your agency's overall or total operating budget for the current year?

$ _____

What is the budget for your department or program area?

$ _____

23. Approximately what percentage of the agency's (or department's or program's) total annual budget is assigned to following categories:

_____ % Salary and wages of employees

_____ % Employee benefits (e.g., health insurance premiums, retirement programs, social security, worker's compensation, and unemployment insurance)

_____ % Travel

_____ % Staff training

24. Is the agency's budget or income fairly predictable and stable from year to year, or is it uncertain and unpredictable?

_____

25. Of the budget, about what percentage is derived from each of the following sources:

_____ % Allocations by the U.S. Congress

_____ % Allocations by the state legislature

_____ % Allocations by the county commissioners

_____ % Allocations by the city council

_____ % Allocations by the United Way or other combined giving program

_____ % Grant from a federal agency

_____ % Grant from a state agency

_____ % Grant from a private foundation

_____ % Fees paid by the clients or consumers of services

_____ % Fees paid by a third party (e.g., insurance)

_____ % Purchase of a service contract

_____ % Private donation made directly to the agency

_____ % Other

26. What types of problems, concerns, or needs bring people to your agency or cause them to be brought to the attention of your agency (e.g., child abuse, delinquency, and marital conflict)?

_____

_____

_____

_____

27. Do the clients served by your agency often fall into certain demographic categories such as age, sex, ethnicity, socioeconomic class, level of education, religion, or language?

_____

_____

_____

28. What statistics are recorded on a regular basis by agency personnel (e.g., number of clients served each month, number of cases opened and closed, or characteristics of clients)?

_____

_____

_____

29. By what process does the agency determine if it is effective (e.g., recidivism, client's completion of treatment plans, number of clients served, level of client satisfaction, specific legislation passed, and objectives reached)?

_____

_____

_____

_____

30. Is the effectiveness of your agency's services and programs evaluated by agency staff or by persons from outside the agency?

_____

31. Do your agency's clients or consumers participate in the evaluation process? If yes, in what way?

_____

_____

_____

32. If your agency ceased to exist next week, who would care? Who would be harmed? Who would complain? Who would cheer?

_____

_____

_____

33. What state or federal agencies or regulatory bodies have a significant impact on your agency's policy and operation (e.g., a state's department of health, department of social services, department of mental health, department of education, or the federal government's Department of Health and Human Services, Department of Labor, and Department of Education)?

_____

_____

_____

_____

34. Is your agency required to submit reports to a state or federal agency regarding its programs and services?

_____

If yes, what is the nature and the purpose of those reports?

_____

_____

_____

35. Is your agency regularly subjected to on-site inspections, surveys, or reviews by personnel from an oversight or regulatory body?

_____

If yes, what is the purpose of these reviews?

_____

_____

_____

36. Is your agency accredited by a national organization (e.g., Joint Commission on the Accreditation of Health Care Organizations and Commission on Accreditation of Rehabilitation Facilities or licensed by a state organization)?

_____

If yes, what is the name(s) of this accrediting body? How often is your agency reviewed by this accrediting body? How does your agency prepare for these reviews?

_____

_____

_____

37. What community agencies frequently refer clients to your agency?

_____

_____

_____

38. To what agencies does your agency frequently refer its clients?

_____

_____

_____

39. Is your agency often in conflict with other agencies?

_____

If yes, why?

_____

_____

_____

_____

40. Does your agency compete with other agencies for funding?

_____

If yes, with what other agencies?

_____

_____

_____

_____

_____

41. In what interagency planning and coordinating bodies is your agency an active participant?

_____

_____

_____

_____

_____

42. How many people are employed by your agency or in the division, department, or program that serves as your practicum setting?

_____

43. Of the professionals employed by your agency, (division, department, or program) about what percentage have the following types and levels of education:

_____ % DSW or Ph.D. in social work

_____ % Doctoral degree in field other than social work

_____ % Masters degree in social work

_____ % Masters degree in field other than social work

_____ % Bachelors degree in social work

_____ % Bachelors degree in field other than social work

_____ % A.A. degree in human services

_____ % Other

44. Do the employees in your agency belong to a union?

_____

If yes, what union represents the agency employees? In what ways does the existence of a union affect the operation of the agency and the assignment of work to agency personnel?

_____

_____

_____

_____

45. Do staff tend to stay with the agency for a long time, or is there a high rate of staff turnover? What explanations are given by the agency and administrators for either the high or low rate of turnover?

_____

_____

_____

46. How do staff members describe the state of morale among agency personnel? What factors contribute to high or low morale?

_____

_____

_____

_____

47. What efforts or programs are in place within the agency to help reduce job-related stress and worker burnout?

_____

_____

_____

_____

48. Are the salaries paid by the agency lower, about the same, or higher than those paid by similar agencies in the community?

_____

49. To what extent and in what ways, if any, are unpaid volunteers utilized within your agency?

_____

_____

_____

_____

Additional notes and comments:

_____

_____

_____

_____

SUGGESTED LEARNING ACTIVITIES

- Study your agency's organizational chart. Locate on this chart your practicum supervisor and/or the department or unit in which he or she works.
- Study your agency's policy manual. Ask your supervisor to identify those portions of the manual that are of highest priority for you to read. Also examine your agency's employee handbook. Give special attention to sections on job performance, personnel evaluations, and unacceptable behavior.
- Ask your supervisor or other administrative personnel to explain how the agency's budget is established. Also ask about the problems faced by the agency in securing the funds it needs.
- Attend meetings of the agency's board of directors or advisory board and consider how the topics discussed relate to the agency's mission, goals, programs, and funding.
- Examine your agency's monthly, quarterly, or annual reports to better understand your agency's goals and performance.
- Seek to discover how ordinary citizens or the general public view your agency. Speak with friends and acquaintances who know little about social work or the human services in your community and ask what they know or have heard about your agency.
- Attend legislative hearings at which legislation relevant to your agency's programs is being considered.
- Attend public meetings sponsored by the United Way organization or other social welfare planning groups in order to better understand how your agency fits into the overall social welfare system.
- Accompany a client applying for services at another agency and identify attitudes reflected in how agency staff treat clients and handle client requests.
- Ask your practicum instructor what changes he or she would like to see in how the agency operates and is structured.

ADDITIONAL SUGGESTIONS AND HINTS

- Ask for an orientation on how to use your agency's phone and e-mail system.
- Ask for instruction on procedures related to the use of various office machines (e.g., copy machine, fax, or computer).
- Ask for instruction and guidance on agency procedures, format and protocol related to record keeping, record storage, and client confidentiality.
- Collect a set of agency pamphlets, brochures, newsletters, and other materials used to inform the public about your agency and its services.
- In Sheafor, Horejsi, and Horejsi (2000), read the sections on "Learning about Your Agency," "Preparing a Budget," and "The Process of Agency Planning."

SELECTED BIBLIOGRAPHY

Edwards, Richard, and David Austin. "Managing Effectively in an Environment of Competing Values." In *Skills for Effective Human Services Management.* Ed. Richard Edwards and John Yankey. Washington, DC: NASW Press, 1991.

Lauffer, Armand. *Understanding Your Social Agency.* 2nd ed. Newbury Park, CA: Sage, 1984.

Morales, Armando, and Bradford Sheafor. *Social Work: A Profession of Many Faces.* 9th ed. Boston: Allyn and Bacon, 2001.

Netting, F. Ellen, Peter Kettner, and Steven McMurtry. *Social Work Macro Practice.* 2nd ed. New York: Longman, 1998.

Weinbach, Robert. *The Social Worker as Manager.* 2nd ed. Boston: Allyn and Bacon, 1994.

9

THE COMMUNITY CONTEXT OF PRACTICE

Goals for Learning

- To understand the impact of the community on the social functioning of clients
- To identify and analyze community resources and needs
- To understand community forces that impede or support social change
- To develop community analysis and organization skills

The previous chapter focused on the agency, or organizational context of social work practice. This chapter will draw your attention to the community context. There are several reasons why it is important to study the community in which your practicum agency is located. First, it is obvious that agencies do not exist in a vacuum. In fact, an agency's mission, programs, and operation are often a reflection of the community's characteristics, such as its values, politics, history, and special problems.

Second, most of your clients live and work in this community. It is not possible to understand your clients without understanding their wider social environment and both the positive and negative conditions and forces within that environment. If you work within a direct services agency, the client assessments and intervention plans you develop must consider your client's interactions with others in the community, as well as the resources available in the community.

Third, your informal study of the community will allow you to begin identifying unmet human needs as well as the gaps in the service network that should be addressed in order to better serve the people of the community. Finally, by gathering information about the community's values, history, power structure, economic base, demographics, and decision-making processes, you will be able to identify those groups or individuals who have the power and influence to either facilitate or block needed social change.

Learning about a community takes time and effort. However, you will find this to be an invaluable experience. You will become fascinated as you begin to observe and understand the interplay between the functioning of individuals and families and their neighborhood and community. If your practicum is in an agency concerned mostly with micro-level practice, you will soon see how your clients' lives are either enriched or harmed by community factors. If your practicum is in an organization heavily involved in macro-level practice, you will come to understand that every community has its own personality, and that in order to deal effectively with social problems and bring about needed social change, you must understand and appreciate that uniqueness.

BACKGROUND INFORMATION

The term *community* refers to a group of people brought together by physical proximity or by a common identity based on their shared experiences, interests, or culture. There are two major types of communities: communities of place or location, and communities of interest and identification.

A *community of interest and identification* can be described as a group of individuals who share a sense of identity and belonging because they share a characteristic, interest, or life experience such as ethnicity, language, religion, sexual orientation, or occupation. We are referring to this type of community when we speak of the "social work community," "the business community," "the gay community," "the African American community," the "Islamic community," "the Catholic community," "the Italian community," the "university community," and so forth.

The second type of community, a *community of place or location,* is defined mostly by geography and specified boundaries. Such communities include neighborhoods, suburbs, barrios, towns, and cities. The boundaries of a community of place might be a legal definition, a river, or a street. They may have formal or informal names such as "Woodlawn," "the South Bronx," "Orange County," "the Blackfeet Reservation," "the university area," and the "warehouse district." The people living in these areas or places may share some level of identification, but typically they are more diverse in terms of values, beliefs, and other characteristics than are the people of a community of interest and identification. Also, it is common for the people within this type of community to be in conflict over a variety of issues. Living in proximity to others, in and of itself, does not create a social bond and a sense of belonging. Within a given community of place, there may be many different communities of interest and identification.

It can be useful to examine communities of location in terms of their usual functions. Sheafor, Horejsi, and Horejsi (2000, 296–297) describe these functions as follows:

- *Provision and distribution of goods and services.* Water, food, housing, garbage disposal, medical care, education, transportation, recreation, social services, information, and the like are provided.
- *Location of business activity and employment.* Commerce and jobs exist from which people earn the money needed to purchase goods and services.
- *Public safety.* Protection from criminal behavior and hazards such as fires, floods, and toxic chemicals is provided.
- *Socialization.* Opportunities are available to communicate and interact with others and to develop a sense of identity and belonging beyond that provided by the family system.
- *Mutual support.* Tangible assistance and social supports beyond those provided by one's family are available.
- *Social control.* Rules and norms necessary to guide and control large numbers of people (e.g., laws, police, courts, traffic control, and pollution control) are established and enforced.
- *Political organization and participation.* Governance and decision making related to local matters and public services are in place (e.g., streets, sewer, education, public welfare, public health, economic development, and zoning of housing and businesses).

Social workers and social agencies must be alert to how power and influence are used in the community. *Power* is the ability to make others do what you want them to do, whereas *influence* is the capacity to increase the chances that others will do what you want. Successful efforts to develop a new agency program, pass a law, modify social policy, and bring about social change all depend on the skilled use of power and influence. By themselves, social workers possess little power or influence. Thus, in order to promote social change, they must have access to and relationships with those individuals and organizations that have power and influence and are willing to use it on behalf of the social agency or its clients.

There are various forms of power and influence. Different types are more or less important, depending upon the issue being addressed and the kind of change desired. Below are examples of various forms and sources of power and influence:

- Those who control credit, loans, and investments (e.g., banks)
- Those who control information (e.g., newspapers or television stations)
- Those who hold elected offices (e.g., mayor, members of city council, county commissioners, or state legislators)
- Those in charge of corporations that employ large numbers of people
- Respected religious and moral leaders
- Recognized experts in their profession or field
- Longtime and respected residents of the community
- Natural leaders (i.e., persons who are charismatic, articulate, and have attracted a loyal following)
- Advocacy organizations that are known for their solidarity, persistence, and devotion to a cause

---

Food for Thought

Individuals who are isolated, unaffiliated, with little knowledge, and without influence, often see themselves as "objects" susceptible to social forces and circumstances over which they have little or no control. These self-perceptions induce destructive social and psychological adaptations such as deprecatory self-images, anomie, and fatalism. Engagement in community life through political action can be the antidote by which such individuals gain a modicum of influence over some aspects of their lives. (Grosser and Mondros 1985, 159)

◆◆◆

Each community has unmet needs. That is true. It is also true that no matter how poor or frightened or lacking in immediate power, each community has resources to meet many of these needs, including the most important resource, people. In fact, a crucial element for success is your ability to recognize and build on actual and potential capabilities that exist in your community. This, not concern over limitations, will be the foundation of your work. An overemphasis on liabilities is a serious error that colors problem solving in shades of inadequacy and dependence, undermining any attempt at empowerment. (Homan 1999, 121)

◆◆◆

I have the audacity to believe that peoples everywhere can have three meals a day for their bodies, education and culture for their minds, and dignity, equality, and freedom for their spirits. I believe that what self-centered people have torn down, people-centered people can build up.

—*Martin Luther King, Jr.*

◆◆◆

Never doubt that a small group of thoughtful and committed citizens can change the world; indeed it is the only thing that ever has.

—*Margaret Mead*

◆◆◆

The community must protect our individuality; in turn, we are the only ones who can shape communities that will ensure that result.... The tension between individual and group is healthy, but the deepest threat to the integrity of any community is the incapacity of citizens to lend themselves to any worthy common purpose. Individualism that degenerates into anarchism, self-indulgence, or dog-eat-dog exploitation of others is individualism gone wrong. The end to be sought is developed, creative individuals who expend their talents in the service of shared values. (Gardner 1978, 75)

It is important to remember that the "movers and shakers" of a community (i.e., those with real power and influence) are not always the visible leaders. Many key decision makers work behind the scenes.

Community dynamics differ depending on the size of a community. For example, in a large community, those with power tend to be more specialized and exercise their power only in relation to selected issues. By contrast, in smaller and more rural communities, those with power tend to become involved in a wide range of issues and decisions.

Community size also affects how individuals experience the push and pull of social forces and prevailing attitudes. For example, an individual who is gay or lesbian is more likely to experience discrimination and rejection in a small, rural community and feel more isolated than if he or she lived in an urban area. In a larger city, he or she may have access to a more clearly identified gay community to provide positive role models, socialization, and a nurturing environment that can buffer negative societal attitudes toward homosexuals.

GUIDANCE AND DIRECTION

As you think about the community context of practice, appreciate that we are all shaped in positive and negative ways by our life experiences. We are supported or undermined, protected or put at risk, guided or controlled, served or stressed, and encouraged or discouraged by our interactions with the individuals, groups, and organizations that make up the communities in which we live. These interactions have a profound effect on our social functioning and quality of life.

Always be conscious of the fact that the clients or consumers served by a social agency are members of a particular community of place and probably members of several communities of interest and identification. You need to understand their meaning for and their impact on clients.

When working directly with clients, identify their social roles (e.g., spouse, parent, or employee) and then consider how specific community characteristics may make it easier or more difficult to fulfill role expectations. As you examine the influence of a community on the social functioning of individuals and families, consider the following questions:

- Has my client had the benefits and opportunities provided by schools that are intellectually stimulating and physically safe?
- Does my client have adequate employment opportunities to support himself or herself and a family?
- Does my client live in adequate, safe, and affordable housing?
- Does my client feel safe when at home and on the street, and feel adequately protected by the law enforcement agencies of the community?
- Is my client subjected to rejection, discrimination, or stereotyping by others in the community?
- Does my client feel encouraged, supported, and empowered by his or her interactions with others in the community?
- Is my client's social functioning limited by a lack of public transportation, education and training, or accessible and affordable health care in the community?
- What services or programs are needed and wanted by my client but not available in the community?
- Is my client aware of groups or organizations in the community that can act as advocates for his or her needs?

- What natural helpers and informal resources of the community or neighborhood are used by or available to my client?
- Is my client a real or imagined threat to others in the community?
- Has my client chosen to live in this neighborhood or community? If so, why? If not, what social and economic circumstances necessitate that he or she live in a particular neighborhood or community?
- What significant life experiences have shaped my client's attitudes toward the community and toward my practicum agency, its services and programs?

As social work students gain experience and carefully observe and participate in a given community, they often become aware of factors that are common to many communities. For example, be alert to the following:

- Social support networks and informal helpers exist in all communities and neighborhoods. However, special effort may be required to identify and access these resources.
- There is a degree of overlap and duplication in the functions and programs of various agencies in the community. Sometimes this duplication is unnecessary and wasteful, but in many cases the duplication is beneficial to clients and healthy for the total system of services.
- There are "turf" issues and conflicts between agencies, brought on, in part, by their competition for funding and differences in how they define and explain problems.
- The people of the community expect agencies to cooperate and collaborate. However, this can be inherently difficult when the agencies must compete with each other for funding and because cooperation and collaboration are time consuming and labor intensive.
- An agency that has the support of powerful and influential individuals is able to secure funding and gain recognition, even when its mission and program are less important and worthy than that of other agencies in the community.
- Negative community attitudes toward a certain client group or a certain type of agency can be a major obstacle to developing and providing needed services to a particular group.
- Certain groups in the community are better organized and better able to act as advocates for themselves than are others.
- Community attitudes and values can negatively or positively affect social agencies and their ability to carry out their mission.

Be cautious regarding the conclusions you reach about why the people of the community do not fully utilize the services available in the community, such as the ones offered by your agency. For example, you might assume that they are not fully informed or sufficiently motivated, when in reality they see your agency as culturally insensitive or irrelevant to their needs. Perhaps the agency's hours of operation do not mesh with their hours of employment or their lifestyle. They may also see your agency as representing a set of values and beliefs significantly different from their own.

Use critical thinking skills in your community analysis so that your conclusions are well founded and not a result of first impressions, hasty judgments, faulty assumptions, or poor data gathering. It is as important to do good community assessments as it is to do good client assessments. Community level social work needs to be based on a thorough, careful, and ongoing assessment.

BEGINNING A COMMUNITY ANALYSIS: A WORKBOOK ACTIVITY

The following questions are designed to help you understand the community and its effects on your agency and its clients. Answer each one to the degree that you can, recognizing that you will obtain additional information over time. You can obtain some of this information from other social workers or administrators in your agency and some from organizations such as the U.S. Census Bureau, local chambers of commerce and economic development groups.

1. What geographical area is served by your agency?

    _____

    _____

2. What are the names of the communities, neighborhoods, or areas served by your agency?

    _____

    _____

3. How many people live in the area served by your agency?

    _____

4. What is the population density of the area (i.e., people per square mile or per city block)?

    _____

5. Of the people in the community, about what percentage is in various age groups (e.g., preschool, grade school, teen, young adult, middle age, and old age)?

    _____

    _____

    _____

6. About what percentage falls into the various categories used to identify racial and ethnic background or identity? (Note: The categories listed below were used in U.S. Census 2000 materials.)

    _____ % White (Caucasian)

    _____ % Black (Afro-American)

    _____ % American Indian or Alaska Native

    _____ % Mexican, Mexican American, Chicano

    _____ % Puerto Rican

    _____ % Cuban

_____ % Other Spanish/Hispanic/Latino _____

_____ % Asian Indian

_____ % Chinese

_____ % Filipino

_____ % Japanese

_____ % Korean

_____ % Vietnamese

_____ % Other Asian _____

_____ % Native Hawaiian

_____ % Guamanian or Chamorro

_____ % Samoan

_____ % Other Pacific Islander

_____ % Other _____

7. What languages are spoken by the people of the community?

   _____

   _____

8. About what percentage of the people now living in the community:

   _____ % Grew up in the community

   _____ % Moved to the community from another city or state

   _____ % Moved to the community from another country

9. Of the people living in the area served by your agency, what can be said about their income levels?

   _____ Median per person income

   _____ Median household income

   _____ Percentage of families receiving some form of public assistance

10. How do these data on income compare with the state and national averages?

   _____

   _____

   _____

11. How does the cost of living in this community compare with communities or cities of similar size in the state or region?

_____

_____

_____

12. What are the major types of employers, occupations, and jobs available to people living in the area served by your agency?

_____

_____

_____

13. What is the percentage of unemployment in the community? How does this compare with figures for the state, region, and nation?

_____

_____

_____

14. What types of training and education are necessary to secure and maintain employment in the major industries and occupations of the area?

_____

_____

_____

15. Of the adults living in the community, about what percentage are in each of the following categories of educational achievement? (Consult U.S. Census data.)

_____ % 8th grade or less

_____ % 12th grade (no diploma)

_____ % High school graduate

_____ % Some college

_____ % Associate arts degree

_____ % Bachelors degree

_____ % Graduate degree

16. To what extent are the people who use the services of your agency representative of the wider community population? For example, are clients served by

your agency similar to or different from most others living in the community in terms of the following:

Age _____

Income _____

Race/Ethnicity _____

Religion _____

Language _____

Education _____

Marital status _____

Family or household composition _____

17. What groups wield considerable power and influence in the community? What is the source of their power and influence?

_____

_____

_____

_____

18. Are certain economic interests, business organizations, or occupational groups particularly influential in the community?

_____

_____

_____

19. Are certain ethnic, racial, or religious groups particularly influential in the community?

_____

_____

_____

20. What groups are underrepresented in the community's decision-making process and structures? Why?

_____

_____

_____

21. Does one political party or a particular ideology dominate decision making at the community level?

_____

_____

22. To what media sources (e.g., newspapers, television, and radio) do people turn for news and information about what is happening in their community?

_____

_____

_____

23. What significant problems (e.g., crime, pollution, lack of affordable housing, and poverty) is the community experiencing?

_____

_____

_____

_____

24. To what extent has the community experienced intergroup conflict related to differences in race, ethnicity, religion, language, and social class?

_____

_____

_____

25. Of what is the community especially proud (e.g., physical beauty, history, climate, schools, and sports teams)?

_____

_____

_____

26. About what is the community especially fearful or embarrassed (e.g., environmental problems, corruption, violence, poor roads, and high taxes)?

_____

_____

_____

27. What minority groups live within the community, including refugees and immigrants? What special services, if any, are available to them?

_____

_____

_____

28. What community needs, conditions, or problems does your agency address in its goals or mission statement?

_____

_____

_____

29. In what ways do the community's characteristics (e.g., demographics and values) support the work and purpose of your agency?

_____

_____

_____

30. In what ways are the community's characteristics a barrier to the work and purpose of your agency?

_____

_____

_____

31. What other agencies or organizations in the community have a purpose or program similar to your agency? How is your agency different from these others?

_____

_____

_____

_____

32. What community welfare planning councils or interagency coordinating bodies exist in the community? How might you observe or participate in their work?

_____

_____

_____

_____

33. What self-help groups exist in the community that might be especially helpful to the clients you serve in your practicum agency (e.g., Alcoholics Anonymous, fetal alcohol syndrome support group, Alliance for the Mentally Ill,

Alzheimer's support group, and Parents Anonymous)? Can you attend and observe their meetings?

_____

_____

_____

_____

34. Does your community have a United Way or other combined fund-raising program that raises money for numerous human service agencies? If yes, does your agency receive funds raised in this manner? By what process does this fund-raising organization (e.g., United Way) decide which agencies it will support?

_____

_____

_____

_____

35. What significant gaps exist in the array of human services and programs within the community? Why do they exist?

_____

_____

_____

_____

_____

36. Are there significant, unnecessary, or wasteful duplications among the human service programs of the community? If yes, what are they and why does this situation exist?

_____

_____

_____

_____

_____

37. What "turf" conflicts and unhealthy competitions exist between human services agencies within the community? How do they affect your clients?

_____

_____

_____

_____

38. To what extent do the people of the community volunteer their time and talent to work with human services agencies? To what types of agencies, activities, and causes are these volunteers most attracted?

_____

_____

_____

_____

39. In the opinion of experienced human services professionals and experts of the community, how adequate are the community's:

Programs of low-cost housing _____

_____

Schools _____

_____

Police and fire protection _____

_____

Recreational programs _____

_____

Public transportation _____

_____

Health care and hospitals _____

_____

Mental health services _____

_____

Day care of children _____

_____

Family support programs _____

_____

Programs for the treatment of alcoholism and drug abuse _____

_____

Programs for troubled youth _____

_____

Programs for the elderly _____

_____

Additional notes and comments:

_____

_____

_____

_____

_____

SUGGESTED LEARNING ACTIVITIES

- Observe and participate in interagency committees or task groups that are made up of representatives of various community organizations.
- Read grant proposals and reports written by your agency to see how they claim to meet community needs.
- Analyze the community's need for a service that your agency might be able to develop and offer. What factors would your agency need to consider before deciding if it could or should offer this new service?
- Locate and study community resource directories, census data, and historical materials to help deepen your understanding of a particular social problem addressed by your agency.
- Use the Internet to examine census data related to the area served by your agency. The home page for the U.S. Census Bureau is http://www.census.gov/. Once there, click on Access Tools, then click on American FactFinder.

ADDITIONAL SUGGESTIONS AND HINTS

- In Sheafor, Horejsi, and Horejsi (2000), read the sections on "Learning about Your Community" and "Community Decision-Making Analysis."

SELECTED BIBLIOGRAPHY

Fisher, Robert, and Howard Jacob Karger. *Social Work and Community in a Private World: Getting Out in Public.* New York: Longman, 1997.

Gardner, John. *Morale.* New York: Norton, 1978.

Grosser, Charles, and Jacqueline Mondros. "Pluralism and Participation: The Political Action Approach." In *Theory and Practice of Community Social Work.* Ed. Samuel Taylor and Robert Roberts. Irvington, NY: Columbia University Press, 1985.

Hardcastle, David, Stanley Wenocur, and Patricia Powers. *Community Practice.* New York: Oxford University Press, 1997.

Homan, Mark. *Promoting Community Change.* 2nd ed. Pacific Grove, CA: Brooks/Cole, 1999.

Sheafor, Bradford, Charles Horejsi, and Gloria Horejsi. *Techniques and Guidelines in Social Work Practice.* 5th ed. Boston: Allyn and Bacon, 2000.

10

THE SOCIAL PROBLEM CONTEXT OF PRACTICE

Goals for Learning

- To understand the conditions, needs, and problems faced by your clients
- To understand the human and social conditions, needs, and problems that have given rise to the programs and services provided by various human services agencies
- To understand how various theories concerning the cause of social problems influence the development of social policies and social programs
- To understand how particular explanations and theories of causation may influence the operation and administration of human services organizations
- To understand how political power and influence can determine whether a particular condition comes to be defined as a social problem that elicits community or societal efforts to solve or minimize this condition

In order for you to understand your agency's purpose, policies, and operation, it is important to carefully examine the social problems or conditions on which it focuses its attention and resources. Most of the agencies and organizations that employ social workers were created in response to a specific social problem or need as perceived and understood by elected officials (in the case of public agencies), by powerful and committed community leaders (in the case of private non-profit agencies), or by investors (in the case of for-profit organizations).

The definition and conceptualization of a social problem is a complex process that is shaped by historical, political, and cultural forces as well as by existing scientific knowledge. There can be intense disagreement over whether a particular condition is to be defined as a problem. Even when there is agreement that a problem exists, there can be much debate over its cause, and over what can and should be done about it.

How a problem or need is defined and the predominant beliefs about its causation have a profound effect on the formulation of social policies and the design of social programs that are intended to address the problem. Moreover, as our understanding of the problem changes, agencies must modify their guiding principles and adapt their services and interventions to these new interpretations.

BACKGROUND INFORMATION

To analyze the beliefs and assumptions that shape a social agency and its programs, begin by making a distinction between a social *condition* and a social *problem.* Sullivan (1997) offers the following insight:

> A *social problem* exists when an influential group defines a social condition as threatening to its values; when the condition affects a large number of people; and when the condition can be remedied by collective action. . . . An *influential group* is one that can have a significant impact on public debate and social policy. . . . *Values* are people's ideas about what is good or bad, right or wrong. (5)

A *social condition* is a factual reality. Examples include the fact that about 50 percent of marriages in the United States end in divorce, the fact that between two and three million people in the U.S. are homeless, the fact that about one in four high school students (mostly minorities) never graduate, the fact that many teenagers have babies, and the fact that many children are beaten and injured by their parents. These are facts, but are they actually social problems? If yes, why? Who decides that this condition is a problem that requires action by the community or government? Whose values, norms, and beliefs are to be used in forming a judgment?

Some people may view a given condition as a problem that demands collective action and an investment of resources, whereas others presume that it is simply an aspect of life that requires no special response. A condition becomes a problem when it threatens the values, the sense of morality, the security, or safety of those in a community or a society who have the power and influence to bring forth collective action and, eventually, the new policies, programs, and agencies that will address this problem. For example, powerful leaders in business may come to define the performance of our educational systems to be a serious problem because their businesses are threatened by the lack of a skilled and well-educated workforce.

When powerful and influential individuals and groups come to view a social phenomena or condition as a problem and a threat to what they value, they must decide what social policies and actions are needed to solve this problem or lessen its negative impact. Many different solutions or actions may be proposed. Each will rest on a particular set of assumptions and beliefs about the cause of the problem and what interventions will be feasible and effective. There may be several competing theories of causation, each of which purports to explain why the problem exists and what can be done about it.

Those in decision-making positions may sponsor research into the causes of the problem and seek the advice of experts, but in the final analysis, the decisions about the nature and cause of the problem will be heavily political and will reflect the views and preferences of those who have power and influence. For example, in recent years powerful political forces have redefined poverty as a problem caused by an unwillingness of people to work and by the existence of welfare programs thought to create dependency. Their approach is to reduce access to welfare benefits and thereby force poor people into taking jobs. Not addressed in this approach are questions of whether the jobs exist, whether those who are poor have the skills needed to obtain and hold such jobs, and whether the available jobs provide health insurance and pay a wage high enough to support economic independence.

The decisions made concerning which actions should be taken to address a social problem eventually give rise to specific *social policies.* In turn, these shape the programs and services provided by social agencies and other human services organizations. Many of the social agencies that serve as social work practicum settings have been assigned the responsibility of carrying out these social policies and designing specific programs and interventions to solve the problem.

The specific actions by agency employees can be viewed as their *practices*. The relationship between a social condition, a social policy, a social program and practices is outlined in Figure 10.1.

GUIDANCE AND DIRECTION

In any community or society, there is great variety in the perspectives of its members as they seek to understand and explain the social problems they observe and experience. These different viewpoints will be based on personal experiences, attitudes, values, information, misinformation, and stereotypes. You may think that some of these perspective are biased or uninformed, but it is important to realize that the beliefs make sense and seem valid to those who hold them.

These differences and the political debate which arises from them will sometimes result in social policy that you support and, at other times, in policy that you see as ineffective or harmful. Remember that the democratic political process is influenced by public attitudes, values, information, and power.

As our society becomes more diverse and pluralistic, there will be even more differences in how people think about social conditions and social problems. Strive to understand perspectives that are different from your own. Expect increasing numbers of lively discussions, heated debates, and serious conflicts between groups with very different views about what constitutes social problems

---

SOCIAL CONDITION (an existing situation or phenomena)

SOCIAL PROBLEM

The people of a community or society judge the social condition to be unacceptable and are motivated to do something about it. The condition is now perceived as a social problem.

For a condition to "become" a social problem, its existence must somehow threaten or disturb those groups that have the power or influence to bring about a collective and political response and move others to address the problem.

SOCIAL POLICIES

The existence of a social problem calls forth or requires some type of action. A social policy is an agreed upon course of action. Policy makers (e.g., legislators) propose various policy options based on their values and their beliefs and knowledge about the nature and cause of the problem.

A political process determines which of the possible options is chosen. These policies are then expressed in laws, in administrative rules and regulations, and in the budgeting process and the allocations of monies.

Policies change over time in response to new knowledge or a shifting political climate.

SOCIAL PROGRAMS

Social programs flow from, or are expressions of, social policy. A program is a planned and organized effort that reflects the social policies. A program is designed to accomplish a certain outcome.

A program exists as an organization or as a component of a formal organization. Programs require funds for staff, office space, travel, staff training, equipment, various client services, etc.

PRACTICES

Practices are actions performed by those hired to perform the tasks and activities required by the social policies and social programs.

Figure 10.1   The Evolution of Policies, Programs, and Practices

Food for Thought

[Elements of subjectivity are involved in defining a social problem.] To identify a phenomenon as a problem implies that it falls short of some standard. But what standards are to be used? . . . In a pluralistic society like ours there is no uniform set of guidelines. People from different social strata and other social locations (such as region, occupation, race, and age) differ in their perceptions of what a social problem is, and once defined, how it should be solved. Is marijuana use a social problem? Is pornography? Is the relatively high rate of military spending a social problem? Is abortion a social problem? There is little consensus in U.S. society on these and other issues. All social observers, then, must be aware of differing viewpoints and respect the [various] perspectives. . . . (Eitzen and Baca Zinn 1994, 5)

◆◆◆

Definitions of social problems are expressed in terms that describe the condition, reflect attitudes toward the condition, and give numerous other hints as to how that condition is considered offensive or problematic. Groups vie for control of the definition of a problem. When one group wins, its vocabulary may be adopted and institutionalized while the concepts of the opposing group fall into obscurity. When terminology changes, when new terms are invented, or existing terms are given new meaning, these actions signal that something important has happened to the career or history of a social problem. (Spector and Kitsuse 1977, 8)

◆◆◆

[Problems of adolescent crime, dropouts, school-age childbearing, etc.] . . . can be studied separately, but in the real world they interact, reinforce one another, and often cluster together in the same individuals. Increasingly, the individuals also cluster, and the damage that begins in childhood and becomes so visible in adolescence reverberates throughout a neighborhood as part of an intergenerational cycle of social devastation. (Schorr 1989, 15).

◆◆◆

Poverty by itself, does not necessarily generate violence; it is the loss of hope that creates violence. When the children of my neighborhood are planning their funerals instead of their futures, it is a sure sign that we, as a society, have lost our sense of hope. (Wallis 1994, 6)

◆◆◆

I don't think of all the misery, but of the beauty that still remains.

—*Anne Frank*

◆◆◆

Every bigot was once a child free of prejudice.

—*Mary De Lourdes*

◆◆◆

There may be many times when we are powerless to prevent injustice, but there must never be a time when we fail to protest it.

—*Elie Wiesel*

and what ought to be done about them. If you wish to address social problems at the community or societal level, you will need to contribute reason, solid data, and political influence to this debate.

To a large extent, your understanding of social conditions and social problems will be rooted in your liberal arts background and in course work in sociology, psychology, economics, political science, anthropology, and history. You may have had personal experiences that deepen your understanding of certain problems, or perhaps these experiences serve to bias your viewpoint, particularly if the associated pain and conflict have not been satisfactorily resolved at an emotional level. Strive to develop an awareness of what you truly believe and why.

It is important to remember that clients who are experiencing problems firsthand may view them very differently from the way you do. A situation that you or other professionals define as a problem may not seem like a problem to your client or vice versa.

If you have never struggled with poverty, were not raised in an unsafe home or neighborhood, or have not been affected by racism, you may not fully appreciate the profound effects these experiences can have on people. Listen sensitively to client accounts of their life experiences so that you can better understand their importance.

Continually deepen your knowledge about how social problems such as poverty, violence, or racism develop not only so you can help clients improve their social functioning, but so you can also work toward the prevention of these social problems. If you are familiar with the multitude of individual, family, community, and economic factors associated with various social problems, you will be better equipped to devise effective strategies of intervention and prevention.

Draw upon your understanding of the ecosystems perspective and social systems theory to examine how social problems develop and change over time. Identify the many factors, conditions, and circumstances that interact to create a social problem. As you gain experience, you will see more clearly how one social problem can lead to or exacerbate others, or how several problems clustered together can overwhelm clients and have devastating consequences. You will also see that social change at the macro level must take place in order to enhance the social functioning of individual clients and families.

Give serious thought to the concept of prevention. What changes at the community and societal level are needed in order to prevent adverse conditions and social problems from developing in the first place? Do existing prevention programs appear to be effective? Do we have the knowledge, the resources, and the political will to launch effective programs of prevention? What would various solutions cost and from where would this money come? As you ponder various strategies, consider the advantages, disadvantages, feasibility, and probable effectiveness of various prevention efforts at the micro, mezzo, and macro levels. What groups might oppose prevention programs and why?

During your practicum, you will most likely meet clients who are truly remarkable, positive human beings despite the fact that they grew up in very destructive environments. For reasons that we are just beginning to understand, some individuals are resilient and able to resist the negative influences of a corrosive environment. Seek to understand why the same environment affects people differently. Learn from your clients about the strengths and resiliency factors that have made it possible for them to overcome adversity.

THE PROBLEMS AND NEEDS ADDRESSED BY YOUR AGENCY: A WORKBOOK ACTIVITY

1. What specific human and social conditions, needs, or problems does your practicum agency attempt to address?

_____

_____

_____

_____

2. Within the geographical area served by your agency, how many people are estimated to have the specific condition(s), problem(s), or need(s) addressed by your agency?

_____

3. How do these numbers and data compare with state and national statistics regarding the prevalence of this social problem or condition?

_____

_____

_____

4. What particular subpopulations are most likely to experience these problems, needs, or conditions? For example, is there a particular age group, gender, racial or ethnic group, socioeconomic class, or occupational group that is most likely to experience the problems or conditions addressed by your agency?

_____

_____

_____

5. In what way does the existence of these social conditions, problems, and needs violate the values, beliefs, norms, or safety and security of the community or society? How will the community be harmed if these conditions or problems grow larger and more serious?

_____

_____

_____

_____

6. In what way does the existence of these social conditions, problems, and needs violate your own core values, beliefs and norms, or your own safety and security? How are you personally affected by such conditions or problems?

_____

_____

_____

_____

7. What groups and organizations in your community have argued that the concerns or conditions addressed by your agency should indeed be defined as problems that require action in the form of programs, services, and interventions? In other words, who believes in and supports what your agency is trying to do?

_____

_____

_____

8. What groups and organizations in your community have argued that the concerns or conditions addressed by your agency should not be viewed as real or significant problems and that the programs and services provided by your agency are unnecessary, misdirected, or of low priority? In other words, who does not believe in and support what your agency is trying to do?

_____

_____

_____

9. What groups or organizations, if any, stand to benefit economically or politically from the continued existence of these social conditions, problems, and needs?

_____

_____

_____

10. What groups or organizations, if any, might be penalized or in some way harmed (e.g., by higher taxes and loss of power or status) by a more extensive or successful effort to eliminate or reduce these social conditions, problems, and needs?

_____

_____

_____

11. Was there a time within the past twenty-five to fifty years when the community or society paid little or no attention to the conditions, problems, or needs now addressed by your agency? If yes, what has happened to bring about a change in viewpoint or opinion? Why are these conditions or problems now of concern to the community or society?

_____

_____

_____

_____

12. Has the problem or concern addressed by your agency become more or less serious in the past ten years?

_____

_____

_____

_____

13. What criteria are used to measure the seriousness of the problem or condition?

_____

_____

_____

_____

14. Are there different opinions and perspectives about the seriousness of the problem? If so, are these differences based on different definitions of the problem, different statistics, or differences in attitudes toward the problem?

_____

_____

_____

_____

15. In what ways are the problems and concerns addressed by your agency related to other broad social problems such as poverty, crime, racism, violence, high rates of divorce, substance abuse, lack of affordable health care, lack of jobs, or changes in societal values and attitudes?

_____

_____

_____

_____

_____

16. What differing opinions, beliefs, and theories of causation are offered to explain the existence of the human and social conditions, problems, and needs that are addressed by your agency?

   a. Opinions and beliefs held by persons and groups in your community who fund and support your agency?

   _____

   _____

   _____

   b. Opinions and beliefs held by persons and groups in the community who oppose your agency and its programs and services?

   _____

   _____

   _____

   c. Opinions and beliefs held by the clients or consumers who use your agency's services and programs?

   _____

   _____

   _____

   d. Opinions and beliefs held by the professionals and staff who are employed within your practicum setting?

   _____

   _____

   _____

17. How do the various professional groups in the community and society differ in their explanation of and the solutions proposed for the problems and concerns addressed by your agency (e.g., the views of physicians, nurses, lawyers, police, economists, business people, psychologists, clergy, teachers, sociologists, and social workers)? On what points do they agree?

   _____

   _____

   _____

   _____

18. In what ways, and to what degree, are the ordinary citizens of the community or society divided in their opinions over what can and should be done in relation to these problems and concerns?

_____

_____

_____

_____

19. In what ways, if any, are new research findings in the social and behavioral sciences changing the way your agency conceptualizes and explains the problems, conditions, and needs that it attempts to address?

_____

_____

_____

_____

20. Given the results of various demonstration programs, experimental approaches, and research projects around the country, what approaches to these problems, conditions, and needs appear to be most effective and efficient?

_____

_____

_____

_____

21. What specific steps and actions would be needed to prevent these problems or conditions? Why these actions rather than others?

_____

_____

_____

_____

22. In what specific areas and on what questions would you recommend that research and demonstration projects focus in order to build knowledge about the social problem your agency addresses (e.g., genetic influence on addictions, resiliency factors for adolescents, child abuse prevention principles, effects of racial discrimination on social functioning, and indicators of wellness)?

_____

_____

_____

23. What local, state, or federal monies or funding programs are available to combat the problem your agency addresses (e.g., United Way funding, government grants, line items in state budgets, private foundations, and service organizations with specific human service priorities)?

   _____

   _____

   _____

24. What national resources or organizations address or provide help for this social problem (e.g., clearinghouses, advocacy groups, and toll free hotlines)?

   _____

   _____

   _____

   Additional notes and comments:

   _____

   _____

   _____

   _____

   _____

   _____

SUGGESTED LEARNING ACTIVITIES

- Review agency manuals, annual reports, and other documents in order to identify the specific human and social problems addressed by your agency.
- Attend meetings of client groups that focus on the social problems addressed by your agency (e.g., Narcotics Anonymous or agency advisory councils) to determine their theories of causation for problems they have experienced personally.
- Conduct interviews with experienced professionals within the agency to better understand the theories of causation that shape the agency's programs, procedures, and staff interactions with the agency's clients and consumers.
- Attend public meetings (e.g., city council meetings) and read the letters to the editor of the local newspaper in order to better understand the various ways in which people explain the existence of social problems and the variety of solutions that may make sense and seem logical to them.
- Attend the meetings of a group or organization that defines the problem addressed by your agency much differently than does your agency.

ADDITIONAL SUGGESTIONS AND HINTS

- Look through several textbooks that focus on human and social problems in search of information about the problems and conditions addressed by your practicum agency. For example, if your agency provides services to abused children, read chapters that present various theories that have been developed to explain the growing problem of child abuse and neglect.
- Examine the *Encyclopedia of Social Work* for chapters that offer a summary of basic information related to the various problems addressed by social workers and social agencies.
- Seek out and read recent community needs assessments to better understand how and why certain problems and needs are judged to be most serious and of highest priority in the community.
- Examine the most recent edition of the *Social Work Almanac* or a similar book that presents national statistics to determine how the problem addressed by your agency at the community level fits into a larger context at the national level.

SELECTED BIBLIOGRAPHY

Edwards, Richard L., ed. *Encyclopedia of Social Work.* 19th ed. Washington, DC: NASW Press, 1995.

Eitzen, D. Stanley, and Maxine Baca Zinn. *Social Problems.* 6th ed. Boston: Allyn and Bacon, 1994.

Ginsberg, Leon. *Social Work Almanac.* Washington, DC: NASW Press, 1995.

Schorr, Lisbeth. *Within Our Reach: Breaking the Cycle of Disadvantage.* New York: Doubleday, 1989.

Spector, Malcolm, and John Kitsuse. *Constructing Social Problems.* Menlo Park, CA: Cummings, 1977.

Sullivan, Thomas. *Social Problems.* 4th ed. Boston: Allyn and Bacon, 1997.

Wallis, Jim. *The Soul of Politics.* New York: New Press, 1994.

Zastrow, Charles. *Social Problems.* 5th ed. Belmont, CA: Wadsworth, 2000.

11

THE SOCIAL POLICY CONTEXT
OF PRACTICE

Goals for Learning

- To identify, become familiar with, and analyze the social policies that most directly influence the operation and activities of your practicum agency
- To identify, become familiar with, and analyze the social policies that most directly affect the clients or consumers served by your agency
- To become aware of the difference between an agency policy and a social policy, and of the interplay between these two types of policy
- To understand how social policies are formed and how they change over time

In the previous chapters we focused on the agency context, the community context, and the social problem context of social work practice. In this chapter we examine a fourth context, the social policy context. The clients or consumers served by your practicum agency, the other social workers and staff within this agency, and even your practicum experiences are affected, directly and indirectly, by social policy.

The study of social policy can be an exciting activity because it involves the examination of what we as a society believe about people, the problems experienced by people, and what can and should be done about these problems. It forces us to carefully examine our own beliefs and values and in the process we are sometimes surprised by what we discover about ourselves. While stimulating, the study of social policy is a complex undertaking. For example, the analysis of a particular social policy requires students to know how to locate relevant governmental documents and legal codes, understand the legislative process, and acquire a basic understanding of the many historic, political, cultural, and economic forces that shaped the development of a particular policy. The study of social policies and social policy development is further complicated because an agreed upon terminology does not exist. Consequently, those who discuss and write about social policy often use different words for basically the same concepts.

In this chapter we attempt to clarify the nature of social policy by defining and distinguishing between various terms and by explaining the impact of social policy on a social agency and on those that it serves. In addition, we offer specific suggestions on how you can identify and locate information concerning the social policies most relevant to your practicum setting.

BACKGROUND INFORMATION

Soon after beginning his or her practicum, the social work student discovers that the typical human services agency has an abundance of policies and procedures. Very often, as a matter of fact, one of the first assignments the student receives from his or her practicum instructor is to read the agency's policy manual. It is important for the student to recognize the difference between the policy statements found in an agency's policy manual and a social policy. In many settings, agency policies will reflect the influence of social policy, but an agency policy is not a social policy.

For purposes of this chapter, we offer a definition of a social policy:

> A *social policy* is a decision, made by public or governmental authorities, regarding the assignment and allocation of resources, rights, and responsibilities and expressed in laws and governmental regulations.

In this definition, the term *resources* refers to various social and economic benefits and opportunities, both tangible and intangible. Our use of the terms *assignment* and *allocation* implies that a policy may either offer or curtail these resources. The term, *responsibilities* refers to such matters as tax burdens, service in the military, payment for public services, and other duties common to citizenship.

Needless to say, lawmakers and government officials formulate policies on a wide variety of topics. Thus, there are public policies on international relations, economics and the monetary system, the tax structure, interstate and international commerce, military and defense, highways, public lands, environmental safety, education, and the like. For the most part, social policies address matters or issues related to the social well-being of people and the relationships between various groups within society. Thus, social policies focus on such concerns as marriage, divorce, adoption, domestic abuse, the special needs of the elderly, juvenile delinquency, mental health, discrimination against minority groups, training and job opportunities for the disadvantaged, economic assistance to the poor, availability of affordable housing, immigration, and other similar concerns. The term *social welfare policy* is often applied to those social policies that focus primarily on the distribution of economic benefits to those in need (e.g., public assistance, food stamps, subsidized housing, Medicaid, or subsidized child care).

Lowy (1991, 377–379) explains that public social policies are derived from four dichotomous approaches to the legislative process:

1. *Generic vs. Categorical Approach.*   A generic approach to social policy development seeks a particular outcome for an entire population, such as health care or housing for all people in society. By contrast, a categorical approach focuses on only one segment of the population, such as housing for the elderly or health care for children.
2. *Holistic vs. Segmented Approach.*   A holistic approach to policy development attempts to address the needs or concerns of the total person or the whole family, while a segmented approach focuses on only a single factor, such as an individual's income or nutrition. A segmented approach gives rise to a fragmented and confusing service system in which clients must approach several different agencies in order to secure the services or results they need in a system that completely fails to address some important needs.
3. *Rational vs. Crisis Approach.*   The rational approach places a heavy emphasis on deriving social policy from a careful and thorough study of the problem and issues. By contrast, the crisis approach creates policy as a hurried and usu-

ally highly political reaction to a crisis or serious problem. Very few of our country's social policies have grown out of the rational planning process.

4. *Future Planning vs. Political Context Approach.* The future planning approach gives careful consideration to social trends and probable future developments and tries to anticipate how the various policy options would fit with what can be expected in the future. By contrast, the political context approach is mostly concerned with solving an immediate problem and allows the policy to be determined mostly by popular opinion, political interests, and pragmatic assumptions about what will be supported and tolerated by dominant forces in society.

A social policy is created when a legislative body enacts a law, usually at the federal or state level but in some cases, at the county or city level. Once the law is enacted, high-level governmental officials and various governmental legal departments will usually prepare a set of rules and regulations that clarify the provisions of the law and describe in detail how the law is to be implemented. These directives are often called *administrative rules and regulations*. Subsequently, key provisions of the law and many of the rules and regulations are written into a public agency's manual of policy and procedure which guides its day-by-day operation and the decisions and actions of agency staff.

Statements of social policy are found in legal codes, in executive orders issued by the president and state governors, in administrative rules and regulations issued by governmental officials, and sometimes in statements and speeches made by high-ranking public officials. In some instances, legal decisions handed down by appellate courts have the effect of creating social policy.

Thus far we have spoken only about public social policies or those that were developed by elected officials and governmental bodies. Clearly, the vast majority of social policies are public policies. However, some social policies fall into a category that can be called *private social welfare policy* (or *nongovernmental social policy*). In this category are the national-level policies of large private agencies (e.g., YWCA), the policies of fund-raising organizations (e.g., the United Way), and policies formulated by community-wide social welfare planning bodies and perhaps school districts.

At the local or community level, such private social welfare policies can have a significant impact on the operation of voluntary agencies and on the establishment of their service priorities. For example, a local United Way organization may decide (i.e., formulate a policy) that because it can fund only a limited number of agencies and programs, its priority will be to fund those that address basic needs such as emergency food and shelter and consequently, other types of programs such as Boy Scouts or Big Brothers and Big Sisters would be assigned a lower priority in the allocation of funds raised by the United Way campaign.

As indicated above, an agency policy is not a social policy, but social policies do filter down to the level of a local or community agency and find their way into the agency's policy manual. At the local level, social policies have a significant impact on an agency's services and programs and on what a social worker actually does or does not do in his or her work with clients. The impact of social policy on agency policy is most evident in the operation of a public agency where one will find that many of the statements found in a public agency's manual are a direct response to specific legal codes and various governmental rules and regulations.

The far-reaching and sometimes subtle effects of a national or state level social policy on a social agency, on the practice of social work in that agency, on the

Food for Thought

Demands for public programs, services, subsidies, and supports continue to outstrip revenue derived from taxes. Large annual deficits and growing national debt make enactment of new initiatives extraordinarily difficult. At the same time, the United States is wealthier than ever before, and the government is spending a higher proportion of the gross national product on public programs than ever. Thus, for contemporary America, the question may not be how much is spent, but how the funds collected by government are allocated. The real poverty in American government may not lie in its lack of wealth but in its inability to amend or eliminate old programs and its concomitant difficulty in agreeing on policies and finding sufficient funds for new ones. Government is becoming increasingly paralyzed because of special interest groups that hamper reallocation of existing program dollars. Over time, programs that were once innovative and progressive become part of established government structure, and program employees, as well as outside interests, fight to retain programs long beyond their time of need. (Dear 1995, 2230–2231)

◆ ◆ ◆

Students sometimes think that time spent in [social policy] courses could be more effectively devoted to the development of practitioner skills. I believe the reverse is true. It is precisely because policy makers have so little understanding of the impact of policy on clients that practitioners need to have an understanding of the limits and problems of the policy makers. The social worker called upon to implement particular kinds of decisions needs to understand that, for the most part, regulations are not made with indifference to the welfare of clients. Social workers also need to understand the policy processes so that they can effect change when policy makers have been ill informed or have acted capriciously. Only by understanding the range of choices that are economically efficient and politically feasible, while still being responsive to the underlying social problem, can social workers do this successfully. Proposed alternatives to a flawed policy must take into account what the current policy offers, as well as the values, both implicit and explicit, in the alternatives. (Heffernan 1992, 4)

◆ ◆ ◆

Policy shapes and delineates what the practitioner does, how he or she relates to the client group, and the manner in which discretion is allowed or exercised. Policy also provides the priorities within which the practitioner can allocate time and other resources and, consequently, provides a structure for how one's professional role is to be carried out. . . . it also shapes the nature of things at the program level, setting the agency's direction, the content of services, and the tone and quality of the milieu within which work is accomplished and services provided. The workers . . . have many opportunities to set, modify, and even negate social policy in both formal and informal ways. Thus, we may infer that social practitioners undertake policy analysis at all times, at least at some level of consciousness, as evidenced by their dutifully or creatively carrying out policy mandates or by their purposefully engaging in social action at various system levels to modify or even resist those mandates. (Flynn 1992, 21)

◆ ◆ ◆

If a free society cannot help the many who are poor, it cannot save the few who are rich.

—*John F. Kennedy*

◆ ◆ ◆

A government that robs Peter to pay Paul can always depend on the support of Paul.

—*George Bernard Shaw*

◆ ◆ ◆

The test of our progress is not whether we add more to the abundance of those who have too much, it is whether we provide enough for those who have too little.

—*Franklin D. Roosevelt*

◆ ◆ ◆

Policy advocates need perspective to avoid pessimism and self-recrimination in the wake of defeats or partial successes. No single person or group is likely to prevail on the complex playing field of policy deliberations. Advocates must realize that defeats are more likely when people champion the needs of stigmatized and relatively powerless groups, which lack the clout of more powerful interests. (Jansson 1999, 23)

◆ ◆ ◆

The social worker in public settings carries out programs created by the public through elected representatives. Although members of the public are rarely aware of the intricacies of social programs, the programs do represent the choice, considered or not, of the voters. Inadequate financing or discriminatory programs may represent the wishes of an electorate choosing among the conflicting demands for tax money. The social worker who protests is risking a less-than-enthusiastic response. (Schroeder 1995, 5–6)

individual social worker employed by the agency, and on the agency's clients is illustrated in the following sequence of concerns, decisions, and responses:

- The problems, concerns, and unmet needs of people and various political responses and economic considerations at the state and national level give rise to a social policy.
- The nature of the social policy shapes the programs that are created to respond to human needs and problems.
- The nature and purpose of the programs shape the function, structure, and funding of those agencies or organizations that are to administer the programs.
- Organizational function, structure, and the funding mechanisms and restrictions shape the formation of the agency's policies, operational procedures, and the writing of the agency manual to be followed by the agency's personnel (i.e., the social workers employed by the agency).
- Agency policy and procedure shape and influence the social worker's selection of a practitioner role, theoretical frameworks for practice, tasks to be performed, and the relative priorities among those professional tasks and activities.
- The roles, tasks, and activities of the social worker shape and influence the relationships he or she forms with the agency's clients or consumers and the nature of the services provided to them.
- The services provided by the social workers shape and influence the behavior and needs of clients and consumers.

Social policies are a reflection of values and what is believed to be right and wrong, desirable and undesirable. They are mostly shaped by those having power and influence. As explained in Chapter 10, the formulation of social policy is basically a political process and politics is primarily about power. It is the art of gaining, exercising, and retaining power.

If social policies are ill conceived, because the decision makers either do not understand the problem or have erroneous beliefs about its causes, the resulting social programs will also be flawed. Those who understand the concerns being addressed and understand the inadequacies of existing policies and programs, have both an obligation and an opportunity to provide accurate information to the decision makers so they can develop appropriate and effective social policies.

GUIDANCE AND DIRECTION

Social work students differ widely in their level of interest in social policy. You may be very interested in learning about social policy so that you can take part in its formulation. You may be excited at the prospect of working at the macro level to design social policies and social programs that could improve the lives of many people. You may see social change and social policy development as the most efficient way to help large numbers of people and promote social justice.

On the other hand, you may see yourself as primarily a direct services provider and have less interest in social policy. You may prefer to help clients and families, one by one, and in a very personal way. The idea of becoming involved in political action and social change efforts may have little appeal. But even if that is the case, it is still imperative for you to understand social policy and how it affects your clients, positively or negatively. In order to be an informed advocate for your clients and a skilled provider of direct services, you must understand specific social policies, their strengths and limitations, and why they exist in their current form.

Depending on your practicum setting, you will need to become familiar with a cluster of social policy issues and concerns. You must acquire a basic or working understanding of the social policies that most directly influence the operation of your agency, its own agency policies, and its clients or consumers. Below is a list of social policy domains that are of interest to many social workers and many social agencies.

Abortion	Homelessness
Adolescent pregnancy	Housing
Adult protection (abuse and	Immigration and refugees
neglect of older persons)	Job creation and unemployment
Child protection (abuse and neglect	Juvenile delinquency and adult
of children)	crime
Community and neighborhood	Long-term care
development	Marriage and divorce
Day care for children	Mental health and mental illness
Discrimination and racism	Physical and mental disabilities
Domestic violence	Preschool, elementary, and
Economic development	secondary education
Family planning	Public assistance/welfare
Foster care and adoption	Public health and safety
Health care and rehabilitation	Substance abuse

Social policy is constantly evolving as a result of changing societal needs, changing values, changes in financial resources available to implement policy, and, of course, political forces. You will need to keep abreast of proposed legislative changes and find ways to have input into the political process. During your practicum, make a special effort to involve yourself in the following activities:

1. Participating in task forces or committees working to pass a law
2. Participating in grassroots or advocacy groups seeking to change social policy
3. Giving testimony at public meetings or legislative hearings that solicit public input before social policy decisions are made

As you participate in such activities, always be aware of the fact that when social workers do not engage in the politics of forming social welfare policy and allocating funding for social welfare programs, many client needs and concerns are overlooked by the decision makers, and the insights and values of the social work profession are omitted from the policy development process.

You will need to develop and utilize a model or conceptual framework to guide your examination of the social policies that impact the operation of your agency and either support or undermine the social functioning of your clients. Examples of such models can be found in textbooks on social welfare policy. The questions listed in the workbook activity in this chapter are ones often addressed in the various models and conceptual frameworks used in policy analysis.

Sources of information regarding a social policy include the original code or statute, administrative rules and regulations, and other governmental documents that describe and explain the policy. Various professional and advocacy organizations (e.g., Child Welfare League of America, National Association of Social Workers, American Association of Retired Persons, Children's Defense Fund, American Public Welfare Association, American Hospital Association, Mental Health Association) distribute reports of their analysis of social policies relevant to their particular concerns. In addition, the observations of social workers and of clients will give you insight into how a given policy affects the lives of individuals and families. The social workers in your agency will have opinions about how social policy could be improved, how it benefits or harms clients, and how it complements or conflicts with other social policies.

As a way of learning about social policy, we suggest that you identify a social problem (e.g., child abuse) which your agency addresses. Next, identify a specific social policy related to that problem (e.g., child abuse reporting laws or permanency planning laws). Using the questions found in the workbook activity, analyze this social policy and determine if it is adequate, effective, and positive in its effects.

During your analysis, consider the following categories of social policies, each of which reflects a philosophy, a set of values, and a belief system about how society should deal with social problems:

- *Policies of social and financial support* are intended to help or encourage people to carry out their roles and responsibilities and meet their basic needs for food, shelter, and so on. Examples include policies related to financial assistance, medical care for the poor, and subsidized day care for the children of parents who are poor.
- *Policies of protection* are those that seek to protect people from harm and exploitation, especially those who are most vulnerable. Examples are policies related to child abuse and neglect, domestic violence, the frail elderly, and to groups often subjected to discrimination and oppression.
- *Policies of rehabilitation and remediation* are intended to correct or minimize the impact of certain disabling conditions such as serious mental illness, severe physical disabilities, developmental disabilities, and chronic illness.
- *Policies of prevention* attempt to prevent certain social and health problems from developing or increasing. Examples are those that encourage immunizations, parent education, family planning, proper nutrition, and curfews for youth.
- *Policies of punishment and correction* seek to punish and control those who violate laws and societal norms. Examples are policies related to crime and delinquency, probation and parole, and the monitoring of convicted sex offenders.

The social policy you are analyzing will probably be one of these types, and thinking about it this way will help you understand the overall intent of the policy, the values which drive it, and how it may reflect public attitudes and political ideology.

As you study a social policy, you will soon be able to describe it in terms of:

- Its authority and auspices (federal, state, or local law)
- Its history and the reasons for its development
- Its stated purpose and goals
- Its key principles and main provisions
- Its impact on your agency's operation
- Its impact on your clients
- Its positive effects and advantages
- Its negative effects and disadvantages
- Its relationship to other social policies

After you have become familiar with a specific social policy and its effects, consider how it could be improved and what steps or actions would be necessary to achieve those improvements, such as changes in existing legislation, changes in administrative rules, or the creation of incentives to adhere to the policy.

SOCIAL POLICY ANALYSIS: A WORKBOOK ACTIVITY

Identify one public social policy that has a significant impact on the operation of your agency and/or on the clients or consumers served by your agency. Then, in relation to that specific policy, answer the questions presented below.

1. What is the official name of the social policy being studied?

   _____

2. What is the legal citation of the policy (e.g., public law number or state statute code number)?

   _____

3. When was the social policy enacted or established and when was it significantly modified?

   _____

   _____

   _____

4. What programs are commonly associated with this policy?

   _____

   _____

   _____

   _____

   _____

5. What conditions, problems, or needs does this social policy address (e.g., crime, poverty, lack of adequate housing, mental illness, lack of child care, or child abuse)?

   _____

   _____

6. What are the overall goals of this social policy (e.g., protection of children, provision of public assistance, and social control)?

   _____

   _____

7. Does this social policy apply to all people in society or to only a segment of society? If only certain people, which ones?

   _____

   _____

8. If this policy creates certain benefits or services, what are the criteria for eligibility? Why do some people receive benefits, services, or protection while others do not?

_____

_____

_____

_____

9. What underlying values, beliefs, or assumptions about people and their needs or problems are reflected in this policy?

_____

_____

_____

_____

10. Who benefits from this social policy?

_____

_____

11. Who loses or is placed at a disadvantage as a result of this social policy?

_____

_____

12. Have aspects of the social policy been challenged in a state or federal appeals court? If so, what was the basis for the legal challenge and how have the courts ruled on the matter?

_____

_____

_____

_____

13. What is the source of the funds used to provide these benefits or services (e.g., federal or state income taxes, property tax, sales tax, and voluntary donations)?

_____

_____

14. Does the funding required to implement this social policy need to be reauthorized regularly (e.g., each year or every two years)?

_____

15. Is this social policy doing what it was supposed to do? If not, why not?

_____

_____

_____

_____

16. In what ways could this social policy be changed to better address the needs and concerns of those it is designed to assist (e.g., close gaps in services, coordinate with related programs, increase funding, and change eligibility criteria)?

_____

_____

_____

_____

17. What would it take to actually change this policy (e.g., legislation, amendments, and coalition building)?

_____

_____

_____

18. Does one political party support this policy more than another? If yes, why?

_____

_____

_____

19. Who opposes this policy and would like to change or eliminate it? Why?

_____

_____

_____

20. What interest groups, advocacy groups, or grassroots organizations support this social policy? Why?

_____

_____

_____

21. What interest groups, advocacy groups, or grassroots organizations oppose this social policy? Why?

_____

_____

_____

_____

22. What administrative and organizational arrangements are used to deliver the social policy's protections, benefits, or services (e.g., administered and provided directly by a governmental agency and provided by private agencies under contract with a governmental agency)?

_____

_____

_____

23. How are the roles and duties of social workers in your agency shaped, constrained, or expanded by this social policy?

_____

_____

_____

_____

24. To what degree and in what ways do agency staff at the local level have an opportunity to use professional judgment and discretion in deciding to whom and how the protections, services, and benefits associated with this policy are made available to clients and consumers?

_____

_____

_____

_____

25. What measures, if any, are in place to make sure the benefits or services are provided in a fair and equitable manner and not influenced by such factors as staff preference and bias, racial discrimination, or friendship?

_____

_____

_____

_____

26. What other social policies are interrelated with this particular policy? Do they fit together well or are they in conflict with each other?

_____

_____

_____

_____

Additional notes and comments:

_____

_____

_____

_____

_____

_____

SUGGESTED LEARNING ACTIVITIES

- Interview a social worker in your agency about a social policy that most directly affects his or her clients and obtain his or her recommendations for improving the social policy.
- Review the NASW *Code of Ethics* (1997) guidelines regarding the social worker's responsibility in the area of social policy. (http://www.socialworkers.org)
- Examine the most recent edition of *Social Work Speaks,* which describes NASW's stance or position on a wide variety of social issues.
- Attend legislative or public hearings that gather public input before a social policy is enacted or modified.
- Identify your personal position regarding a controversial area of social policy, such as abortion. Attend meetings of an organization that takes an opposing position to try to understand that perspective, including the values, beliefs, knowledge, and assumptions on which it is based.
- Invite a state legislator to discuss the process by which social legislation is proposed, developed, and passed into law.

ADDITIONAL SUGGESTIONS AND HINTS

- Use the Internet to monitor the progress of bill before the U.S. Congress or your state legislature. For information on federal legislation relevant to social work, explore NASW's legislative page at http://naswca.org/legis.html.

SELECTED BIBLIOGRAPHY

Dear, Ronald. "Social Welfare Policy." In *Encyclopedia of Social Work.* 19th ed. Ed. Richard Edwards. Washington, DC: NASW Press, 1995.

Flynn, John. *Social Agency Policy.* 2nd ed. Chicago: Nelson-Hall, 1992.

Gilbert, Neil, and Paul Terrell. *Dimensions of Social Welfare Policy.* 4th ed. Boston: Allyn and Bacon, 1998.

Ginsberg, Leon. *Conservative Social Welfare Policy.* Chicago: Nelson-Hall, 1998.

Heffernan, W. Joseph. *Social Welfare Policy.* New York: Longman, 1992.

Jansson, Bruce. *Becoming an Effective Policy Advocate.* 3rd ed. Pacific Grove, CA: Brooks/Cole, 1999.

Lowy, Louis. *Social Work with the Aging.* 2nd ed. Prospect Heights, IL: Waveland, 1991.

National Association of Social Workers. *Social Work Speaks.* 5th ed. Washington, DC: NASW Press, 2000.

Popple, Philip, and Leslie Leighninger. *The Policy-Based Profession.* Boston: Allyn and Bacon, 1998.

Schroeder, Leila. *The Legal Enviornment of Social Work.* Washington, DC: NASW, 1995.

Seccombe, Karen. *So You Think I Drive a Cadillac? Welfare Recipients' Perspective on the System and Its Reform.* Boston: Allyn and Bacon, 1999.

12

CULTURAL DIVERSITY

Goals for Learning

- To become familiar with how human services agencies and programs adapt programs and practices to address the concerns and needs of minority groups
- To understand how client experiences with minority status and discrimination might influence their lives and their use of human services and programs
- To become aware of the legal and ethical prohibitions against discrimination
- To understand your own values and beliefs and how they might affect relationships with persons from different backgrounds

We live in an increasingly diverse and pluralistic society. Our nation is made up of many distinct ethnic, religious, and cultural groups. Consequently, its people have different values, beliefs, traditions, and languages. Social workers and human services agencies are being challenged to find ways of recognizing, respecting, and accommodating differences while treating all clients and consumers with fairness and equality under the law.

Public and private human services agencies must be thoughtful and fair as they make decisions concerning who is eligible for the services they offer and how best to allocate limited resources. In keeping with federal law, agencies must avoid discrimination based on race, color, sex, national origin, age, religion, creed, and physical and mental disability.

Members of the social work profession believe that all people have worth, simply because they are human beings. All possess certain fundamental human rights and all have basic responsibilities, including the responsibility to treat others with respect, dignity, and fairness. These beliefs are prerequisites to peaceful relations among people, to social justice, and to the effective and proper operation of human services organizations.

BACKGROUND INFORMATION

Culture refers to the learned patterns of thought and behavior that are passed from generation to generation. One's culture consists of the unspoken and unquestioned assumptions and ideas about the nature or reality, the human condition, and how life should be lived. Everything we do, or think about doing, is influenced by the ways of thinking, values, beliefs, expectations, and customs that make up our culture. All of our professional knowledge and practice, all legal codes, and all agency policies and procedures are shaped by culture.

Whittaker and Tracy (1989) observe that every contact between a social worker and client is, at some level, a cross-cultural encounter.

> On the one hand, the worker brings a particular knowledge base, set of value components, and methods of helping—all of which have been shaped in part by his or her own cultural background, by that of the dominant culture, and by the values and ethics of the professional helping community. These influences shape the manner in which a social worker will define social problems, what aspects will be considered relevant to assess, and what specific interventions will be employed to ameliorate the problem. On the other hand, the client also brings cultural elements to the social work relationship, including culturally determined patterns of help seeking and service utilization. (147)

Ethnocentrism is the tendency to assume that one's own culture, including one's beliefs and way of life, is superior and an appropriate standard for judging the beliefs and behaviors of other people. Needless to say, we cannot avoid being ethnocentric to some degree because our own beliefs, values, and patterns feel natural and normal and seem rooted in common sense. These are such an integral part of us that it is difficult to realize that there can be other ways of thinking and living. However, we must strive to become more aware of how our own culture is influencing our thoughts, decisions, and actions in order to avoid misunderstanding our clients and failing to recognize and respect their unique culture.

Most people are prejudiced to some degree. The word *prejudice* means to prejudge or to judge before one has a factual basis for forming a judgment. It refers to evaluating a person in a negative way, simply because that person belongs to a group or category, such as an ethnic minority.

Prejudice can breed *discrimination*, which refers to decisions, behaviors, or actions that deprive an individual or a whole group of certain rights and opportunities. It should be noted that prejudiced beliefs and attitudes do not always give rise to discriminatory behavior. Moreover, it is possible to engage in discrimination without being prejudiced, as in the case of an employee or a professional who follows a culturally insensitive and unjust policy or is truly ignorant of how his or her decisions and behaviors are causing harm to a group.

Discrimination can be either intentional or unintentional, depending on whether it was motivated by prejudice and the intent to harm. Discrimination can be personal or institutional. In *personal discrimination*, an individual behaves in ways that cause harm to the members of a group. In *institutional discrimination*, the harm is the result of the beliefs and practices that are embedded in law, in social and economic systems, and in governmental or organizational policy. Examples of laws that seem discriminatory to many people include those requiring English as a primary language, those restricting refugees' or illegal immigrants' access to basic services, and those that disallow insurance and governmental benefits to domestic partners.

For both legal and ethical reasons, social workers must avoid discriminating. Section 4.02 of the NASW *Code of Ethics* (1997) states that:

> Social workers should not practice, condone, facilitate, or collaborate with any form of discrimination on the basis of race, ethnicity, national origin, color, sex, sexual orientation, age, marital status, political belief, religion, or mental or physical disability.

Sheafor, Horejsi, and Horejsi (2000) explain that:

It is difficult to completely rid ourselves of the prejudices we all acquire during our upbringing. However, it is possible and necessary for social workers to become aware of their prejudices and refrain from acts of discrimination. Certain behaviors are characteristic of professional helpers who are prejudiced in their thinking:

- Stereotyped explanations are given for the behavior of persons of a specific ethnic or minority group.
- The same helping strategies are used for all clients who are members of a particular ethnic or population group.
- The importance of culture and ethnicity in a person's life are easily dismissed or, on the other extreme, they are used to explain nearly all behavior.
- Discussions of race and culture are avoided or are talked about continuously. (175)

Clients' membership in a minority group is often a more significant influence on their interaction with a social worker or agency than is their membership in a specific cultural group. A *minority group* is one whose members have significantly less power and control over their lives than the members of the dominant or majority groups of the society. Typically, the members of a minority group experience some level of discrimination and, according to Schaefer (1996, 6), ". . . a narrowing of life's opportunities—for success, education, wealth, the pursuit of happiness—that goes beyond any personal shortcoming he or she may have."

Schaefer (1996) identifies several *characteristics of a minority group*. For example:

1. Members . . . share physical or cultural characteristics that distinguish them from the dominant group such as skin color or language. . . .
2. Members . . . experience unequal treatment and have less power over their lives than members of a dominant group have over theirs. Social inequality may be created or maintained by prejudice, discrimination, segregation, or even extermination.
3. Members . . . are born into the group. [Membership is not voluntary.]
4. Members . . . have a strong sense of group solidarity. [They] make strong distinctions between members of their own group (the in-group) and everyone else (the out-group). When a group is the object of long-term prejudice and discrimination, the feeling of "us versus them" can and often does become extremely intense. (7)

Minority status is not simply of function of numbers. In a given society, a particular group may be in the majority in terms of percentage of the overall population, but still have minority status. For example, even though females are slightly more numerous than males, women are often considered a minority group because they have less power and control over their lives than do men, and because they experience prejudice and discrimination based on gender. Minority status may also be tied to age, sexual orientation, physical or mental disability, socioeconomic status, educational background, or religion. If people perceive themselves as different from others or as less powerful and more vulnerable, these perceptions have an impact on help-seeking behavior, on how they expect to be treated, and on what they consider to be a useful and relevant service or program.

Social agencies vary in their capacity to respond effectively to culturally diverse clients. Cross (1988, 1–4) suggests that the various levels of cultural competency

Food for Thought

I have a dream that my four little children will one day live in a nation where they will not be judged by the color of their skin, but by the content of their character.

—Martin Luther King, Jr.

◆◆◆

In spite of their training, behavioral science students, researchers, and practitioners are no more immune to racism than is the average person. (Lum 1992, 133)

◆◆◆

Cultural Competence and Social Diversity

a. Social workers should understand culture and its function in human behavior and society, recognizing the strengths that exist in all cultures.

b. Social workers should have a knowledge base of their clients' cultures and be able to demonstrate competence in the provision of services that are sensitive to clients' cultures and to differences among people and cultural groups.

c. Social workers should obtain education about and seek to understand the nature of social diversity and oppression with respect to race, ethnicity, national origin, color, sex, sexual orientation, age, marital status, political belief, religion, and mental or physical disability. (NASW *Code of Ethics* 1997, Section 1.05)

◆◆◆

Regardless of your cultural heritage, it is essential that you honestly examine your own expectations, attitudes, and assumptions about working with various cultural and ethnic groups. . . . One mistake is to deny the importance of these cultural variables; another mistake is to overemphasize such cultural differences to the extent that helpers lose their spontaneity and thus fail to be present for their clients. . . .

It is essential that you do not get into the trap of perceiving individuals as simply belonging to a group. Remember that the differences among individuals within the same group are often greater than the differences between groups. (Corey and Corey 1993, 111–112)

◆◆◆

Empathy, which requires openness to the reality of another person's feelings, experiences, and perceptions, facilitates the conscious efforts of [social] workers in establishing relationships with clients of a different culture. Work with clients of a culture different from that of the workers' requires, in addition, an openness on the part of workers to values, norms, and world views that their own culture may not share. This requires of the workers the capacity to under-

stand and respect their own culture and the role it has played in their development, and to feel free to respect the culture of the other. It demands from workers a belief that no culture is inherently better than or superior to another, but that each is merely different. Such an attitude will allow workers to attempt to perceive situations from the point of view of the minority client. (Velasquez, Vigil, and Benavides 1994, 174)

◆◆◆

A person of color often approaches a formal, professional social service organization with varying degrees of resistance. The person may feel anxiety and uncertainty over the unknown, shame and guilt over failure to solve his or her own problems, or anger when there is legal coercion to use the service. Moreover, going to a helping agency may represent the last resort after the client has asked family, friends, and the community's natural support systems for help. (Lum 1992, 102)

◆◆◆

. . . the world view of the culturally different client who comes to counseling boils down to one important question: "What makes you, a counselor/therapist, any different from all the others out there who have oppressed and discriminated against me?" (Sue and Sue 1990, 6)

◆◆◆

Racism is a scholarly pursuit; it's taught, it's institutionalized.

—Toni Morrison

◆◆◆

Cultural self-awareness is a vital skill for social work practice. This includes recognition of one's own cultural influences upon values, beliefs and judgments, as well as the same influences derived from the professional culture of social work. Awareness of the effects of these personal and professional influences upon client relations is necessary for the implementation of an ethnic sensitive approach. Without self-awareness, biases will be unconsciously imposed and client self-determination will be compromised. The commitment of the social work profession to equal treatment of all groups requires an approach which is not "color blind," but rather sensitive to the particular situations of each individual, including the impact of their group membership on their lives. (Winkelman, 1999, 7)

◆◆◆

Generalizations are generally wrong.

—Mary Wortley Montague

and cultural sensitivity among human services agencies exist along a continuum. Six levels are identified on this continuum:

1. *Destructiveness*—The agency's policies, programs, practices, and attitudes are destructive to cultures and hence, to the individuals of the culture. The agency is aware of its negative effect on the peoples' culture and believes its actions are desirable or justified.
2. *Incapacity*—The agency's policies, programs, and practices are destructive but these negative effects are unintended and unrecognized.
3. *Blindness*—The agency does not recognize important differences. It assumes that all people are the same and that all clients can and should be treated the same without consideration of different customs and belief systems.
4. *Pre-Competence*—The agency recognizes its inability to properly serve minorities or those who are culturally different and is working to improve service to a specific population. Efforts may include recruiting minority personnel, seeking cultural knowledge, and building linkages with the minority community.
5. *Basic Competence*—The agency recognizes and respects cultural differences and conducts ongoing self-assessments of its policies and practices and continually works to expand its cultural knowledge and the special resources needed to adequately serve minority groups.
6. *Advanced Competence*—In addition to activities of basic competence, the agency strives to develop new knowledge of culturally competent practice and is an advocate for changes within the wider human services system and throughout society.

GUIDANCE AND DIRECTION

Many social work students work hard at being culturally sensitive and respectful of differences among people. However, they, like other people, may not always recognize their own biases, prejudices, or ignorance regarding diverse groups. The practicum offers an important opportunity for self-examination and self-correction. Use it well.

You may believe that people are more alike than different, and also that treating all clients alike is fair and reasonable. However, these beliefs do not recognize the importance of diversity, and may cause you to overlook unique aspects of a client's background and the powerful impact of minority status. While it is true that people have much in common, it is also true that there are differences and these can greatly affect social work practice. Sue and Sue (1990, 165) remind us that "In counseling, equal treatment may be discriminatory."

Be alert to the positive experiences resulting from minority group status, such as ethnic pride, bilingual abilities, community solidarity, extended family cohesion, and a strong sense of history. These experiences are strengths on which a professional relationship and a possible intervention can be built. Do not assume that membership in a minority group has only negative implications.

Work to understand any negative experiences your clients may have had because of their minority status, such as discrimination in school, housing or employment, inappropriate placement in foster homes, or threats and violence in the form of hate crimes. Remember that many personal problems such as depression, suicide, dropping out of school, substance abuse, criminal behavior, and even physical illness may have some roots in the stress and inner turmoil a person feels when subjected to discrimination or oppression.

If you are the member of a minority group, you may be better able to understand the effects of prejudice and discrimination. However, it is important for you to have satisfactorily resolved any related personal issues, anger, and resentment in order to be objective and to perceive the uniqueness of every situation and individual. A social worker who, for whatever reason, is bitter and has a personal agenda will be of little help to clients.

Social work with diverse clients is complex and demanding. Simple adaptations of usual approaches or slight changes in the agency's standard operating procedures are not likely to be effective. Rather, you will need to develop distinct methods that are acceptable, relevant to, and appropriate for the specific group with which you are working.

If the clients you serve are more comfortable with a language different from your own, make a genuine effort to learn at least some of their language. This demonstrates your respect for their language and your desire to understand and communicate.

Be alert to the fact that misunderstandings and misinterpretations in cross-cultural interactions can occur in many areas and situations including:

* Spoken language (e.g., misunderstanding words, accent, and nuances)
* Nonverbal communication (e.g., misunderstanding of gestures, facial expressions, and tone of voice)
* Judgments concerning what is an appropriate level of directness, assertiveness, and disclosure of personal information
* Male–female relations and in judgments concerning what is appropriate touching and appropriate expressions of attraction for another person
* Judgments concerning appropriate dress, body decorations, and level of modesty
* Importance assigned to punctuality, use of time, and planning ahead
* Work habits, ways of organizing and approaching work to be done, and level of formality in communication between employees in organization
* Use of physical space and judgment as to what is an appropriate distance between people
* Ways of learning and teaching and in giving and taking direction
* Ways of negotiating, handling conflict, and expressing emotion

Strive to learn about differences in worldview and how you and your clients may differ in the value and meaning assigned to, for example, loyalty and obligation to family and friends, time, money, mealtimes, independence, health and wellness, and religious practices.

Seek to understand your clients' beliefs about the appropriateness of asking for help and receiving help from professionals and agencies. The members of some ethnic groups may believe that personal and family problems should not be discussed with a person outside the family. Some may feel great shame if they must seek help from a stranger.

Recognize that different groups may hold very different beliefs about the nature and cause of personal problems. For example, some ethnic groups may view depression or physical illness as primarily a problem of spirituality (e.g., a consequence of eating a taboo food, having broken one's relationship with God, or of a lack of balance between one's spirit and body).

Appreciate that different groups have different ideas about what constitutes an appropriate method of helping and about who has the capacity and authority to help with or treat certain types of problems. For example, some people may choose to use informal helpers and spiritual leaders, prayer, purification ceremonies, and religious rituals rather than the services of a physician or psychotherapist. As a professional you will need to learn how to work cooperatively with spiritual leaders, healers, and clergy.

Be alert to the fact that clients from a minority group may have had or may expect negative experiences when they must have contact with social workers or social agencies, based on their group's history with the dominant culture. Clients may also be fearful of interacting with social workers because they fear legal recrimination for themselves (e.g., illegal immigrants and homosexual clients living in states that have laws prohibiting homosexual sexual activity). Their fears may be a barrier to their development of trust and their willingness to invest themselves in a professional helping relationship. Be careful not to interpret such mistrust, fear, or anger as client resistance. Do not automatically interpret client quietness, reticence, or anxiety as pathology or dysfunction.

When working with a client of a different cultural background, it is especially important to individualize that client. Miller (1982) emphasizes this point as she provides guidelines for cross-cultural interactions:

> Consider all clients as individuals first, as members of a minority status [second] and as members of a specific ethnic group [third]. Never assume that a person's ethnic identity tells you anything about his or her cultural values or patterns of behavior.
>
> Treat all "facts" you have ever heard or read about cultural values and traits as hypotheses, to be tested anew with each client . . .
>
> Remember that all minority group people in this society are bicultural, at least. The percentage may be 90–10 in either direction, but they still have had the task of integrating two value systems that are often in conflict. The conflicts involved in being bicultural may override any specific cultural content. (182)

CULTURAL AWARENESS IN YOUR AGENCY: A WORKBOOK ACTIVITY

1. What specific actions has your agency or organization taken to make sure it is in compliance with federal law that prohibits discrimination on the basis of race, color, sex, national origin, age, religion, creed, physical or mental disability, and (in matters of housing) familial status?

    _____

    _____

    _____

    _____

2. Does your state's anti-discrimination law include protected classes or categories in addition to those listed in federal law? If yes, what additional classes are included?

    _____

    _____

    _____

3. In what ways does your agency make accommodations for clients or consumers who have a physical or mental disability?

    _____

    _____

    _____

    _____

4. In what ways does your agency make accommodations for clients or consumers who have limitations of vision and hearing?

    _____

    _____

    _____

    _____

5. In what ways does your agency make accommodations for clients who are not fluent in or comfortable with the English language?

    _____

    _____

    _____

    _____

6. About what percentage of your agency's clients or consumers could be described as members of a cultural, ethnic, religious, or racial minority?

_____

What groups are they?

_____

_____

_____

_____

7. What special efforts has your practicum agency made to reach out to and provide relevant services or programs to members of minority groups?

_____

_____

_____

_____

8. What specific actions, if any, has your agency taken to make sure it does not discriminate on the basis of sexual orientation? On the basis of clients' political beliefs?

_____

_____

_____

_____

9. To what extent are members of minority groups represented on your agency's board of directors or on advisory boards?

_____

_____

_____

10. What culturally sensitive assessment instruments or practice techniques, if any, does your agency use with clients who are members of minority groups?

_____

_____

_____

_____

11. Is there anything about your agency which might discourage minorities from using its services (e.g., the racial, ethnic, or gender makeup of staff; location; office hours and days of operation; reputation in community; and perceived attitude toward minorities)?

_____

_____

_____

_____

12. What state or federal laws or regulations may affect minority clients negatively (e.g., anti-immigration laws and laws which prohibit same sex marriage)?

_____

_____

_____

_____

13. What grievance procedures are available to clients or consumers if they believe they have experienced discrimination by the agency or its staff?

_____

_____

_____

_____

14. About what percent of the personnel assigned to professional and administrative jobs within your agency are:

_____ % Members of a racial or ethnic minority

_____ % Persons with physical or mental disabilities

_____ % Women

_____ % Members of a religious minority

_____ % Over 65 years of age

_____ % Fluent in a second language

15. Does your agency or organization have an affirmative action program that is applied when hiring new staff? If yes, does the program achieve its purpose?

_____

_____

_____

_____

16. What types of accommodations are made within your agency to permit the employment of qualified persons with physical or mental disabilities?

_____

_____

_____

_____

17. Where on the cross-cultural continuum described by Cross (see Background Information) would you place your agency? Why?

_____

_____

_____

Additional notes and comments:

_____

_____

_____

_____

_____

_____

IDENTITY AND SELF-AWARENESS: A WORKBOOK ACTIVITY

1. How would you describe yourself in terms of gender? Race? Ethnicity? Socio-economic class? Religion? Age group? Minority group?

_____

_____

_____

_____

2. What are the positive aspects of each of these group identities or memberships for you?

_____

_____

_____

_____

3. What are the negative aspects of each of these group identities or memberships for you?

_____

_____

_____

_____

4. How might your identity, characteristics, and membership in particular groups affect your work with clients who are different from you?

_____

_____

_____

_____

5. What are your most common thoughts and feelings when you encounter people who are different from yourself?

_____

_____

_____

_____

_____

6. Describe a time and place when you were in the minority in terms of your race, skin color, ethnicity, or religion (i.e., most others present were of a different group). What were your feelings about this experience?

_____

_____

_____

_____

7. Describe your earliest memories of realizing your own identity in terms of your gender, race, ethnicity, socioeconomic class, and religion.

_____

_____

_____

_____

8. What positive and negative characteristics were ascribed to your gender, race, ethnicity, socioeconomic class, and religion by your family? Your relatives? Your neighbors? Your classmates in elementary school and high school?

_____

_____

_____

_____

9. What steps can you take to improve your skills in working with diverse clients?

_____

_____

_____

_____

Additional notes and comments:

_____

_____

_____

_____

_____

CULTURAL FACTORS IN CLIENT BEHAVIOR: SITUATIONS TO DISCUSS

Many factors influence the behavior and decisions of clients. One important set of factors, but certainly not the only one, is the client's cultural and ethnic background. Below, is a list of situations that a social worker might encounter. Read each one carefully, and identify possible cultural beliefs, values, and customs or issues in cross-cultural interaction that might be operating in this situation. Consider how cultural differences might result in a misunderstanding of the client's behavior. What additional information might be needed by the social worker in order to avoid such misunderstandings and to respond in a culturally sensitive manner?

1. A couple with six children hopes to have additional children. They live in a small and crowded house and have great difficulty paying their bills and handling expenses related to food, rent, and health care.

   _____

   _____

   _____

2. A man who needs his job and wants to keep it, did not report to work today. Instead, he drove 200 miles to be with a relative who had phoned him last night and requested his assistance.

   _____

   _____

   _____

3. A client did not appear for a scheduled appointment and did not submit an application form, even though these two actions are prerequisites for receiving government benefits that the client wants and desperately needs.

   _____

   _____

   _____

4. A male client touches the neck and shoulders of a female social worker and tells her that she is sexually attractive.

   _____

   _____

   _____

5. Without first checking with her counselor, a client brings two of her relatives to a scheduled individual counseling session.

   _____

   _____

   _____

6. When a social worker arrives at her client's home for a scheduled and critically important half-hour interview, the client greets the social worker and then invites her to sit at a table, meet two relatives and a friend, and have coffee and cake.

_____

_____

_____

7. The father and mother of a 16-year-old girl become very angry when their daughter asks if she can go on a date with a 17-year-old boy who is a high school classmate. The parents then restrict the daughter from all social activities for three months.

_____

_____

_____

8. The adults in a family that immigrated to this country three years ago avoid learning the English language, even though this decision erects a serious barrier to their economic advancement.

_____

_____

_____

9. A man is consistently fifteen to thirty minutes late for work even though he insists that he likes his job and wants to keep it.

_____

_____

_____

10. During the first meeting with a social worker, a client asks the worker many personal questions about the worker's parents, children, marriage, religion, and family history.

_____

_____

_____

11. A client who lives in near poverty and expresses a strong desire to obtain a decent job, refuses to take a well-paying job in another city 100 miles away.

_____

_____

_____

12. A woman whose husband restricts her movement, and verbally and physically abuses her, returns to live with her husband after seeking shelter for herself and her children in a domestic violence shelter.

_____

_____

_____

13. A husband and wife have been caring for the husband's elderly father for six years. The father is very ill and dependent, and requires round the clock care and supervision. A doctor and medical social worker suggest that the couple seek the help of a home attendant or consider placing the father in a nursing home. The couple becomes very angry and flatly refuses to even discuss such options.

_____

_____

_____

14. Parents who recently immigrated to this country refuse to authorize recommended corrective surgery for their daughter, a decision that will result in permanent disability.

_____

_____

_____

15. A woman whose 12-year-old daughter was sexually molested and impregnated by the child's uncle refuses to report this matter to authorities and wants to avoid making an issue out of the situation.

_____

_____

_____

16. An immigrant family who was robbed of several valuable possessions refuses to report the crime or speak with police.

_____

_____

_____

17. A community organizer hopes to bring people of a particular neighborhood together for a meeting to discuss actions that would improve health and safety in the area. Several members of one ethnic group say they are very interested in such a meeting. However, they tell the community organizer that they will

attend only if he makes sure that members of another ethnic group do not attend the meeting.

_____

_____

_____

18. An enrolled member of an American Indian tribe is in need of social services, but is reluctant to accept them from an agency that provides these services to individuals and families from many different backgrounds.

_____

_____

_____

SUGGESTED LEARNING ACTIVITIES

- Attend cultural and religious celebrations and activities that are meaningful to many of the clients or consumers served by your agency (e.g., powwows, religious celebrations, and gay pride events).
- Invite respected members of various ethnic and religious groups to explain how cultural and religious factors might influence clients' perceptions of the agency's programs and services and whether they would be inclined to use those services.
- Listen to music and read books and poetry by members of cultural or minority groups served by your agency.
- Study the history of the diverse groups your agency serves.
- Visit agencies that specifically serve members of minority groups (e.g., refugee programs, women's centers, and advocacy groups for persons with disabilities). Ask about how their programs differ from yours.
- Seek special training designed to help human services personnel respond more effectively to diverse clients.

ADDITIONAL SUGGESTIONS AND HINTS

- In Sheafor, Horejsi, and Horejsi (2000) read the section on "Cross-Cultural Helping."
- Read articles in the *Journal of Multicultural Social Work* and *Journal of Gay and Lesbian Services*.

SELECTED BIBLIOGRAPHY

Child Welfare League of America. *Cultural Competence Self-Assessment Instrument.* Washington DC: Child Welfare League of America, 1993.

Corey, Marianne, and Gerald Corey. *Becoming a Helper.* 2nd ed. Pacific Grove, CA: Brooks/Cole, 1993.

Cross, Terry. "Services to Minority Populations: Cultural Competence Continuum." *Focal Point* 3.1 (Fall, 1988): 1–4.

Lum, Doman. *Social Work Practice with People of Color: A Process-Stage Approach.* 2nd ed. Pacific Grove, CA: Brooks/Cole, 1992.

Miller, Nancy. "Social Work Services to Urban Indians." In *Cultural Awareness in the Human Services.* Ed. James Green. Englewood Cliffs, NJ: Prentice-Hall, 1982.

National Association of Social Workers. *Code of Ethics.* Washington, DC: NASW Press, 1997.

Schaefer, Richard. *Racial and Ethnic Groups.* 6th ed. New York: HarperCollins, 1996.

Sheafor, Bradford, Charles Horejsi, and Gloria Horejsi. *Techniques and Guidelines for Social Work Practice.* 5th ed. Boston: Allyn and Bacon, 2000.

Sue, Derald, and David Sue. *Counseling the Culturally Different: Theory and Practice.* 2nd ed. New York: John Wiley, 1990.

Velasquez, Joan, Marilyn E. Vigil, and Eustolio Benavides. "A Framework for Establishing Social Work Relationships across Racial/Ethnic Lines." In *Social Work Processes.* Ed. Beulah Compton and Burt Galaway. Pacific Grove, CA: Brooks/Cole, 1994.

Whittaker, James, and Elizabeth Tracy. *Social Treatment.* 2nd ed. New York: Aldine De Gruyter, 1989.

Winkelman, Michael. *Ethnic Sensitivity in Social Work.* Dubuque, IA: Eddie Bowers, 1999.

13

PROFESSIONAL SOCIAL WORK

Goals for Learning

- To understand the purpose and nature of the social work profession
- To clarify how social work is similar to and different from other helping professions
- To distinguish between professional and nonprofessional behavior
- To become aware of the challenges of adhering to principles of professional practice within a bureaucratic agency with many regulations and restrictions

Social workers see themselves as professionals. They describe their occupation as a profession. As a social work student you are expected to behave in a professional manner during your practicum, but what exactly is a profession and what does professional behavior look like? How does one decide whether clients are being treated in a truly professional manner and receiving a truly professional service? Does the presence of professionally trained social workers in an agency have an observable and positive effect on the nature and quality of the services received by clients or consumers?

Social work is one of many helping professions. Social workers often work closely with other helpers such as physicians, nurses, speech therapists, psychologists, substance abuse counselors, school counselors, and others. What do social workers do that is not done by the members of other helping professions? Is there anything unique or special about what social workers know or do? How is social work different?

This chapter will review basic information about the unique nature of our profession and offer criteria for judging whether your own work and the work you observe in your practicum setting is of a professional nature.

BACKGROUND INFORMATION

All professions and all professionals *profess* to have special knowledge and skills. They profess to understand certain phenomena better than those who do not have this special training. Because they profess to adhere to a code of ethical conduct, they expect to be trusted by their clients and by the public at large. They profess to be accountable for their decisions and actions. Professionals lay claim to a certain domain of activities. This is the basis for professional licensing and certification. From a legal perspective, professionals are responsible for providing their clients with a certain standard of care, and if they fail to do so, they may be sued for malpractice or professional negligence.

Broadly speaking, a *profession* is an occupation that possesses certain characteristics:

- A unique body of knowledge and theoretical underpinnings from which special skills and techniques are derived
- Methods of teaching this body of knowledge and skills to persons entering the profession
- Recognition by society that the members of the profession possess a special expertise
- Sanction by the community or state to perform certain activities
- Practitioners who share a distinct culture, specialized language or terminology, sense of purpose, identity, history, and set of values
- A writen code of ethics that guides practice activities
- A professional organization whose members are bound together by a common purpose
- Capacity and authority, usually by law, to regulate practice
- Ability to control the admission of new members to the profession
- Individuals entering the profession who usually feel a "calling" by virtue of their values, interests, or natural abilities

The NASW (1970, 2) defines *social work* as "the professional activity of helping individuals, groups, or communities enhance or restore their capacity for social functioning and creating societal conditions favorable to this goal." The term *social functioning* refers, in general, to the social well-being of people and especially their capacity and opportunity to *meet their basic needs* such as food, shelter, safety, self-worth, and to satisfactorily *perform their social roles* such as spouse, parent, student, employee, and citizen.

Social work professionals focus primarily on the interactions or transactions between the individual and his or her social environment. That environment is composed of a multitude of units and systems such as family; support networks; neighborhood and community groups and organizations; workplace; and various legal, educational, health, and human services systems. This is often referred to as the *person-in-environment* focus of the social work profession.

The Council on Social Work Education (1994) explains that professional social work practice serves the following purposes:

- The promotion, restoration, maintenance, and enhancement of the social functioning of individuals, families, groups, organizations, and communities by helping them to accomplish tasks, prevent and alleviate distress, and use resources
- The planning, formulation, and implementation of social policies, services, resources, and programs needed to meet basic human needs and support the development of human capacities
- The pursuit of policies, services, resources, and programs through organizational and administrative advocacy and social or political action, so as to empower groups at risk and promote social and economic justice
- The development and testing of professional knowledge and skills related to these purposes (135)

The first of these purposes is concerned with enhancing social functioning and preventing impediments to effective social functioning. The other three seek to create conditions and social policies that ensure that people receive appropriate human services when needed and to prevent social problems from developing. Stated somewhat differently, we can say that a social worker will perform tasks and activities aimed at achieving the following:

- Restoring and maintaining the social functioning of people
- Enhancing the problem-solving and coping capacities of people
- Preventing the occurrence of serious personal and social problems
- Linking people with those systems and resources that can provide needed support, services, and opportunities
- Promoting humane and effective social policy and human services programs
- Planning, developing, and administering social agencies and social programs
- Promoting the effective and humane operation and administration of organizations and human services delivery systems that provide people with resources, services, and opportunities
- Protecting the most vulnerable members of society from destructive social influences
- Protecting the community from persons who consistently behave in ways that harm others
- Conducting research, developing and disseminating knowledge relevant to the practice of social work

Social work is often described as a value-driven profession because so much of what a social worker does is guided by a particular set of core values. However, at a fundamental level, all professions are rooted in a particular set of values. For example, the medical profession values health and the education profession values learning. Thus, the physician strives to develop knowledge and methods that can be used to maintain and restore health, and the educator strives to develop knowledge and methods that facilitate learning.

A profession can be viewed as an organized effort to actualize its core values. This idea is reflected in the definition of *social work practice* offered by *The Social Work Dictionary* (Barker 1995, 95): "The use of social work knowledge and social work skills to implement society's mandate to provide social services in ways that are consistent with social work values."

The NASW *Code of Ethics* (1997, 5–6) identifies six core values that should inform and guide the decisions and actions of a social worker. These values and their implications are described as follows:

Value: *Service*

Ethical Principle: *Social workers' primary goal is to help people in need and to address social problems.*

Social workers elevate service to others above self-interest. Social workers draw on their knowledge, values, and skills to help people in need and to address social problems. Social workers are encouraged to volunteer some portion of their professional skills with no expectation of significant financial return (pro bono service).

Value: *Social Justice*

Ethical Principle: *Social workers challenge social injustice.*

Social workers pursue social change, particularly with and on behalf of vulnerable and oppressed individuals and groups of people. Social workers' social change efforts are focused primarily on issues of poverty, unemployment, discrimination, and other forms of social injustice. These activities seek to promote sensitivity to and knowledge about oppression and cultural and ethnic diversity. Social workers strive to ensure access to needed information, services, and resources; equality of opportunity; and meaningful participation in decision making for all people.

Value: *Dignity and Worth of the Person*

Ethical Principle: *Social workers respect the inherent dignity and worth of the person.*

Social workers treat each person in a caring and respectful fashion, mindful of individual differences and cultural and ethnic diversity. Social workers promote clients' socially responsible self-determination. Social workers seek to enhance clients' capacity and opportunity to change and to address their own needs. Social workers are cognizant of their dual responsibility to clients and to the broader society. They seek to resolve conflicts between clients' interests and the broader society's interest in a socially responsible manner consistent with the values, ethical principles, and ethical standards of the profession.

Value: *Importance of Human Relationships*

Ethical Principle: *Social workers recognize the central importance of human relationships.*

Social workers understand that relationships between and among people are an important vehicle for change. Social workers engage people as partners in the helping process. Social workers seek to strengthen relationships among people in a purposeful effort to promote, restore, maintain, and enhance the well-being of individuals, families, social groups, organizations, and communities.

Value: *Integrity*

Ethical Principle: *Social workers behave in a trustworthy manner.*

Social workers are continually aware of the profession's mission, values, ethical principles, and ethical standards and practice in a manner consistent with them. Social workers act honestly and responsibly and promote ethical practices on the part of the organizations with which they are affiliated.

Value: *Competence*

Ethical Principle: *Social workers practice within their areas of competence and develop and enhance their professional expertise.*

Social workers continually strive to increase their professional knowledge and skills and to apply them in practice. Social workers should aspire to contribute to the knowledge base of the profession.

These six core values are the foundation of social work practice.

Although social work is a profession, social workers may or may not behave in a professional manner. Nonprofessional behavior leads to diminished quality of services and may also violate the NASW *Code of Ethics*. Sheafor, Horejsi, and Horejsi (2000, 200–201) offer a comparison of professional and nonprofessional behavior in the table below.

Professional and Nonprofessional Behavior

Professional Behavior	Nonprofessional Behavior
Decisions and actions are based primarily on a body of knowledge learned through a process of formal education and training.	Decisions and actions are based primarily on personal opinions, personal preferences, or on agency rules and regulations.
Principles of good practice are followed, regardless of other pressures.	Political and fiscal pressure and other forces are allowed to dictate decisions and actions.
Objectivity is emphasized and decisions are based on the facts of the situation.	Decisions are based mostly on personal bias and personal convenience.
The profession's values, principles, and *Code of Ethics* are used to identify and resolve ethical issues.	Only personal moral judgments are used to resolve ethical questions. Many ethical issues go unrecognized or are ignored.
Knowledge and skills are continually developed so that services to clients can be improved.	Only what is required to keep the job is learned.
The relationship with the client is purposeful, goal-oriented, and time-limited.	The relationship with the client resembles a friendship.
The well-being and needs of the client are of primary concern; worker's personal needs are not expected to be met within work-related relationships.	The well-being and needs of the worker are of primary concern; worker expects to have personal needs met through contact with the client and within work-related relationships.
Review of performance by peers is expected and invited.	Peer review is threatening and is avoided.
Self-discipline in decision making and action is exercised; when with an angry or frustrated client, personal reactions are under control; personal feelings are expressed in a helpful and purposeful manner.	Emotions shape decisions and actions; when with an angry or frustrated client, reacts with anger and frustration; emotions may be expressed in a thoughtless and hurtful manner.
The client's expressions of negative emotion are not taken personally; worker seeks to understand the reasons behind the client's frustration and anger.	The client's frustrations and anger are taken personally.
Accurate and complete records of decisions and actions are kept.	Record keeping is avoided; records are incomplete or inaccurate.
Responsibility is taken for seeking new knowledge and information and for sharing it with peers.	The worker does not see self as responsible for the development of new knowledge or for teaching peers.
Personal responsibility is assumed for examining the quality of services delivered and for working to make the agency, program, or policy changes that would improve services to the client.	The worker is concerned only about doing the job as assigned or described by others; worker does not see self as responsible for agency, policy, or program changes.
Social work is regarded as a lifelong commitment; the occupation and work are seen as a "calling."	Social work is seen as a job that can be easily abandoned if something better comes along; another occupation or type of work could easily be sought.

Social workers must be alert to the possibility of *professional drift*. This occurs when a social worker begins to neglect or avoid traditional social work values, purposes, and functions in favor of ones associated with another helping profession or discipline. This is evident, for example, when social workers abandon or avoid the title of social worker and prefer to be identified as psychotherapists. Shulman (1991, 10) explains that when social workers align themselves with the purposes and knowledge base of another profession that gives little attention to issues of social justice and service to disadvantaged groups, it results in social workers ". . . who adopt a view of themselves as therapists first and social workers second, or not even social workers at all." Professional social workers, including those who perform the roles of counselor and psychotherapist, want to be known as social workers and identified with the social work profession.

For the most part, social work is an agency-based profession. Most social workers are employed by some type of social agency or social welfare–related organization. Social workers often experience a push and pull between loyalty to their organization and its managers and loyalty to their profession and its values and principles. On the one hand, they want the benefits that come from being an employee within an organization, and on the other hand they want the freedom and status that come from being an independent professional. This tension is illustrated in the table below.

Employee Orientation	Professional Orientation
Employees are to follow all policies and rules.	Rules and policies may need to be adapted and changed to serve the best interests of clients.
Salary is to be determined by years of service to organization.	Salary is to be determined by level of knowledge, skill, and performance.
Loyalty and duty to superiors and organization are highest value.	Duty to clients is highest value.
Employees place their jobs in jeopardy if they openly criticize agency's operation and policy.	Professionals must speak out and question agency operations and policy if necessary to better serve clients.
All employees are to be supervised, and major decisions require approval from a higher level.	Professionals must have and are entitled to autonomy in their decisions and practice. Supervision is not always needed or appropriate.

Much of what a social worker does is shaped—and sometimes driven—by agency policy. For this reason, social workers must be attentive to the nature and purpose of their agency's policies and how these impact clients. From the perspective of professional social work, an agency policy should have the following characteristics:

- It promotes the well-being of clients and of the community as a whole.
- It is respectful and fair to those most directly affected by the policy.
- It serves to empower clients and it recognizes and builds upon their strengths.
- It promotes social and economic justice, directly or indirectly.
- It is consistent with the core values and principles found in the *Code of Ethics*.
- It reflects the principle of effective social work based in current knowledge and research findings.
- It holds social workers and other agency employees accountable for the work they perform and the services they are to provide.
- It is clearly written, realistic, and consistent with relevant legal codes and regulations.

Food for Thought

It has been said that a professional is someone who knows what to do and can be counted on to do what needs to be done, even when he or she does not feel like doing it. There is much wisdom in that description. It suggests that a professional knows what should be done, can be trusted to do it, and does not let matters of personal convenience or personal feelings interfere with his or her performance. (Sheafor, Horejsi, and Horejsi 2000, 200)

◆ ◆ ◆

Social work practice consists of the professional application of social work values, principles, and techniques to one or more of the following ends: helping people obtain tangible services; providing counseling and psychotherapy with individuals, families, and groups; helping communities or groups provide or improve social and health services; and participating in relevant legislative processes. The practice of social work requires knowledge of human development and behavior; of social, economic, and cultural institutions; and of the interaction of all these factors. (Barker 1995, 357)

◆ ◆ ◆

A social worker:

- has recognized professional preparation (i.e., education in the requisite knowledge, ethics, and competencies);

- is sanctioned by society to provide specific services targeted primarily at helping vulnerable populations (e.g., children, the aged, the poor, minorities, women, families) engage in efforts to change themselves, the people around them, or social institutions; and

- has the purpose of helping others meet social needs or eliminate difficulties so that they might make maximum use of their abilities to lead full and satisfying lives and contribute fully to society. (Sheafor, Horejsi, and Horejsi 2000, 1)

◆ ◆ ◆

Everybody was asked to do it.
Everybody was sure somebody would do it.
Anybody could have done it.
But nobody did it.

—Author unknown

◆ ◆ ◆

There is an important difference between being effective and being efficient. We must strive to be *effective* in our work with our clients. We must strive to be *efficient* in our work with things and objects such as agency records, monthly reports, and computers. If we emphasize efficiency in work with clients, we will end up treating them as things and objects.

GUIDANCE AND DIRECTION

A primary purpose of the practicum experience is to help you develop a professional identity as a social worker. To possess this identity means that you have a clear understanding of the purpose of the profession, your roles and responsibilities as a social worker, the profession's core values and ethical guidelines, and the skills and knowledge needed to perform social work tasks and activities. Most students begin developing a professional identity by observing other social workers and reflecting on their behavior, decisions, and attitudes.

As you meet social workers employed in various agencies, consider whether they possess the hallmarks of a professional person. Drawing on ideas presented by Gambrill (1997, 13–16) these hallmarks include the following:

- The social worker takes responsibility for his or her decisions and actions.
- The social worker helps the client attain outcomes that the client desires and values.
- The social worker does not cause harm to the client.
- The social worker uses methods and approaches that are the least restrictive and least intrusive for the client.
- The clients (or representatives) are fully informed of the social worker's decisions and intentions and involved in decision making to the greatest extent possible.

- The social worker possesses knowledge and skills relevant to the client's problems and concerns.
- The social worker's decisions and interventions are thoughtful and well reasoned.
- The social worker values truth and is alert to the dangers of personal prejudice, ignorance, and the human desire to be certain. The worker engages in a critical examination of ideas and decisions and tests all claims of truth and effectiveness.
- The social worker's decisions are based on observations and data as well as on theory.
- The social worker values and respects individual and cultural differences.
- The social worker strives to develop self-knowledge.
- The social worker's words correspond to his or her actions.

Read the job description for social workers in your agency, and determine if it is consistent with the profession's stated purposes, values, and practice roles. Watch for variation between how social workers define their own roles and responsibilities and how their roles may be defined by administrators or funding sources. Ask your practicum instructor or other social workers how they attempt to meet the expectations of high-level administrators and fiscal managers while still adhering to the mission and purpose of the profession and fulfilling their obligations to their clients.

Recall and review the variety of social work roles and activities described in social work textbooks. Common social work roles include counselor, broker, advocate, organizer, facilitator, case manager, mediator, program planner, and policy analyst or researcher. Because BSW-level social workers and many MSW-level social workers are expected to be generalists, we recommend that you gain experience in many of these roles.

Identify the roles that the social workers in your agency perform and observe how social workers may select and shift their practice roles in response to individual situations and client needs. Become skilled at moving from one role to another, matching your actions to each situation and its requirements.

Strive to clarify how the values, knowledge base, and approach of the social work professional are different from those of other helping professionals such as clinical psychologists, nurses, school counselors, physicians, occupational therapists, and vocational counselors. Social work's uniqueness will become apparent if you truly understand the profession's core values and ethical principles, as well as the concept of social functioning. You will discover that social work's uniqueness lies in its commitment to the overall social functioning of people as well as its commitment to working for social change and social justice. Contrary to the beliefs of many social work students, social work is not unique because it pays attention to the "whole person," the client's environment, and the ecological perspective. These are ideas also commonly discussed in textbooks for nursing, education, counseling, and occupational therapy.

You will encounter stereotypes and misconceptions about social workers and the social work profession, and you will need to learn how to respond to them appropriately. Such stereotypes may include ideas such as:

- The job of social workers is to remove children from their homes and hand out welfare checks to the poor.
- Social workers create dependency in their clients.
- Social workers like to meddle in other people's lives.
- Social workers are soft-headed, low-level bureaucrats, and wild-eyed liberals.

- Anyone can do social work, including nonprofessionals and those with degrees in other related fields.
- Because many social workers are generalists, they are "jacks of all trades and masters of none."

Hearing these misconceptions about your chosen profession will be frustrating, and you may need to inform others about the profession's real purposes and values. You might also ask yourself where these perceptions of social work originated, and consider whether some social workers may speak or behave in ways that perpetuate the stereotypes.

The image of the profession, when negative, is often based on limited information about social work and sometimes on experiences with ineffective or unethical social workers. It could also be based on negative experiences with persons who are assumed to be social workers, but who are not. While in your practicum, give careful thought to whether social workers are recognized and respected as true professionals within your agency and community. Consider why the social workers in certain agencies behave and are viewed as professionals, whereas in other agencies they neither behave as professionals, nor are they treated as professionals.

Finally, you will probably find it helpful to remember that for all the emphasis on social work knowledge, theory, and research, you will not be effective if you do not pay close attention to what many consider the "art" of social work. As Sheafor, Horejsi, and Horejsi (2000, 37–41) note, the "social worker as artist" has several components:

- *Compassion and courage to confront human suffering.* You will daily confront the pain of others, and must join with them in a compassionate manner. You must also develop the inner strength to repeatedly face human suffering and frustration without being consumed by it.
- *Capacity to build a meaningful and productive helping relationship.* Your most fundamental tool in practice is the professional relationship, which is rooted in your capacity for demonstrating empathy, genuineness, and nonpossessive warmth.
- *Creativity to overcome barriers to change.* You must be innovative, imaginative, flexible, and persistent as you work for change.
- *Hopefulness and energy.* You will need to believe in the basic goodness and ability of people, to continue working without becoming discouraged, and to bounce back from failures and mistakes.
- *Sound judgment and critical thinking.* You will need to develop critical thinking skills, thoughtful decision-making abilities, and the ability to reflect upon and learn from successes and failures.
- *Appropriate personal values.* Your personal values must be compatible with the core values of social work, including respect for basic rights, a sense of social responsibility, commitment to individual freedom, and support for self-determination.

The social worker's professional identity is formed as he or she blends these artistic elements with the science of the profession. Sheafor, Horejsi, and Horejsi (2000) explain that:

the social worker must combine his or her personal qualities, creative abilities, and social concern with the profession's knowledge in order to help clients enhance their social functioning or prevent social problems from developing. Each person has unique personal qualities that represent the artistic component of social work practice. Professional education cannot teach these artistic features, although it can help the learner identify such strengths and develop the ability to focus and apply them in work with clients. Professional education can also assist the learner in developing a beginning understanding of the knowledge (or science) that is necessary for effective practice. This merging and blending of one's art and the profession's science is initiated in social work education programs, but it is a life-long activity, as social work knowledge is constantly expanding and the worker is being continually changed by life experiences. (36)

THE IMAGE AND IMPACT OF SOCIAL WORK:
A WORKBOOK ACTIVITY

It is important to examine the impact of the profession's values, ethical code, practice principles, and knowledge base on the behavior and performance of the social workers in your practicum agency.

1. Is the NASW *Code of Ethics* frequently mentioned and discussed by the social workers in your practicum agency?

_____

2. Does the NASW *Code of Ethics* appear to have a significant impact on decision making and practices within your practicum agency? If yes, in what ways? If no, why not?

_____

_____

_____

_____

3. To what extent and in what ways, if any, do political pressures and a push to hold down operating costs keep agency staff from following principles of good social work practice and adhering to basic principles of the NASW *Code of Ethics?*

_____

_____

_____

_____

4. In what ways and to what degree are the six core values of the social work profession reflected in the mission of your agency and in the behavior of the social workers you observe (see Background Information)?

_____

_____

_____

_____

5. Which of the six core values of social work are most lacking in your agency?

_____

_____

_____

6. Which of the six core social work values are most central to your own practice?

_____

_____

_____

7. Which of social work's purposes are most apparent in the goals and activities of your agency and its social workers?

_____

_____

_____

_____

8. Which of the following social work roles are most often assumed by the social workers in your agency?

_____ Broker of services

_____ Case manager

_____ Advocate

_____ Social activist

_____ Counselor/Therapist

_____ Collaborator/Networker

_____ Group Leader/Facilitator

_____ Program planner

_____ Educator/Trainer

_____ Community organizer

_____ Social policy analyst

_____ Researcher/Program evaluator

_____ Administrator/Manager/Supervisor

_____ Other

9. About what percentage of the social workers in your agency are members of NASW?

_____

About what percentage are active members of NASW?

_____

About what percentage of the social workers in your agency have a social work license?

_____

What are the requirements for obtaining and retaining a social work license in your state (e.g., degree required, examination, years of experience, and hours of supervised practice)?

_____

_____

_____

_____

_____

10. What governmental agency or body issues social work licenses and receives complaints about the practice of social workers?

_____

_____

11. Does your agency require a social work degree (BSW or MSW) as preparation for certain positions or jobs? If yes, for what jobs?

_____

_____

_____

_____

12. Do the administrators of your agency prefer to hire persons with degrees in social work rather than persons with training in other fields? If yes, why?

_____

_____

_____

_____

13. If the administrators have no preference for trained social workers, why is social work training not especially valued (i.e., the belief that a specific educational background is of little importance in staff selection)?

_____

_____

_____

_____

14. If the administrators prefer to hire persons with backgrounds other than social work, why do they have this preference?

_____

_____

_____

_____

15. Do the employees in your agency who have a degree in social work call themselves social workers?

_____

If not, why not? If they do not use the title "social worker," what title do they use and why (e.g., therapist, case manager, program coordinator, and client advocate)?

_____

_____

_____

_____

16. Do you see evidence of "professional drift" in your agency? If yes, describe and explain.

_____

_____

_____

_____

17. What professional journals do the social workers in your agency read on a regular basis?

_____

_____

_____

_____

18. What is the public image of social workers in your community? What forces and experiences have shaped this image?

_____

_____

_____

_____

19. What agency policies, procedures, and expectations reinforce and encourage social work professionalism within your agency (e.g., continuing education is expected and rewarded, workers are expected to take personal responsibility for decisions and actions, and constant attention is given to professional ethics)?

_____

_____

_____

_____

20. What agency policies, procedures, and behavioral norms undermine and discourage social work professionalism within your agency (e.g., lack of sanctions for sloppy work, political concerns drive decision making, or bureaucratic regulations take precedence over individual client needs)?

_____

_____

_____

_____

21. Do factors of staff convenience and personal preferences take precedence or priority over the needs of the client in service delivery? If so, how and to what extent?

_____

_____

_____

_____

Additional notes and comments:

_____

_____

_____

_____

_____

_____

SUGGESTED LEARNING ACTIVITIES

- Attend local chapter meetings of the NASW or the meetings of other social work–related professional organizations and decide what issues are of greatest concern to the social workers in your community.
- Review flyers of social work conferences and workshops to determine what topics are of interest to social workers.
- Watch for media portrayals of social workers in newspapers, magazines, and on television to determine how social work is described and whether it is usually presented in a positive or negative light.

ADDITIONAL SUGGESTIONS AND HINTS

- In Sheafor, Horejsi, and Horejsi (2000), read and discuss the section "Improving the Social Work Image."

SELECTED BIBLIOGRAPHY

Barker, Robert L. *The Social Work Dictionary.* 3rd ed. Washington, DC: NASW Press, 1995.

Council on Social Work Education. *Handbook of Accreditation Standards and Procedures.* 4th ed. Alexandria, VA: CSWE, 1994.

DuBois, Brenda, and Karla Miley. *Social Work: An Empowering Profession.* 3rd ed. Boston: Allyn and Bacon, 1999.

Gambrill, Eileen. *Social Work Practice.* New York: Oxford University Press, 1997.

National Association of Social Workers. *Model Statute Social Workers License Act.* Silver Spring, MD: NASW Press, 1970.

National Association of Social Workers. *Code of Ethics.* Washington, DC: NASW Press, 1997.

Payne, Malcolm. *Modern Social Work Theory.* 2nd ed. Chicago: Lyceum, 1997.

Sheafor, Bradford, Charles Horejsi, and Gloria Horejsi. *Techniques and Guidelines for Social Work Practice.* 5th ed. Boston: Allyn and Bacon, 2000.

Shulman, Lawrence. *Interactional Social Work Practice.* Itasca, IL: F. E. Peacock, 1991.

Specht, Harry, and Mark Courtney. *Unfaithful Angels: How Social Work Has Abandoned Its Mission.* New York: Free Press, 1994.

14

PROFESSIONAL ETHICS

Goals for Learning

- To identify the ethical questions and dilemmas that arise most frequently in your practicum setting
- To articulate various ethical positions and principles that are related to an ethical question or dilemma
- To become familiar with how your agency and its staff attempt to resolve ethical dilemmas
- To become aware of how the NASW *Code of Ethics* may affect the decisions and actions of social workers within your agency setting
- To become aware of how your own moral and ethical standards may differ from those identified in the NASW *Code of Ethics*

Every day, social workers make decisions and take actions based on ethical principles. These principles have a profound and far reaching impact on practice. They also have a significant impact on a student's social work practicum.

Prior to beginning your social work practicum, you have studied the NASW *Code of Ethics* and devoted classroom time to the discussion of ethical questions and issues. Up to this point, the topic of professional ethics may have seemed rather abstract. In your practicum you will meet these questions and dilemmas "face to face."

In this chapter we will briefly review the nature of professional values and ethics, discuss the content of the NASW *Code of Ethics*, and offer guidance on resolving ethical dilemmas. The workbook activity will heighten your awareness of ethical concerns within your practicum setting.

BACKGROUND INFORMATION

The National Association of Social Workers (NASW) was formed in 1955 by the merging of several separate social work organizations, some of which had developed a code of ethics for their members. In 1960, the NASW adopted its first *Code of Ethics*. It has been revised several times. In this section we will be referring to the NASW *Code of Ethics* that became effective in January 1997.

Ruggiero (1992) explains that

Ethics is the study of right and wrong conduct. . . . The focus of ethics is moral situations—that is, those situations in which there is a choice of behavior involving human values. [Values] are those qualities that are regarded as good and desirable. (4–5)

Social work ethics are rooted in six values (listed in Chapter 13). A *value* can be defined as a consistent preference that affects one's decisions and actions and is based on one's deepest beliefs and commitments. A value reflects one's fundamental beliefs about what is right and wrong. Typically, emotions are attached to our values. Thus, if we do not experience a stirring of our emotions when we think or speak about our values, we are probably not talking about a genuine value.

According to NASW (1997), the *Code of Ethics* serves six purposes:

1. Identifies core values on which social work's mission is based (see Chapter 13)
2. Summarizes broad ethical principles that reflect the profession's core values and establishes a set of specific ethical standards that should be used to guide social work practice
3. Is designed to help social workers identify relevant considerations when professional obligations conflict or ethical uncertainties arise
4. Provides ethical standards to which the general public can hold the social work profession accountable
5. Socializes practitioners new to the field to social work's mission, values, ethical principles, and ethical standards
6. Articulates standards that the social work profession itself can use to assess whether social workers have engaged in unethical conduct (1)

NASW (1997) explains that while the *Code of Ethics* provides principles and standards, it

does not provide a set of rules that prescribe how social workers should act in all situations. Specific applications of the *Code* must take into account the context in which it is being considered and the possibility of conflicts among the *Code*'s values, principles, and standards. (1)

Included in the *Code of Ethics* are hundreds of separate statements of general principle, some of which may be in conflict in a specific practice situation. The term *ethical dilemma* describes a situation in which the social worker has two or more ethical obligations (e.g., to take action to protect the client from imminent harm and also to protect the client's right to privacy) but cannot adhere to one principle without violating another. The *Code of Ethics* does not offer guidance on how to resolve an ethical dilemma. NASW (1997) explains that its ethical code

does not specify which values, principles, and standards are most important and ought to outweigh others in instances when they conflict. Reasonable differences of opinion can and do exist among social workers with respect to the ways in which values, ethical principles, and ethical standards should be rank ordered when they conflict. (1)

Because much of the *Code of Ethics* focuses on the social worker's responsibilities to clients, every application of the *Code* must begin by answering the question: Who is my client? Sometimes that question is difficult to answer, especially when working with an involuntary client or with a group that has been targeted for change but has not requested specific services. A dictionary defines a *client* as the party for whom professional services are rendered and/or a customer or patron. Thus, the social work client is the person, group, or organization who has requested the social worker's services and expects to benefit from what the worker does.

Thus far, we have focused on the NASW *Code of Ethics* as one set of principles and values that may govern a social worker's behavior. There are two others of importance to the social worker. A worker's *moral code* consists of his or her personal beliefs and judgments as to what is right and wrong. In addition, there is a *legal code* that regulates practice.

The social worker must sometimes struggle to sort out the relevant issues and resolve conflicts related to the interplay of these three standards of behavior. Often there is an overlap among these codes. For example, the act of murder would violate all three codes. However, an individual may view a specific action as immoral

---

Food for Thought

Ethical self-knowledge has been a neglected dimension in discussions of self-awareness in social work. Although a great deal of attention has been focused on the development of self-awareness in the psychological and sociological realms of social work practice, little attention has been paid to the development of ethical self-knowledge in the profession. Ethics in social work has focused on decision making rather than on the decision maker. (Abramson 1996, 195)

◆◆◆

Social workers cannot be non-judgmental and they should not attempt to be. They are merchants of morality and should acknowledge this fact openly. (Pilseker 1978, 55)

◆◆◆

The judgment of [moral and ethical] issues within our own culture is easier in the sense that it does not require learning about another people and a different value system. But it is more difficult in that it demands that we look objectively at ideas and beliefs to which we have developed strong emotional attachments. [Our] . . . attitude can influence the way we analyze issues. If for example, we are alienated from our culture and reject its moral perspective, we will be inclined to overlook its virtues. On the other hand if . . . we accept its perspective consciously or unconsciously, we will be inclined to overlook its shortcomings. In addition, when we share our culture's perspective, one crippling assumption is liable to run through all our evaluations: Its view is right because it is familiar to us and we feel comfortable with it or because it is modern. Neither familiarity nor modernity is a valid measure of an idea.

Another problem . . . is the special reluctance we feel about examining issues close to our everyday lives. . . . When the actions are those of our relatives and friends, our teachers and roommates, the writers and media personalities we revere, we feel obligated to forego moral judgment. . . . "To each his own" we say. "Who am I to judge?" . . .

Judging an action is not the same as judging the person who performs it. "Love me, love my idea" is not a reasonable demand; and mature people know better than to make it. We can disagree with the conclusions of others without straining mutual respect . . . because, though courtesy is a civilized requirement for dealing with other people, it does not extend to ideas.

It is true, of course, that judgment of others' views involves not only the risk of error, but also the risk of offending others. However, the alternative is to evade judgment when judgment is needed, which is unworthy of thinking individuals; or to feign approval where we secretly disapprove, which is deceitful. (Ruggiero 1992, 23–24)

◆◆◆

For many years, the practice principle of value neutrality found wide acceptance among social workers. . . . Yet there are critical questions about this value-neutral stance that must be considered. Many have asked whether value neutrality or value suspension is a realistic option for social workers. They point out that social workers are human beings, not robots. What are they to do with the values they hold when working with clients who hold contrary values? Can they really avoid imposing their own values by either subtle or nonverbal communications? . . .

Social workers have to make moral judgments. There is no escaping moral and ethical issues at each step of social work processes. . . . [Can] we honestly say that we do not care what a client does? Can we accept child molestation, neglect, violence, cheating, stealing, or lying? Dare social workers not condemn physical and sexual abuse, rape and beatings, irresponsible sexual activities, and similar antisocial behaviors? (Loewenberg, Dolgoff, and Harrington, 2000, 125–126)

even though it is legal. Examples might be abortion, capital punishment, depriving someone of welfare benefits, and paying taxes that finance a war. On the other hand, an individual might find nothing wrong or immoral with some acts that are illegal (e.g., certain forms of drug use, assisted suicide, and the theft of needed food). On a personal level, an individual might not see anything wrong with having sex with a client, but such an action is a very clear violation of the NASW *Code of Ethics*.

GUIDANCE AND DIRECTION

Read the NASW *Code of Ethics* carefully and often. Pay particular attention to those ethical principles that apply most directly to your agency setting. If you do not understand a principle or its application, seek consultation.

Ask your practicum instructor to identify the ethical concerns most often encountered in the agency. It is important to recognize that many ethical concerns and questions have been anticipated by the agency, and guidance on how to handle them has been written into the agency's policy manual or employee handbook. Thus, to the student, some ethical issues appear to be matters of agency policy and procedure, rather than of ethics.

Inquire about the agency's process or procedures for resolving ethical dilemmas. These procedures may be written or informal. Your agency may utilize ethics committees, staff discussions, and outside legal and ethics consultations to help staff members make difficult decisions. Observe and participate in such meetings as often as possible, as this will help you develop awareness of and skill in identifying and resolving ethical dilemmas.

You can expect to observe disagreement over situations involving ethics. Each situation is unique to some degree, and there is seldom only one right way to deal with it. Over time, you will become more comfortable with this uncertainty and better able to sort out the competing values and potential consequences of each decision. Baird (1996) reminds us that

> ethics cannot be boiled down to a simple "cookbook" of dos and don'ts. Ethical conduct requires a continuous process of self-monitoring, reflection, and careful thought. . . . As a professional it is incumbent upon you to know and understand not only the letter of the ethical codes, but their spirit, rationale, and practical implications. (30)

When you encounter an ethical dilemma, we recommend that you consider the guidelines offered by Sheafor, Horejsi, and Horejsi (2000, 219–220) and begin by seeking answers to questions such as the following:

- What ethical principles and obligations apply in this situation?
- Which, if any, ethical principles are in conflict in this situation and therefore create an ethical dilemma?
- Would certain ethical obligations be more important than others?
- What aspects of the agency's activity or worker's roles and duties give rise to the dilemma (e.g., legal mandates, job requirements, agency policy, questions of efficient use of limited resources, or possible harm caused by an intervention)?
- Who can or should resolve this dilemma? Is it a decision to be rightfully made by the client? Other family members? The worker? The agency administrator?
- For each decision possible, what are the short-term and long-term consequences for the client, family, worker, agency, community, and so on?
- Who stands to gain and who stands to lose from each possible choice or action? Are those who stand to gain or lose of equal or of unequal power (e.g., child

versus adult)? Do those who are most vulnerable or those with little power require special consideration?

- When harm to someone cannot be avoided, what decision will cause the least harm or a type of harm with fewest long-term consequences? Who of those that might be harmed are least able to recover from the harm?
- Will a particular resolution to this dilemma set an undesirable precedent for future decision making concerning other clients?

You will encounter some very troublesome situations in which all available choices or options are in some way and to some degree harmful and destructive to your client and other people. In such cases you must decide which option is the least harmful. Essentially, you are forced to choose the lesser of two or more evils.

In order to function effectively as a social worker you must be able to distinguish between your values and morals and those of the client. As a general principle, you should not impose your values and beliefs on the client. However, this is a challenging principle because the social work profession and social agencies are built on and represent a set of values and beliefs about what is good for people and desirable in human relationships. Moreover, some clients engage in behaviors that are clearly wrong and a danger to themselves and others (e.g., assault, rape, robbery, and child neglect). In such situations, attempting to be value free or value neutral is extremely dangerous.

Avoiding the imposition of one's own values on a client is especially difficult when the client's perspective and behavior is rooted in uncommon or unusual cultural or religious beliefs. For example, parents may decline needed medical treatment or surgery for their child because of their religious beliefs, and you may have to decide between honoring the family's religious beliefs and requesting legal action to protect the physical well-being of the child. Fundamentally, the resolution of this dilemma revolves around the answer to the questions: Who is my client? Will a certain decision or action cause significant harm to another person?

In keeping with the *Code of Ethics*, the social worker's primary responsibility is to his or her client. In general, *client* can be defined as the person who requested the social worker's assistance and expects to benefit from the services provided by the social worker or his or her agency.

You may find that your personal moral code conflicts with the values of your clients, your practicum instructor, your agency, or even the NASW *Code of Ethics*. For example, you and your client or you and other professionals may hold very different views on the morality of abortion or of requiring new parents to place their children in day care in order to work. When you encounter such conflicts, do not ignore them. They are important questions and dilemmas that must be faced honestly and squarely. You will need to decide when you can and cannot suspend your personal moral code.

When you encounter a troublesome practice situation, you must be able to distinguish between questions of preferred method and questions of ethics. The former has to do with ideas about what actions will work best in a given situation to bring about a desired change. Ethical questions are about what is right and wrong from a moral perspective. Many of the conflicts and disagreements between professionals have to do with differences of opinion about the intervention method and are not true ethical dilemmas.

There may be times when you conclude that your agency violates certain ethical principles or violates the rights of certain clients. If this occurs, discuss your concerns with your practicum instructor or faculty supervisor in order to sort out the issues and determine whether or not an ethical principle is being violated.

In general, practicum students most commonly make mistakes in the following areas of ethical conduct:

- *Violating client confidentiality and privacy.* Do not release information regarding your clients without their consent, or reveal their identity by carelessness in casual conversation or in how you handle and store written documentation.
- *Violating client autonomy and self-determination.* Be careful not to violate your clients' right to autonomy by overprotecting vulnerable populations such as youth or the frail elderly. Be prepared to accept your clients' choices, even when you disagree with them.
- *Violating client right to information and informed consent.* Do not withhold from clients information that they request and are entitled to have. Keep your clients fully informed of decisions and plans that will have a significant impact on their situation.
- *Violating client right to competent services.* Be careful not to practice beyond your abilities or knowledge level. When a situation calls for knowledge and skills that you do not possess, consult your practicum instructor and consider referral to someone who can provide the needed service.
- *Entering into dual relationships.* Maintain a proper professional relationship with your clients. Be friendly, but realize that a professional relationship is not a friendship. Never date or become romantically involved with a client. Do not enter into a buying, selling, lending, or renting agreement with a client.

An ethical area of special concern for you may be the limits to client confidentiality. Clients have a right to privacy. However, this right is not absolute; there are limits and exceptions to a client's right to confidentiality. You may need to release client information, without your client's permission, in the following situations:

- Your client is abusing or neglecting a child or an elderly person.
- Your client is planning a serious and dangerous illegal act that places others at risk of harm.
- Your client is threatening to harm himself or herself or another person.
- You receive a court order requiring the release of client information.
- You are required by contract to share information with third party entities (e.g., managed care and insurance) that pay for the services received by your client.
- Your client is a minor.

When you encounter these or similar situations, consult with your practicum instructor on how to handle the matter.

Be certain that you understand the laws in your state that apply to confidentiality as well as related agency policy on this matter. Make sure that you also understand the concept of privileged communication so you can accurately explain to your client whether client information can ever be revealed to others or to the courts.

VALUES, ETHICS, AND YOUR PRACTICUM:
A WORKBOOK ACTIVITY

1. What are the two or three ethical concerns or dilemmas most frequently encountered in your practicum setting?

_____

_____

_____

2. How do the personnel in your agency go about dealing with ethical questions and resolving ethical dilemmas (e.g., discussions at a staff meeting, presentations to an ethics committee, and consultations with experts)?

_____

_____

_____

3. Does your agency have its own code of ethics or a code of conduct for its employees? If yes, how is it similar to and different from the NASW *Code of Ethics*?

_____

_____

_____

4. To what degree and in what way does the NASW *Code of Ethics* influence the decisions and behavior of the social workers employed by your agency (e.g., is the *Code* referred to during case conferences and staff meetings and do the social workers have a copy of the *Code* in their office)?

_____

_____

_____

5. Are there specific items or sections in the NASW *Code of Ethics* that are particularly difficult to follow in your agency? If yes, what are they and why are they difficult to follow?

_____

_____

_____

_____

6. Are there particular issues or concerns that are not addressed by the *Code of Ethics* but, in your opinion, should be included? If yes, what are they?

_____

_____

_____

_____

_____

7. Does your agency have policies that, in your opinion, are a violation of the NASW *Code of Ethics?* If yes, describe how the policy is in conflict with specific provisions of the *Code of Ethics.*

_____

_____

_____

_____

_____

8. Are there specific items or sections in the NASW *Code of Ethics* that appear to be in conflict with the state or federal laws and regulations that your agency is expected to follow? If so, describe the conflict and explain how you and other agency social workers attempt to resolve this matter.

_____

_____

_____

_____

_____

9. Section 1.01 of the *Code of Ethics* (1997) states that the social worker's primary responsibility is the well-being of his or her clients. As you observe the day-to-day operation of your agency and the day-to-day activities of the social workers in your agency, does it appear as if the well-being of the client is the primary concern? On what basis do you reach this conclusion?

_____

_____

_____

_____

10. The answer to the question "Who is my client?" is critical to making ethical decisions in social work practice. Who are your agency's clients or consumers? In other words, who is asking for and expecting to benefit from the services and activities of your agency and to whom is your primary ethical obligation?

_____

_____

_____

_____

11. How does your agency handle reports of ethics violations on the part of its staff (e.g., written incident reports, temporary suspensions of staff, formal investigations, grievance policies, and reports to state licensing bodies)?

_____

_____

_____

12. Within the past five years, have any agency social workers or other agency personnel been dismissed or reprimanded for ethics violations? If so, what was the nature and type of misconduct?

_____

_____

_____

_____

13. Does your agency have policies that are in conflict with your personal moral code? If yes, how will you handle or resolve these conflicts?

_____

_____

_____

_____

14. Are there statements or sections in the NASW *Code of Ethics* that are in conflict with your personal moral and ethical standards? If yes, describe the conflict and explain how you will attempt to resolve this conflict.

_____

_____

_____

_____

15. What ethical principles in the NASW *Code of Ethics* do you feel most strongly about? Why?

_____

_____

_____

_____

16. What is the name of the agency in your state that is responsible for handling formal complaints about ethics violations by licensed social workers?

_____

_____

17. What is the process used by this agency to investigate possible ethics violations?

_____

_____

_____

_____

18. What are the possible sanctions in your state for social workers who commit ethics violations (e.g., loss of license, civil action for monetary damages, criminal prosecution, and sanctions by the NASW)?

_____

_____

Additional notes and comments:

_____

_____

_____

_____

_____

_____

SUGGESTED LEARNING ACTIVITIES

- Read and study the NASW *Code of Ethics*. It can be downloaded from the NASW's Website (http://www.naswdc.org). The *Code of Ethics* issued by the Canadian Association of Social Workers (CASW) can be downloaded from the CASW's Website (http://www.intranet.ca/~casw-acts/code2-e.htm).
- If members of other professions (e.g., psychologists, nurses, or teachers) work in your practicum setting, secure a copy of their profession's code of ethics and compare it to the NASW *Code of Ethics*.
- Conduct interviews with experienced social workers and ask them to describe the ethical issues they most often encounter and the issues that are especially difficult for them to resolve.
- Review your agency's policy manual and identify policy principles that are very similar to the NASW *Code of Ethics*. Identify policies that appear to be in opposition to the *Code of Ethics*.
- In a small group, discuss and share your beliefs regarding the following questions:

  1. How do you decide when the good of the community is more important than the good of the individual?
  2. What is your image of a truly ethical social worker?
  3. What should a social worker do when his or her personal morals are in conflict with agency policy? With the NASW *Code of Ethics?*

ADDITIONAL SUGGESTIONS AND HINTS

- In Sheafor, Horejsi, and Horejsi (2000), read the section on "Making Ethical Decisions."

SELECTED BIBLIOGRAPHY

Abramson, Marcia. "Reflections on Knowing Oneself Ethically: Toward a Working Framework for Social Work Practice." *Families in Society* (April, 1996): 195–200.

Baird, Brian N. *The Internship, Practicum, and Field Placement Handbook: A Guide for the Helping Professions.* Upper Saddle River, NJ: Prentice-Hall, 1996.

Gambrill, Eileen, and Robert Pruger, eds. *Controversial Issues in Social Work Ethics, Values and Obligations.* Boston: Allyn and Bacon, 1997.

Loewenberg, Frank, and Ralph Dolgoff. *Ethical Decisions for Social Work Practice.* 5th ed. Itasca, IL: F. E. Peacock, 1996.

Loewenberg, Frank, Ralph Dolgoff, and Donna Harrington. *Ethical Decisions for Social Work Practice.* 6th ed. Itasca, IL: F. E. Peacock, 2000.

National Association of Social Workers. *Code of Ethics.* Washington, DC: NASW Press, 1997.

Pilseker, C. "Values: A Problem for Everyone." *Social Work* 23 (1978): 54–57.

Ruggiero, Vincent. *Thinking Critically about Ethical Issues.* Mountain View, CA: Mayfield, 1992.

Sheafor, Bradford, Charles Horejsi, and Gloria Horejsi. *Techniques and Guidelines for Social Work Practice.* 5th ed. Boston: Allyn and Bacon, 2000.

15

LEGAL CONCERNS

Goals for Learning

- To become familiar with the specific state and federal statutes (codes) that are of special relevance to your practicum setting and its programs and services
- To become familiar with the legal terminology frequently used within your practicum setting
- To become aware of the types of cases and practice situations that could give rise to an allegation of wrongdoing or professional negligence
- To become aware of precautionary steps that may reduce the chances of being named in a malpractice suit

Like all professions, social work is profoundly affected by the law. Every human services agency and program is shaped and guided by specific codes or legal considerations. In some agencies, a client's eligibility for services is defined by law. In many instances, a social worker's actions are dictated by law, as in the case of mandated reporting of child abuse. Many social workers are licensed by state law and must conform their practice to the provisions of that law.

The social work practicum student must understand the legal context of his or her professional practice. He or she must be alert to the actions that may violate the law and to the types of situations that might give rise to a lawsuit against an agency, a professional social worker, and even a social work student.

BACKGROUND INFORMATION

The actions of social workers and social agencies are guided, directed, and sometimes mandated by laws in three broad categories:

1. *Laws regulating services or actions related to a specific client.* Such laws may determine whether a client is eligible to receive a certain service or benefit, whether a specific client can be forced to accept intervention (e.g., involuntary hospitalization), or whether a particular family situation can be defined as suspected child abuse or neglect that must be reported to child protection authorities.
2. *Laws regulating a field of practice or type of human services program.* For example, if an agency provides service to youth, many of its policies and procedures for

dealing with young clients will be shaped by laws related to the notification of parents regarding services to be provided to their children. In hospitals, such laws as those related to informed consent, release of patient records, and durable power of attorney for health care are daily concerns to a medical social worker. A social worker in a mental health facility must understand existing laws requiring batterers or sex offenders to pay for their victim's counseling.

3. *Laws regulating professional practice of social work.* Laws guiding professional social work practice dictate how social workers must conduct themselves in order to practice competently. These laws may deal with matters such as confidentiality, informed consent, duties to clients, and requirements for obtaining a social work license.

Social workers must acquire a basic understanding of the laws and legal procedures that most directly impact their practice setting and the clients served. In addition, they must become familiar with specific laws related to their practice roles, duties, and job description. For example, if a social worker has administrative or supervisory responsibilities, he or she must understand the basic laws related to the hiring and firing of employees and employee benefits.

Social workers must be familiar with the court system and know proper conduct when testifying in court. Practitioners in the fields of child welfare (especially child protection) and in probation and parole may testify in court on at least a weekly basis. However, all social workers, regardless of field of practice or agency setting, can expect to be occasional witnesses in court proceedings.

Practitioners and social work students must operate on the assumption that any of their professional records, case notes, reports, and correspondence may eventually become the target of a subpoena, gathered and reviewed by attorneys, and read in court. They need to be thoughtful and cautious about what they put into a written record and how they write it, for at some point they may be asked to explain and defend their statements.

A growing number of social workers are being sued for malpractice. This reality must be considered each and every day. Malpractice and professional negligence fall under a category of law known as tort law. A *tort* is a private or civil wrong or injury that results from actions other than the breach of a formal legal contract and the commission of a crime.

The person who alleges the negligence and brings a malpractice lawsuit against a social worker or agency is termed the *plaintiff*. In this instance, the social worker or agency would be termed the *defendant*.

In order for the plaintiff (e.g., the social worker's client or former client) to be successful in this type of lawsuit, the plaintiff's attorney must prove four points:

1. The social worker had a professional obligation or duty to provide the plaintiff with a certain level of service, a certain standard of care, or a certain manner of professional conduct.
2. The social worker was negligent or derelict in his or her professional role because he or she did not live up to this recognized obligation or duty, standard of care, or expected professional conduct.
3. The plaintiff suffered injury or harm (e.g., physical, mental, emotional or financial) as a result of what the social worker did (act) or did not do (omission) and this act or omission had a foreseeable harmful consequence for the plaintiff.
4. The social worker's act or omission was a direct or proximate cause of the harm experienced by the plaintiff.

Sheafor, Horejsi, and Horejsi (2000) explain how the actions of social workers are judged:

> Whether a breach of duty has occurred is determined by measuring the allegedly harmful act or omission against published standards of practice, agency policy, and the performance of social workers in similar settings. The client's injury must be one that would not have occurred had it not been for the social worker's negligence. Despite this traditional "proximate cause" requirement, juries are increasingly finding liability without fault (i.e., finding providers of health and social services negligent even when they are not the proximate cause of the injury). (226)

A wide variety of acts or omissions can place social workers or the agencies for which they work at risk of being sued and held liable for causing harm to their clients or to individuals harmed by their clients. For example:

- Sexual or romantic involvement with a current or former client
- Failure to warn others when a client discloses clear intent to inflict serious physical harm on them
- Failure to alert others when a client discloses intent to harm self
- Failure to attempt to prevent a client's suicide
- Failure to properly diagnose and treat a client
- Failure to provide proper and appropriate treatment and services to a client
- Failure to ensure continuity of service to a client under the care of a worker or agency
- Failure to maintain and protect confidentiality
- Failure to maintain accurate professional records and a proper accounting of client fees, payments, and reimbursements
- Misrepresentation of professional training, experience, and credentials
- Breach of client civil rights
- Failure to refer clients to other services or professionals when indicated
- Use of harmful or ineffective interventions
- Failure to protect a client from harm caused by other clients in a group, program, or facility
- Failure to report suspected child or elder abuse or neglect

Dealing with certain types of clients and situations place social workers and agencies at a higher risk of being sued. These clients and situations may include:

- Clients who have a history of alleging malpractice and negligence and bringing suits against various professionals
- Clients who are very suspicious of others and quick to blame and accuse others of some wrongdoing
- Clients who may commit suicide
- Clients who are a real physical danger to others
- Clients who are very manipulative and deceptive
- Clients who have a history of using sex as a way of manipulating others
- Clients who have been separated from their child because of actions taken by the social worker or agency (e.g., foster care placement and custody evaluations)

Food for Thought

. . . changes in the law in the past 20 years have dramatically altered the principle of confidentiality. . . . Laws now compel social workers and other professionals to report suspected child abuse, neglect, and threats by clients to harm others. (Barker and Branson 1993, 43–44)

◆◆◆

Social workers . . . are required to respect client confidentiality. But the law also requires them to protect the public if the client constitutes a danger. Malpractice claims are increasingly made against social workers who have failed to warn either the public or intended victims when their clients have indicated their dangerousness. . . .

Malpractice claims have been upheld against social workers who failed to warn intended victims. But so too have claims succeeded when social workers have issued such warnings and the client has not subsequently harmed anyone. Charges of defamation as well as breach of confidentiality are then made. (Barker and Branson 1993, 40–41)

◆◆◆

Even a social worker employed in settings that provide group liability coverage should seriously consider obtaining their own individual coverage. When both a social worker and the worker's employer are named in a liability claim, the employer could argue that the social worker, and not the employing agency, was negligent. Individual coverage would thus protect workers who find themselves at odds with their employers in relation to a liability claim. (Reamer, 1994, 24)

◆◆◆

In many States the law defines who can practice social work and specifies the tasks a social worker may perform. The law . . . may give social workers certain legal rights, may impose certain legal obligations on social workers, or may make social workers accountable for certain actions they take on their jobs. . . .

Social workers have to be aware of the laws that affect their clients in order to assist them effectively. For example, in order to arrange for a patient's aftercare, a hospital social worker may have to know whether or not the law allows an adult child to admit a parent to a nursing home against the parent's will. And, in order to help a battered woman make an appropriate decision, a social worker in a shelter for battered women should know whether or not the woman risks losing custody of her children if she temporarily leaves them with her husband. While the law may influence the choices of social worker's clients, social workers should not act as lawyers and may not dispense legal advice to their clients. However, social workers must know when . . . it is necessary for their clients to consult lawyers. (Saltzman and Furman, 1999, xiii–xiv)

GUIDANCE AND DIRECTION

Make a special effort to become familiar with the laws relevant to your practicum setting, including the laws that regulate the services your agency provides and the laws which regulate professional social work practice.

Depending on the nature and purpose of your agency, you will need to become familiar with federal and state codes, and sometimes local ordinances, that apply to your clients and the services your agency provides. Your clients' lives are affected directly and indirectly by such laws. For example, you may need to understand laws pertaining to the following:

- Marriage and divorce
- Parenthood and child custody
- Domestic violence and abuse
- Voluntary and involuntary termination of parental rights
- Foster care and adoption
- Guardianship, conservatorship, power of attorney, durable power of attorney for health care
- Child abuse and neglect and child protection
- Involuntary hospitalization of the mentally ill

- Detention or involuntary hospitalization of persons who are suicidal or a threat to others
- Prosecution and punishment of adult offenders
- Probation and parole
- Adjudication and treatment of juvenile offenders
- Crime victims assistance
- Immigration
- Health care (e.g., managed care, Medicaid, and Medicare)
- Substance abuse and treatment of chemical dependency
- Buying and selling of illegal drugs
- Welfare assistance
- Family planning
- Abortion
- Education of children with disabilities
- Discrimination in employment and housing
- Social Security and Supplemental Security Income
- Confidentiality for persons with AIDS
- Reporting of contagious diseases and public health hazards
- Personal debt and bankruptcy
- Disability accommodation

If a social worker takes on an administrative role within a human services agency, he or she will need a basic understanding of laws related to employee matters, financial management, and the like. Watch for opportunities to learn about laws pertaining to:

- Contracts
- Leases and rental agreements
- Property and liability insurance
- Employee compensation and benefits
- Workers compensation and unemployment insurance
- Hiring and dismissal of employees
- Employee unions
- Financial record keeping
- Receipt of charitable contributions
- Accessibility for persons with disabilities
- Job classification related to public employees
- Restrictions on political action and lobbying by public employees
- Nonprofit corporations

If social workers in your agency commonly appear in court, request the opportunity to observe their testimony. Determine their role and function in court, how they prepare for a court appearance, what types of questions they are asked by attorneys, what written documents they provide the court, and if their recommendations tend to be followed by judges. Give special thought to legal and ethical issues that may arise when social workers advocate for their clients, when they are asked to participate in involuntary treatment of clients, or when they must testify on behalf of one client and against another.

If possible, read the case records of clients whose cases are heard in court. Read the petitions and other legal documents filed on behalf of or against your agency's clients. Read the court orders found in client records.

Learn about the types of situations and clients that present the highest legal risk to social workers in your agency. Ask how often lawsuits are threatened or actually filed against social workers or the agency. Ask about your agency's policy regarding legal defense expenses for employees who are sued. Find out if practicum students who are sued are covered in your agency's liability insurance policy.

Be alert to the fact that an agency's manual of policy and procedure, in effect, describes a standard of care and service owed to, and expected by, the client. Thus, in a malpractice lawsuit, a social worker's failure to follow agency policy may be used as evidence of professional negligence. An agency places itself at higher legal risk when it has an official policy that is not or cannot be regularly followed by its employees.

Use precautions to avoid becoming involved in malpractice lawsuits. You can protect yourself by acting on the following guidelines:

- Read the NASW *Code of Ethics* regularly and abide by its guidelines.
- Adhere to agency policy, procedure, and protocol.
- Make every effort to practice competently.
- Utilize supervision regularly to ensure that your approaches and techniques are legal, ethical, and therapeutically sound.
- Refer clients to other professionals and programs when you are unable to provide the services they require and document your efforts to make a referral.
- Consult with your agency's legal counsel whenever confronted with troublesome legal issues or questions.
- Recognize situations of high legal risk.
- Obtain malpractice insurance if your agency does not provide it for you.
- Avoid dual relationships with clients.
- Protect client confidentiality.
- Inform clients about the limits of confidentiality.
- Maintain up-to-date, accurate, and complete client records.
- Create client records that are free of judgmental language and hearsay.
- Obtain permission from clients to release information about them to others.
- Document any client complaints or grievances, and the steps you took to resolve them.
- Understand the concept of privileged communication.

You are not likely to become entangled in a malpractice law suit if you follow the guidelines described above. Adhere to what would be considered reasonable, customary, and prudent practices. The actions you take on behalf of clients must be fair, in good faith, and in keeping with how other professionals would tend to act. If you need clarification in any particular area, seek guidance and consultation from your social work supervisor and/or agency legal counsel.

LEGAL ISSUES AND CONCERNS: A WORKBOOK ACTIVITY

The following questions are designed to heighten your awareness of the legal context of social work practice and the legal considerations that are relevant to your practicum agency. Discuss these questions and issues with your practicum instructor and with experienced social workers in your agency. If you are in a large agency, it may have a legal department and staff attorneys who can respond to your questions and explain legal principles.

1. Is eligibility for your agency's services in any way defined by law? If so, what specific codes or statutes and legal rules and regulations are used to determine who is and is not eligible?

   _____

   _____

   _____

   _____

2. Are certain individuals legally required or mandated to involve themselves with your agency and obtain services from your agency (e.g., those on probation and court-ordered treatment)? If so, what specific statutes apply to these individuals and situations?

   _____

   _____

   _____

   _____

3. Do those individuals who are pressured to make use of your agency have a right to refuse to participate? If so, do they face any consequences for that action?

   _____

   _____

   _____

   _____

4. Is your agency program licensed by the state (e.g., a licensed child placing agency, licensed nursing home, and licensed foster care provider)? If yes, identify the specific license(s) and the legal citation of the laws and regulations that apply.

   _____

   _____

   _____

   _____

5. What outside agencies or organizations (e.g., governmental agencies, accrediting bodies, and citizen review boards) are authorized to interview staff about their practices and review the records kept by your agency (e.g., client records, client services, and financial records)?

_____

_____

_____

_____

6. What are the possible legal consequences for a social worker who takes action that conflicts with or violates the agency's written policy?

_____

_____

_____

_____

7. What percentage of the social workers in your agency hold a state social work license?

_____

Another type of professional license?

_____

8. Does your agency have liability insurance that provides employees with legal defense against allegations of wrongdoing and/or pay the assessed damages if found guilty? If so, what limitations and restrictions apply (e.g., must the employee be following agency policy and behave in an ethical manner before he or she can use the insurance policy)?

_____

_____

_____

_____

9. Does the agency's liability insurance cover the actions of social work practicum students? The actions of volunteers? If yes, what limitations and restrictions apply?

_____

_____

10. Do the social workers in your agency carry and pay for individual malpractice insurance in addition to that provided by the agency? If yes, why?

11. From what organizations or companies do social workers purchase their malpractice insurance? About how much does this insurance cost? From what organizations or companies does the agency purchase liability insurance? How much does this cost?

12. Within the past ten years, has the agency or any staff member been sued for negligence or malpractice? If yes, what was the nature of the allegation(s) and the outcome of the lawsuit(s)?

13. Within the context of your agency, what types of clients and what types of situations are associated with high legal risk (i.e., cases most likely to result in a lawsuit alleging agency wrongdoing or professional malpractice)?

14. What attorneys or law firms represent your agency or its staff when someone alleges wrongdoing or professional negligence?

_____

_____

_____

_____

15. What agency policies or procedures apply when you or others encounter the following cases or situations that raise legal questions?

a. The client who appears to be a real threat to self (e.g., possible suicide)

_____

_____

b. The client who appears to be a real threat to others

_____

_____

c. The client who may not be mentally competent to care for himself or herself or make legal, medical, or financial decisions

_____

_____

d. The client who is a minor

_____

_____

e. The client who is injured while in your agency or while participating in an agency program

_____

_____

f. The client who insists on withdrawing from a treatment program or another agency service when doing so will place the client at risk of harm

_____

_____

g. The client who threatens harm to a social worker or other agency staff member

_____

_____

h. The client who is suspected of or known to have committed a serious crime

_____

_____

i. The client who appears to need legal counsel or representation

_____

_____

j. The client who has been ordered by a court to receive certain services from your agency (e.g., assessment, treatment, and intervention)

_____

_____

k. The client who has clearly lied, withheld information, or falsified an application in order to become eligible for the benefits or services provided by your agency

_____

_____

l. The client who states he or she intends to bring a lawsuit against a social worker or the agency

_____

_____

16. What policies or procedures apply when you or others encounter the following situations and legal questions?

a. How to proceed when a client requests the opportunity to read or copy his or her records (case file)

_____

_____

b. How to obtain a client's permission to release his or her records to another agency or professional

_____

_____

c. How to report suspected child abuse and neglect

_____

_____

d. How to obtain a client's informed consent to participate in certain programs and services

_____

_____

e. How to handle and record the receipt of gifts from a client or donations to the agency

_____

_____

f. How to respond when one receives a subpoena for client records or other confidential information

_____

_____

g. How to respond when one receives a subpoena to be a witness in a trial or court action

_____

_____

Additional notes and comments:

_____

_____

_____

_____

_____

_____

SUGGESTED LEARNING ACTIVITIES

- Examine your agency's policy manual and identify policies that refer to the need for staff to conform with specific legal codes or requirements.
- Identify situations in which there might be a conflict between what is required by the NASW *Code of Ethics* and the requirements of a specific state or federal law.
- Spend time observing court proceedings, especially ones in which your agency is involved.

ADDITIONAL SUGGESTIONS AND HINTS

- In Sheafor, Horejsi, and Horejsi (2000), read the sections on "Avoiding Malpractice Suits" and "Testifying in Court."
- Read contracts and legal documents that affect services provided or that are part of your agency's purchase of services agreements (e.g., a state agency agrees to pay your agency for certain services to provide to clients or agreements with managed care companies).

SELECTED BIBLIOGRAPHY

Barker, Robert, and Douglas Branson. *Forensic Social Work.* New York: Haworth, 1993.

Bullis, Ronald. *Clinical Social Worker Misconduct.* Chicago: Nelson-Hall, 1995.

Houston-Vega, Mary, Elane Nuehring, and Elizabeth Daguio. *Prudent Practice: A Guide for Managing Malpractice Risk.* Washington, DC: NASW Press, 1997.

National Association of Social Workers. *Code of Ethics.* Washington, DC: NASW Press, 1997.

Pollack, Daniel. *Social Work and the Courts.* New York: Garland, 1997.

Reamer, Frederic. *Social Work Malpractice and Liability.* New York: Columbia University Press, 1994.

Saltzman, Andrea, and David Furman. *Law in Social Work Practice.* 2nd ed. Chicago: Nelson-Hall, 1999.

Schroeder, Leila. *The Legal Environment of Social Work.* Washington, DC: NASW Press, 1995.

Sheafor, Bradford, Charles Horejsi, and Gloria Horejsi. *Techniques and Guidelines for Social Work Practice.* 5th ed. Boston: Allyn and Bacon, 2000.

16

SOCIAL WORK PRACTICE
AS PLANNED CHANGE

Goals for Learning

- To become aware of the fundamental beliefs about change that may inform and guide your agency's services and programs and the actions of its social workers
- To become aware of the various practice frameworks (perspectives, models, and theories) that are used to plan and guide intervention and agency programs
- To become aware of the data-gathering and assessment tools used in your agency
- To become aware of commonly used interventions in your agency
- To become aware of how the effectiveness of social work interventions is evaluated in your agency

Fundamentally, the practice of social work is about the process of planned change. The verb *process* means to advance, to progress, to move onward. In the practice of social work, the worker takes deliberate and specific steps to encourage and facilitate movement toward a certain goal. Your practicum offers an excellent opportunity to observe and critically examine the values, beliefs, ethical principles, and knowledge base that guide a social worker's efforts to bring about a desired change.

In this chapter we encourage you to think about the nature of change. Strive to identify the assumptions about change that are embedded in your agency's programs and policies as well as in its various approaches to practice. Also, identify your own beliefs about how, why, and under what circumstances desirable change by individuals, families, small groups, organizations, and communities is possible and probable.

BACKGROUND INFORMATION

As explained in Chapter 13, social work is often defined as the activity of helping individuals, families, groups, or communities enhance or restore their capacity for social functioning and for creating societal conditions favorable to these goals.

At the level of the individual, *social functioning* can be viewed as a person's motivation, capacity, and opportunity to meet his or her basic human needs (e.g., food, shelter, health care, education, meaningful work, protection, and self-worth) and carry out his or her social roles (e.g., parent, student, employee, citizen, and neighbor). In order to create conditions favorable for effective social functioning, social workers also seek needed changes in social policy, programs, and services.

To accomplish the goals of their profession, social workers assume a wide variety of roles. *Social work practice roles* include those of client advocate, broker of services, case manager, counselor or therapist, group leader or facilitator, community organizer, administrator, supervisor, researcher, policy analyst, teacher, and trainer. Depending on their practice setting and usual role, social workers are either mostly people changers or mostly system changers, but often they are some of both.

A typical social work intervention involves and affects numerous individuals, groups, and organizations. Pincus and Minahan (1973, 63) suggest the following terminology:

- *Change agent system:* The social worker and the worker's agency.
- *Client system:* The person, group, or organization who has requested the agency's or social worker's services and who expects to benefit from what the agency and worker do. It is the client that enters into an agreement or a contract with the change agent system.
- *Target system:* The person, group, or organization that needs to change in order for the client to benefit from the intervention. (In many situations of direct practice, the client system and the target system are one and the same).
- *Action system:* All of the people, groups, and organizations that the social worker works with or through in order to influence the target system and thereby help the client achieve the desired outcome.

The social worker and client may seek change and formulate interventions at one or more of three levels: micro, mezzo, and macro. The *micro* level refers to human interactions that are fairly intense, very personal, face-to-face relationships such as the interactions between husband and wife, between partners, between parent and child, between brother and sister, and between other family members.

The *mezzo* level (mid-level) refers to interactions between, for example, friends, neighbors, peers at work, members of a treatment group or support group, or members of a church or service club. The interactions and relationships at the mezzo level are less frequent and less intense than those at the micro level.

The term *macro* level refers to interactions between people acting as members of large groups or as representatives of formal organizations such as networks of social agencies, governmental programs, and policy-making bodies. As compared to the micro and mezzo levels, communications and interactions at this level tend to be more formal and structured by an agenda and schedule; they often focus on issues related to laws, regulations, policies, and procedures.

Social work with a client, whether the client is an individual or a community, typically moves through the *phases of a planned change*. These are:

1. Identifying and defining the client's problem or concern and the client's strengths
2. Collecting data and studying the problem or situation
3. Assessing the problem (i.e., deciding what needs to change, what can be changed, how it might be changed, and what resources are available to the client)
4. Establishing goals, objectives, and tasks for change
5. Taking action based on the plan (i.e., intervention)
6. Monitoring of progress and determining if the intervention is achieving the desired outcomes and, if necessary, modifying the plan and trying again
7. Terminating the intervention once goals and objectives have been reached and evaluating the change process to learn for future practice

This list of phases gives the impression that the change process is quite orderly and linear. In reality, that is seldom the case. Typically, the client and worker move back and forth across these phases several times during the intervention process.

While the use of the problem-solving process is pervasive in social work and in many other professions, it has been criticized for being essentially a negative orientation that results in social workers giving too much attention to what is wrong and too little attention to client strengths and situational assets. When thinking about the concept of a problem and its place in the process of change, it is helpful to recall that dictionaries define the word *problem* as a question raised for inquiry, consideration, or solution and as a question or situation that presents uncertainty, perplexity, or difficulty. The word *problem* is derived from the Greek word *proballein* which means to "throw forward." Thus, a problem is a genuine challenge that pushes us to change how we think or act. Giving attention to client strengths does not require a blindness to client problems. Indeed, successful interventions are built on client strengths while also recognizing real client problems and needs.

When considering the various phases of the problem-solving process, it is helpful to make a distinction between data collection and assessment. *Data collection* refers to the gathering of facts and information about the client and/or the situation targeted for change. *Assessment* refers to the worker's interpretation or explanation of these data in a way that lays a conceptual foundation for a plan of action or intervention. Needless to say, several different meanings can be drawn from the same set of facts. The meaning assigned to data is often shaped by the practice perspectives, theories, and models used by the social worker and his or her agency.

Social workers use a variety of orienting theories and practice frameworks to guide their work with clients. As used here, an *orienting theory* is a body of knowledge drawn from the social and behavioral sciences such as sociology, anthropology, psychology, economics, and biology. Such theories help the social worker to understand human behavior and the social environment but, by themselves, do not provide guidance on how to facilitate planned change.

For such guidance, the social worker must look to another type of conceptual framework, which we call a practice framework. A *practice framework* is a set of interrelated beliefs and assumptions about how people and social systems change and what a social worker can do to facilitate change at either the micro, mezzo, or macro level. There is no agreed upon terminology to describe or classify the various practice frameworks. Authors may describe a given framework as either a perspective, an approach, a method, a model, a theory, a paradigm, or a strategy. Sheafor, Horejsi, and Horejsi (2000) suggest three categories: practice perspectives, practice theories, and practice models.

A *practice perspective*, like the focusing of a camera, serves to magnify a particular aspect of the person-in-environment. The general systems perspective and the ecosystems perspective are commonly used in social work for assessing the relationships between people and their environment. The generalist perspective provides a way of looking at practice in ways that broaden the practice roles and consider interventions at various levels (micro, mezzo, and macro) and with various types of clients (individuals, families, groups, organizations, and communities). Others, such as the feminist and ethnic-sensitive practice perspectives, serve to remind the worker that certain client groups face special challenges in our society.

A *practice theory* provides both an explanation of certain behaviors or situations and broad guidelines about how they can be changed. Examples of the micro-level theories include the psychosocial approach, which is based primarily on psychodynamic theory and ego psychology, and the behavioral approach, which is rooted in theories of learning.

A *practice model* is essentially a set of principles used to guide certain interventions. However, by definition, these principles are not tied to a particular explanation of behavior. Examples at the micro level include crisis intervention and the task-centered approach. Examples at the mezzo and macro levels include organizational development, community development, social planning, and social action. Most often, a practice model develops out of a demonstration project or experiment rather than, deductively, from a particular theory of behavior.

The term *model* is also used to describe a conceptual framework or a set of principles that has been borrowed from another field of practice or from another profession. When a particular innovation is successful, other agencies, programs, and professions borrow its key principles. Thus, we hear such terms as the home-builders model, the self-help model, the grassroots model, the 12-step model, the case-management model, and the medical model.

In addition to the practice frameworks mentioned above, there are many others: the strengths perspective, the cognitive-behavioral theory, the person-centered model, the interactional model, the structural model, the solution-focused model, the family systems theory, the narrative approach, the clubhouse model, the various approaches to using the small group, and the various approaches to organizational change and community change.

As a general rule, the practice perspectives, theories, and models utilized in direct services agencies do not give much attention to the roles and activities that would involve practitioners in efforts to change societal systems and institutional structures. The practice frameworks used in macro-level practice do, of course, have such an emphasis, but they differ in their underlying beliefs about how positive social change can be facilitated by a social work practitioner. Payne (1997, 4–5) observes that many social workers' viewpoints on system and institutional change fall into three broad categories:

1. The *reflexive–therapeutic view* has as its goal securing the well-being of individuals, families, groups, and communities. This is accomplished by promoting personal growth and self-fulfillment. As people interact more effectively with each other and with existing systems, they gain competence. As a result of this increased personal power they will rise above their problems and disadvantages. Social workers holding this viewpoint do not directly challenge the existing social order.
2. The *socialist–collectivist view* has as a primary goal the creation of a society characterized by cooperation and mutual support. It seeks to challenge oppression and injustice in the existing social order and to empower people, especially those who have been marginalized or disenfranchised, so they will actively participate in creating new systems and institutions. This approach presumes that those in positions of power and authority will need to be confronted and pressured to make the needed changes.
3. The *individualist–reformist view* has as its primary goal the provision of social services to individuals and the gradual improvement of those services. Social workers holding this view may want to see broad social change but they conclude that working for such change is beyond the scope of their job description and ordinary responsibilities. Consequently, they do not seek social or institutional changes and concentrate instead on making incremental changes in the services they provide to clients.

Food for Thought

I would define change as that which takes place in persons . . . The assertion that change is ultimately lodged in persons is not incongruent with [efforts to change] . . . for instance, social legislation, economic innovations, racial integration, or modifications in a community's structures and institutions. We tend to abstract these phenomena, to see them in nonhuman, institutional, or societal terms as if they were occurring in a self-enclosed sphere. They are, in reality, human endeavors brought about by persons who are committed to the need for change, reform, or modification. (Goldstein 1973, 159)

◆ ◆ ◆

Perhaps the most profound source of resistance to change is simply what we tell ourselves. People who hold onto problems frequently send themselves messages that rob them of their power by stating and confirming current limitations—both real and imagined—in a way that implies that constraints are forever fixed. People who act to improve problem conditions acknowledge current limitations but acknowledge current assets as well. They are willing to use assets to test limitations and to break them down. (Homan 1999, 10)

◆ ◆ ◆

Every change effort requires that someone begin doing something different. Every successful change is the result of action. Distilled to its essence, the process of [community] change involves taking goal-directed action, strengthening your organization through the effective involvement of others, maintaining communication to keep the reality of the change effort and the relationships among members strong, and continuing to make purposeful decisions.

The decision to act and to succeed is the precondition to accomplishment. The more clear that decision, the stronger your actions will be.

It all boils down to this. None of your ideas, desires, or plans amount to a hill of beans unless you act on them. (Homan 1999, 321–322)

◆ ◆ ◆

The professional worker–client relationship is a purposeful one, that is, it is designed to achieve goals of facilitating the client's sense of success, not failure. Its success or failure will depend largely on what kind of goals you agree on and what methods will be used to achieve the goals. If you do not have clear goals, neither of you will know when you have succeeded, and it will be difficult to evaluate the work you and your client are accomplishing. . . .

Goals have two components: *what* you are aiming for and *how* and *what* you are going to do to achieve it. (Berg 1994, 66–67)

◆ ◆ ◆

It is more important to do the right thing than to do things right.

—*Peter Drucker*

◆ ◆ ◆

I don't think we can change society. You can only change individual by individual.

—*Esmeralda Santiago*

GUIDANCE AND DIRECTION

Identify the practice frameworks (perspectives, theories, and models) used in your agency. Whether implicit or explicit, these frameworks influence how your agency designs its programs and services and how it works with clients. Determine why these particular practice frameworks are judged most appropriate and most effective for the clients served by your agency. Consider what your agency's choice of practice frameworks reveals about the agency's beliefs and assumptions concerning:

- The causes of personal and social problems
- How clients and client systems change
- Actions that are most likely to facilitate change

Identify the strengths and weaknesses of the various practice frameworks used in your practicum setting and of those employed by other agencies in your community. To accomplish this analysis, consider the following questions:

- What types of problems, needs, or concerns are addressed by your agency?
- Are the interventions or change efforts conducted by agency staff typically at the micro, mezzo, or macro level? Why at this level of intervention?
- What practice frameworks (perspectives, theories, and models) are used by the professionals in your agency?
- How does the selection of a particular practice framework determine or shape the roles performed by social workers (e.g., the roles of therapist, advocate, organizer, program planner, trainer, and case manager)?
- How is a particular practice framework chosen for a particular client? Is the same one utilized with all clients or based on client characteristics?
- Is the use of a particular practice framework required by law or encouraged by an accrediting body?
- Are the practice frameworks appropriate and relevant for the clients served by the agency?
- When they work, why do they work?
- When they do not work, why not?
- What other practice frameworks might be more effective, and why?
- Is the practice framework used by your agency similar to or different from those used by other agencies with a similar purpose?
- When, if ever, is a client referred to another agency because that agency uses a specific practice framework?
- Does your agency's practice framework work for both voluntary and involuntary clients?
- Does your agency's practice framework work for clients from diverse backgrounds (e.g., ethnicity, religion, language, and sexual orientation)?
- Does your agency's practice framework work for clients who live in severe poverty, those who cannot read, or those who have developmental delays?

It is important that the behaviors and activities expected of you as a social worker are compatible with your own personality, attitudes, and style of interaction. Exposure to real clients and the problems they face is sure to elicit strong feelings in you, both about them and about your own professional role and responsibilities. Pay attention to these feelings and reactions and consider what they may be telling you about your choice of a particular field of practice and even about your choice of social work as a career.

Because social workers, like all people, are unique with regard to their core values, personality, and style of interaction, individual workers usually find some practice perspectives, theories, and models more attractive than others. We urge you to carefully examine the possible reasons behind your attraction to certain ones and your rejection of others. Usually, one's choice of a practice framework is the result of a combination of factors, including beliefs about the causes of human problems, beliefs about what can be changed and what cannot, beliefs about personal and social responsibility, beliefs about how much people should be involved in defining and assessing their own problems, and beliefs about the role and responsibility of the professional in facilitating change.

Examine your preferences for certain practice frameworks, and decide if they are based mostly on your personal beliefs, values, and attitudes, mostly on effectiveness research and empirical data reported in the professional literature, or mostly on what your practicum instructor and school faculty have told you about what does and does not work.

Recognize that your practicum experience is limited to one setting and that other agencies and programs may be quite different from the one you know best. There are significant differences between programs, even when they have similar goals and serve the same types of clients. Strive to learn how and why other agencies have adopted forms of intervention, practice perspectives, theories and models that are different from the ones used in your practicum setting.

Social workers are often drawn to certain practice roles, while preferring to avoid others. For example, some might be attracted to roles related to advocacy and social action because they want to see changes in social structures that can benefit large numbers of people, while others might avoid these same roles because they are uncomfortable with conflict and the use of power and influence. Some might be attracted to the clinician or counselor role because they like intense, face-to-face contact with individual clients, whereas others might be uncomfortable with the discussion of painful personal problems. Still others might either be attracted to or wish to avoid the tasks of budgeting, grant proposal writing, personnel selection, and public relations that are associated with the roles of administration and program planning. Give careful thought to the roles and activities you prefer and ponder the question of why some are more attractive to you than others.

Some of these preferences will be based on your skills, some on your values, some on your previous experiences, and some on your beliefs about what social workers should do. During your practicum, gain experience in as many practice roles as possible in order to understand the nature of these roles and better understand your own abilities. Do not limit yourself to the performance of only a few practice roles. Most likely your career in social work will require that you assume many different practice roles and perform a wide range of tasks and activities.

Observe how the professionals in your agency go about their work of helping clients and providing services. Identify the practice frameworks, approaches, methods, and techniques used during the various phases of their work with clients. Consider the following questions in your analysis:

Engagement and Relationship Building

- What specific techniques are used to facilitate building an effective helping relationship?
- What approaches are used to address the client's possible questions and concerns about utilizing the services offered by the agency?
- What approaches are used to make the client feel more at ease and less fearful about entering a professional relationship?

Clarification of Client's Concern or Request

- What approaches are used to help the client specify, elaborate, and clarify the concerns that brought the client to the agency?
- Are clients actively involved in the process of identifying and defining their problems, concerns, and strengths?

Data Collection

- What information is routinely gathered about clients and their problems, concerns, and strengths?
- What tools or instruments are used to aid the gathering of this data (e.g., interview schedules, checklists, needs assessment instruments, questionnaires, and observation)?

Assessment

- How are available data and information organized, combined, and analyzed in order to arrive at a clear picture of the client's situation and a possible plan of action?

- Are clients actively involved in deciding what needs to change and how it might be changed?
- If clients and workers disagree on what needs to change, how is this difference resolved?

Contracting and Planning of the Intervention

- How are interventions selected?
- Are the interventions highly individualized? Are the same approaches used by the professionals regardless of the client's concern and situation?
- Do clients enter into a formal written contract or service agreement with the agency?
- Are the desired outcomes for change clearly identified and realistic given the client's situation?
- Are the desired outcomes measurable?
- Are time limits set for the achievement of desired outcomes?

Intervention and Monitoring

- What system (e.g., client, family, and community) is typically targeted for change by your agency' programs and professional staff? Why?
- What other agencies or organizations often become involved in the client's intervention plan?
- What practice frameworks (perspectives, theories, and models) guide the change process?
- What specific methods, techniques, or procedures are used to facilitate change?
- What specific methods, tools, or instruments are used to monitor whether the intervention is working as planned and expected?

Evaluation and Termination

- In what ways do the agency and its workers determine if their interventions, programs, and services are effective?
- To what extent are clients involved in determining if interventions, programs, and services are effective?
- Does your agency adequately evaluate its interventions, programs, and services?
- What additional forms of evaluation might you suggest?
- Under what circumstances do clients terminate their relationships with personnel from your agency (e.g., when legal mandates are lifted, when clients no longer wish to receive services, and when their ability to pay for services ends)?
- What specific procedures and techniques are used to bring the professional relationship to a close and terminate the helping process?

THE CHANGE PROCESS: A WORKBOOK ACTIVITY

This workbook activity is designed to facilitate learning by walking through the usual phases of the change process. By answering the questions presented below, you will come to a deeper understanding of a planned change (i.e., a social work intervention).

This exercise presumes that change may need to occur at one or more levels (micro, mezzo, or macro). Moreover, the client may or may not be the target of the planned change. (Review the Background Information section in this chapter for the distinction between the client system and target system and concepts of micro, mezzo, and macro level practice.)

To begin this exercise, select a particular client(s), a case situation, or an episode of practice from your practicum experiences. Then, analyze this situation by answering the questions presented below.

Be careful to protect client confidentiality. *Do not* use real names or list any information that might identify the persons actually involved.

Change Agent System

Briefly describe your agency, its purpose, and your usual role within this social work practice setting.

_____

_____

_____

Identifying the Client

Who is (or was) your client? (Note: The client is that person, group, organization, or community who has requested your services or those of your agency and who expects to benefit from the social worker's actions.)

_____

_____

_____

Identification of Client's Problem or Concern

Why has this client approached your agency and requested your assistance? Or, if the client is nonvoluntary, who is requiring or pressuring this client to use the services of your agency and why?

_____

_____

_____

Briefly describe the client's presenting concern, problem, need, or request.

_____

_____

_____

_____

What are the client's expectations of you and your agency?

_____

_____

_____

Data Gathering and Assessment

What data and information are needed in order to understand the client, presenting concerns, and situation? What are the possible sources of this information? What methods, tools, or instruments were or could be used to collect this information?

_____

_____

_____

Describe the client's current level of functioning. (If the client is an individual, consider the client's motivation, capacity, and opportunity to meet his or her basic needs and perform his or her major social roles and meet other important family and social responsibilities.)

_____

_____

_____

_____

What are the client's special strengths that could increase the chances that needed change will be made or that the desired outcome can be achieved?

_____

_____

_____

What are the client's special challenges or limitations that will be barriers to making needed change and achieving the desired outcome?

_____

_____

_____

What contextual factors (e.g., social and economic conditions, state and federal laws, public attitudes, and political climate) will either increase or limit the possibility of achieving desired outcomes? For example, if the client is an individual, will addressing his or her concern require a change in the policies and operation of a large system such as a school, health care program, human services program, and government program?

_____

_____

_____

What issues of human difference, prejudice, and discrimination need to be considered in assessing the client system and the target system (e.g., sexism, racism, culture and ethnicity, language, religion, age, and disability)?

_____

_____

_____

Given what is known about the client, the client's concern and situation, and wider context, what specific changes and actions are needed in order to address the client's concerns?

_____

_____

_____

What concepts and theories drawn from the social and behavioral sciences help explain the client's functioning, concerns, or problems and predict what type of intervention would be beneficial and effective in this situation?

_____

_____

_____

Prioritizing the Concerns

Of the several issues, problems, and concerns identified above, which ones are most critical and of greatest importance or highest priority to the client?

_____

_____

_____

Which ones are of greatest importance to you or your agency?

_____

_____

_____

Of the concerns, which ones are you, your agency, and your client willing and able to address?

_____

_____

_____

Identifying Desired Outcomes

Given the high priority concerns, identify and specify the desired outcomes (goals and objectives) for the work with the client. (Note: An objective is an outcome that can be measured.)

_____

_____

_____

_____

Identification of Target System

Given the desired outcomes (goals and objectives), what person, group, organization, policy, or program must undergo some type of change?

_____

_____

_____

Given the particular person, group, or organization targeted for change, consider the likelihood of a successful intervention. What issues, difficulties, or resistance may arise when targeting this person, group, or organization for change? Is the desired change likely to occur?

_____

_____

_____

Formulating an Intervention Plan

Given the desired outcomes that have been identified, what are the alternatives or options (i.e., possible interventions) for effecting the needed change and thereby achieving these outcomes? What are the advantages and disadvantages of each option?

_____

_____

_____

Of possible interventions that might bring about the needed change, which one is most feasible and most likely to succeed, given the resources available? (Resources include time, skill, knowledge, funding, sanction to take action, and support from others.)

_____

_____

_____

Of the interventions that are possible, which one is most likely to be successful given the client's motivation, capacity, and other relevant situational and contextual factors?

_____

_____

_____

What legal or ethical concerns, if any, must be considered in formulating an intervention plan?

_____

_____

_____

What other services, programs, or community resources are needed and available to address the client's concerns? Would this client be better served by referral to another agency, program, or professional? Does the client need a particular type of service that does not exist in the community?

_____

_____

_____

_____

Identifying Specific Action Steps and Tasks

Given the desired outcomes (goals and objectives) that have been identified, what specific actions and tasks are necessary to bring abut the required change?

_____

_____

_____

_____

Given the various tasks and activities that need to occur, who will do what? What will the client need to do? What will you do? What is the agency to do? What must others do?

_____

_____

_____

When are these action steps (tasks and activities) to be completed? For example, what must be done during the next three weeks? The next eight weeks? The next six months?

_____

_____

_____

Does the client have the motivation, capacity, and opportunity to perform the tasks and complete the action steps necessary to achieve the desired outcome?

_____

_____

_____

Do you and your agency have the capacity and commitment to perform the tasks and complete the action steps necessary to achieve the desired outcome?

_____

_____

_____

Monitoring Intervention Progress

How is progress toward desired outcomes to be measured? How will you and the client know if the interventions are working? How will you and client decide if the plan must be modified in order to be more effective?

_____

_____

_____

_____

Final Evaluation and Termination

How is the overall effectiveness of the interventions to be measured?

_____

_____

_____

How and when is the professional relationship to be brought to an end?

_____

_____

_____

Additional notes and comments:

_____

_____

_____

_____

SUGGESTED LEARNING ACTIVITIES

- Examine the data-gathering and assessment tools and instruments used in your agency.
- Ask social workers or other professionals in your agency to identify the practice frameworks that guide their practice. Ask why those frameworks are preferred over other possibilities.
- Identify the beliefs, values, and assumptions implicit in the frameworks used in your agency.
- Examine the various evaluation tools and instruments used in your agency.
- Ask social workers or other professionals in your agency to describe how they and the agency determine whether they are being effective in their work with clients.
- Read about three or four different practice frameworks and then attempt to compare and contrast the values, beliefs, and assumptions that are part of each framework.

ADDITIONAL SUGGESTIONS AND HINTS

- In Sheafor, Horejsi, and Horejsi (2000), read chapters on practice frameworks and the process of change.
- In Turner (1996), Dorfman (1988), Payne (1997), Greene (1999), Lehmann and Coady (2000), Allen-Meares and Garvin (2000), and the *Encyclopedia of Social Work,* read chapters on the various practice frameworks used in your agency and by social work professionals.

SELECTED BIBLIOGRAPHY

Allen-Meares, Paul, and Charles Garvin. *Handbook of Social Work Direct Practice.* Thousand Oaks, CA: Sage, 2000.

Berg, Insoo Kim. *Family Based Services: A Solution-Focused Approach.* New York: Norton, 1994.

Dorfman, Rachelle, ed. *Paradigms of Clinical Social Work.* New York: Brunner/Mazel, 1988.

Edwards, Richard L., ed. *Encyclopedia of Social Work.* 19th ed. Washington, DC: NASW Press, 1995.

Goldstein, Howard. *Social Work Practice.* Columbia: University of South Carolina Press, 1973.

Greene, Roberta. *Human Behavior Theory and Social Work Practice.* 2nd ed. New York: Aldine, 1999.

Homan, Mark. *Promoting Community Change.* 2nd ed. Pacific Grove, CA: Brooks/Cole, 1999.

Lehmann, Peter, and Nick Coady. *Theoretical Perspectives for Direct Social Work Practice.* New York: Springer, 2000.

Payne, Malcolm. *Modern Social Work Theory.* 2nd ed. Chicago: Lyceum, 1997.

Pincus, Allen, and Anne Minahan. *Social Work Practice: Model and Method.* Itasca, IL: F. E. Peacock, 1973.

Sheafor, Bradford, Charles Horejsi, and Gloria Horejsi. *Techniques and Guidelines for Social Work Practice.* 5th ed. Boston: Allyn and Bacon, 2000.

Turner, Francis, ed. *Social Work Treatment: Interlocking Theoretical Approaches.* 4th ed. New York: Free Press, 1996.

17

EVALUATING STUDENT PERFORMANCE

Goals for Learning

- To understand the reasons for evaluating student performance in your practicum
- To understand the process of evaluating student performance in your practicum
- To understand the criteria commonly used to evaluate student performance
- To conduct a self-evaluation of performance in order to measure learning and to identify areas for continued learning or remediation

The goal of the social work practicum is to prepare the student for competent and responsible practice. A successful practicum is one that achieves that goal. Ongoing monitoring and frequent evaluations of the student's performance are necessary to determine if the student is making progress, to document learning, to identify strengths, and to identify areas of performance that may need special attention and remediation. It is of critical importance that you become familiar with the procedure and instruments that will be used to evaluate your performance in the practicum.

This chapter will provide basic information on the process of student evaluation used by programs of social work education and encourage you to examine and evaluate your own performance so you can make the best possible use of the practicum as a learning opportunity.

BACKGROUND INFORMATION

Of central importance in a social work practicum is the ongoing evaluation of the student's performance. The term *evaluation* means to examine, judge, appraise, and assign value or worth. The word *performance* refers to the actions of carrying out or completing some function, role, or obligation. Thus, the social work practicum evaluation focuses on the student's behaviors and actions related to the role and obligations of a professional social worker. The primary question addressed is whether the students' performance is meeting the specified standards expected of the beginning (or entry-level) social work practitioner.

Every program of social work education uses some type of rating scale or evaluation tool to monitor and evaluate student progress. The evaluation process compares the student's performance to established standards and criteria and also to the learning goals, objectives, and activities outlined in the student's learning contract (see Chapter 3).

Evaluations of student performance are of two types: formal and informal. An *informal evaluation* consists of the ongoing feedback and suggestions offered by the practicum instructor. This type of evaluation takes place on a weekly or even a daily basis. A *formal evaluation* is a detailed review and comparison of the student's performance with evaluation criteria, standards, and learning objectives for the practicum. It occurs at the end of each academic term or more often, depending on school policy or special circumstances.

The findings or the results of the formal evaluation are placed in a written report. This report typically consists of the ratings assigned to the various items on the school's evaluation tool and a few paragraphs of narrative that describe special strengths and abilities and/or special problems and deficiencies in performance. The report may also describe how needed learning experiences will be secured or deficiencies corrected prior to the next formal evaluation.

Some practicum programs and practicum instructors may ask the student to prepare for this evaluation by compiling a portfolio that includes various reports and documents that describe the student's practicum activities and achievements and serves to illustrate his or her level of performance.

Depending on school policy and the practicum instructor's level of experience, the faculty supervisor may also participate in the formal evaluation. In some cases, other agency staff may be asked to join in the evaluation if they have worked closely with the student and observed the student's performance.

The areas addressed in the practicum evaluation are similar to those addressed in the performance evaluation of the social workers employed by an agency. In order to ensure high-quality performance and reduce their exposure to lawsuits and employee grievances, agencies strive to make their expectations of employees as clear as possible and to use personnel evaluation tools (i.e., rating scales) that are as objective as possible. These same forces have prompted programs of social work education to develop evaluation tools that are as valid and reliable as possible.

However, it must be recognized that it is difficult to develop an evaluation tool that is both clear and specific in its descriptions of standards and criteria, and also flexible enough to accurately and fairly evaluate the practice of social work, which is complex and difficult to observe directly. An evaluation should be objective to the degree possible, but even a well-designed procedure will require judgments by the practicum instructor, and some of these may be open to charges of subjectivity. For example, ratings of a student's level of cooperation, motivation, adaptability, and use of supervision are difficult to assess except when in an extreme form (i.e., very high motivation or very low motivation). Consequently, there will be times when the practicum instructor and practicum student disagree.

An evaluation can be considered fair and relevant when:

- It addresses the areas of performance or competency that are truly important to professional social work and carrying out the agency's mission and goals.
- The criteria used to evaluate the student are clear and objective to the degree possible.
- The evaluation criteria, standards, and the agency's preferred practices and outcomes are made known to the student at the beginning of the practicum or at the beginning of the time period to be evaluated.
- The student's performance is compared to written standards and criteria, rather than to some unstated or implied standards.
- The student has been given ongoing feedback and warnings of poor performance prior to the formal evaluation.
- The performance criteria and standards are realistic given the student's level (e.g., first semester versus second semester and BSW versus MSW).
- The evaluation can cite and describe examples of performance that form the basis of the ratings.

- The evaluation gives consideration to extenuating circumstances that may influence the evaluation (e.g., the student had limited opportunity to learn or demonstrate certain skills and the supervisor had limited time to observe student's performance).
- The evaluation process identifies and records differences in level of performance among students who are different in terms of their motivation, competency, knowledge, and specific skills.
- The evaluation takes into consideration the nature and complexity of the assignments given to the student.
- The evaluation recognizes student growth and performance as well as student problems or need for continued learning.

An unfair or inaccurate evaluation exists when:

- The student did not understand what was expected of him or her, or did not understand the criteria to be used for evaluation.
- The rules, standards, and criteria used to evaluate the student are changed without the student's knowledge.
- The student receives low ratings without being given a description and explanation of the poor performance that resulted in the low ratings.
- The criteria or standards are unrealistically high or not relevant to the student's performance as a social worker.
- Several students receive essentially the same ratings when there were clear differences in their performances.
- The student was not given ongoing feedback, guidance, and suggestions prior to the evaluation.

The practicum instructor and the student must be alert to certain pitfalls that exist whenever one person attempts to rate another person's performance. These are:

- The *halo effect*—tendency to rate a person the same on all items based on the observed performance in only a few areas.
- The *attraction of the average*—the tendency to evaluate every student or employee about the same or about average regardless of real differences in their performance.
- The *leniency bias*—a tendency to evaluate all students or employees as outstanding or to assign inflated ratings so as to avoid arguments or conflict or to avoid hurting their feelings.
- The *strictness bias*—tendency to evaluate and rate all students or employees on the low side because the evaluator has unrealistically high expectations or holds the belief that low ratings will motivate them toward even higher levels of performance.

In some instances the practicum instructor or the practicum coordinator may conclude that the practicum arrangement is unworkable and unsatisfactory for either the student, the practicum instructor, or both. This may happen when it becomes apparent that the setting cannot meet the student's learning needs or because the student's performance is irresponsible or falls far short of expectations. Examples of student behaviors or performance problems that may prompt the practicum instructor or the school to consider terminating the practicum include the following:

- The student's behavior is harmful to clients, agency staff, or the agency's reputation.
- The student's behavior is irresponsible and unprofessional (e.g., late for work, missing scheduled appointments, and unable to spend the required hours in the practicum setting).

- The student is unable to communicate adequately, either verbally or in writing.
- The student is hostile toward supervision and resistant to learning.
- The student displays symptoms of an emotional disturbance that interfere with work (e.g., bizarre behavior, inability to concentrate, aggressiveness, and withdrawal).
- The student inappropriately shares personal views, experiences, and problems with clients after being made aware of this unacceptable behavior.
- The student enters into dual relationships with clients (e.g., dates a client or sells a product to client).

Some behaviors by the student are considered so serious that they may result in the student's immediate dismissal from the practicum. These include:

- Clear and serious violations of the *Code of Ethics* (e.g., sexual relations with a client)
- Clear and repeated insubordination
- Theft or the clear misuse of agency money, equipment, or property
- Concealing, consuming, or selling drugs on agency premises
- Being intoxicated or under the influence of drugs or alcohol when at work
- Reckless or threatening actions that place clients and staff at risk of serious harm
- Deliberately withholding information from a supervisor or from agency personnel that they need to know in order to properly serve clients and maintain the integrity and reputation of the agency and its programs
- Falsifying agency records and reports
- Soliciting or accepting gifts or favors from clients in exchange for preferential treatment

---

Food for Thought

For the mature, adult professional, the idea of being evaluated often is viewed as insulting. It may re-awaken all kinds of humiliating feelings associated with the powerlessness of childhood and of student roles. We tend to think that people should arrive at a point in life where their competence is assumed by all. They should no longer need to be evaluated or to demonstrate their achievements to others. However, if we think about it, we all continue to be evaluated by someone, no matter at what level one is employed. Evaluations provide needed feedback. Consumers of services provide an evaluation of our work when they return or don't return for additional assistance or when they discuss our services in the community. Why, then, should staff be resentful of having to be evaluated by a professional peer who is most likely to be an experienced professional who occupies a higher level in the administrative hierarchy? . . .

We evaluate clients and their situations in our role as practitioner. We evaluate political climates or community strengths and resources. But when it comes to evaluating the work of a colleague with whom we must work, we tend to react with great distaste. (Weinback 1994, 149–150)

◆◆◆

Your field instructor acts as one of the gatekeepers for the social work program. In this capacity, she is responsible for upholding social work standards and ensuring that students who are not yet competent do not pass the practicum until they have achieved the minimum standards (stated as learning goals) required by your social work program. (Collins, Thomlison, and Grinnell 1992, 179)

◆◆◆

It is essential for interns to understand that the internship experience is fundamentally different from the rest of their academic work. In a typical class, lacking knowledge or skill may mean one's grade is lowered, but otherwise little of any real consequence happens. By comparison, at internships, an intern's lack of knowledge or skill has real consequences and those consequences apply not only to the intern but to the clients, supervisor, and agency with whom the intern works. Thus, it is important for interns to go beyond the grade mentality and focus instead on learning. . . . When evaluation [of student performance] is accepted as an essential part of learning, mistakes, successes, and feedback can be understood for what they really should be—learning opportunities—rather than points added or subtracted from an ultimately meaningless grade book. (Baird 1996, 71–72)

GUIDANCE AND DIRECTION

Throughout your practicum, you will be observed, guided, encouraged, assigned tasks, given feedback, and evaluated. Your practicum instructor should provide an informal and ongoing critique so that you know how you are doing from week to week. In addition, you will be evaluated in a more formal and systematic manner at the end of each academic term.

When conducting the formal evaluation, your practicum instructor will most likely use an evaluation tool provided by your school. This tool will rate you on the specific values, attitudes, knowledge, and skills your school defines as important to your professional development. Obtain a copy of this evaluation tool early in your practicum and construct your plan for practicum learning so that you will have opportunities to learn and grow in each of the areas of performance to be evaluated.

You may also be evaluated on the completion of the tasks, projects, and activities you planned at the beginning of your practicum. Review your learning goals for the practicum regularly to determine if you are making satisfactory progress (see Chapter 3).

Your practicum instructor and your faculty supervisor will want to know how you think the practicum is proceeding, as well as hear any suggestions or questions you might have. He or she may ask you the following:

- What aspects of your practicum do you consider to be of highest priority? Lowest priority?
- Are there tasks and activities that you are having to perform that are different from what you were expecting?
- Are the demands on your time reasonable?
- Have there been aspects of your practicum that you have had to neglect for lack of time?
- Have you been able to strike a workable balance between the demands of the practicum, your other academic work, and your personal life and responsibilities?
- How well do you get along with agency staff?
- What suggestions do you have to improve your practicum?
- Do you get enough supervision or too much?
- Is this the right type of social work practice and practicum setting for you?
- What aspects of social work practice in this agency are most appealing, and which are least appealing?
- Which practicum tasks and assignments have you completed most successfully and which have you completed least successfully?
- What do you hope to accomplish in the next month? By the time you complete your practicum?
- What new or additional experiences do you want or need?
- Do you have other comments, complaints, observations, or questions?

When reviewing and thinking about your performance in the practicum, your practicum instructor may ask himself or herself questions such as:

- Has this student demonstrated dependability and professionally responsible behavior?
- Can this individual be counted on in a stressful and demanding situation?
- Would I hire this person for a social work job?
- Would I want this person to be a social worker for my mother? My child? For a good friend of mine?

Behaviors and personal qualities that favorably impress a practicum instructor include the following: initiative, dependability, honesty, punctuality, capacity to meet deadlines, perseverance, ability to handle conflict in interpersonal relations, sensitivity to others, ability to achieve goals and objectives, ability to plan and organize work, clear writing, motivation and willingness to work hard, receptivity to new learning, self-awareness and openness to examining personal values and attitudes, capacity to work under pressure, personal maturity, emotional stability, respect for clients and other students, fairness in decision making, and professionalism.

Behaviors and qualities that cause a practicum instructor to doubt a student's ability to perform as a social worker include the opposite of the above listed behaviors, especially dishonesty, missing deadlines, disrespect for others, manipulation and efforts to "bend" rules and requirements, attempts to secure special concessions or privileges, and the inability to keep personal problems from interfering with professional tasks and activities.

Prepare for a formal evaluation by reviewing your learning agreement and its stated goals and activities, and also the practicum evaluation tool used by your school. Give careful thought to the question of how well you have managed to carry your various responsibilities and completed assigned tasks. Prepare a list of your assigned tasks and responsibilities and assemble documentation of your work and accomplishments so it can easily be reviewed by your practicum instructor. Prior to meeting with your practicum instructor for the formal evaluation, you may be asked to do a self-evaluation using your school's evaluation tool.

Prepare yourself emotionally for the formal evaluation session so that you will be open to hearing feedback about your performance. When receiving feedback on your performance, strive to maintain an openness toward what you are hearing. Although it may be difficult to hear a frank appraisal of your work, avoid being defensive. Consider this feedback carefully and work to improve in the areas noted.

In addition to constructive criticism, you will receive positive feedback related to areas in which you are doing well. Take note of what your practicum instructor sees as your skills and gifts. Review the workbook section of Chapter 1, and determine if the strengths you identified there have been demonstrated in your performance. Build on your strengths—they will form the basis of your professional knowledge and abilities.

Strive to understand what your practicum instructor observed in your performance that led him or her to draw a particular conclusion concerning your performance. Seek descriptions and examples of your poor performance and ask for specific suggestions on how it can be improved. Request descriptions of performances that were rated higher than most others. Reflect on these descriptions and determine why you perform some tasks and activities better than others.

If you and your practicum instructor disagree on the adequacy of your performance, prepare factual documentation supporting your point of view. However, if you agree that your performance is deficient, it is best to acknowledge the problem rather than entering into a pointless argument that can only leave you looking dishonest or lacking in self-awareness.

A common problem experienced by social work practicum students in direct services agencies is for the student to have an unusually strong or unexpected emotional reaction to specific client problems or situations. This is usually rooted in the student's own history of personal or family problems. The student should discuss these reactions with his or her practicum instructor. In some cases it will be necessary for the student to undergo psychotherapy as a way of better understanding these reactions and finding ways to keep them from interfering with social work performance.

It is possible that during your practicum you will discover that you are not well suited to be a social worker, or perhaps you will discover that what you had assumed to be your area of special interest and skill has lost its appeal. While somewhat painful and upsetting, these are very important discoveries. They may open new doors to exploration and opportunity while closing some that need to be closed. To be happy and content in life you need to make career decisions on the basis of accurate information about your particular strengths and gifts and your particular limitations. You need to understand what you can and cannot do.

EXAMINING YOUR PERFORMANCE IN THE PRACTICUM: A WORKBOOK ACTIVITY

Every program of social work education uses some type of evaluation instrument or tool for evaluating student performance in the practicum. Before beginning this workbook activity, carefully examine the instrument that will be used in the evaluation of your performance.

In this activity you are asked to reflect upon and evaluate your own performance in relation to eleven broad categories and fifty-five dimensions or specific areas of social work knowledge and skills. These dimensions are fairly typical of those utilized in various practicum evaluation instruments.* Describe your performance in relation to each of the fifty-five statements.

Category A: Social Work as a Profession

A1. Understands the social work role and purpose as distinct from the role and purpose of other professions.

_____

_____

A2. Demonstrates competence in a variety of social work practice roles (e.g., case manager, advocate, planner, counselor, and broker of services).

_____

_____

A3. Understands social work ethics and conducts self in accordance with the NASW *Code of Ethics* and its underlying values (e.g., client self-determination, confidentiality, human dignity, and social justice).

_____

_____

A4. Demonstrates competence in the various levels of social work interventions from micro- to macro-level practice (e.g., from direct practice with individuals to social change efforts).

_____

_____

A5. Conducts self in a professional manner (e.g., punctual, reliable, efficient, organized, completed assigned tasks, dressed appropriately).

_____

_____

*The authors use the fifty-five items presented here in their program of social work education at the University of Montana.

Category B: Organizational Context of Practice

B1. Understands agency's purpose, mission, history, funding, and structure.

_____

_____

B2. Understands and facilitates the flow of work in the agency and follows established agency policies, procedures, and protocol.

_____

_____

B3. Works creatively and collaboratively within agency guidelines.

_____

_____

B4. Understands the relationship of the agency to other human services organizations in the community.

_____

_____

B5. Analyzes tools and instruments used by the agency to evaluate effectiveness and suggests additional evaluation procedures if needed.

_____

_____

Category C: Community Context of Practice

C1. Is aware of various services, programs, and resources in the community that are relevant to the client population served by agency.

_____

_____

C2. Uses those community resources most appropriate for specific clients.

_____

_____

C3. Uses advocacy, when appropriate, to obtain resources needed by clients and empowers clients to advocate for themselves.

_____

_____

C4. Is able to identify gaps in services within the community.

_____

_____

C5. Understands the effect of community factors on clients and services (e.g., rural/urban environment, demographics, funding priorities, attitudes, and economics).

_____

_____

Category D: Data Gathering and Assessment

D1. Purposefully and selectively gathers relevant data needed for assessments and interventions.

_____

_____

D2. Sorts, categorizes, and analyzes data in order to understand the nature of client concerns, needs, or problems.

_____

_____

D3. Engages and involves the client in the process of data collection and understanding the meaning and implications of those data.

_____

_____

D4. Addresses the client's strengths, capacity, and opportunity for change.

_____

_____

D5. Identifies the major systems related to the problem or concern being addressed (e.g., social institutions, economic structures, and cultural systems).

_____

_____

Category E: Planning and Intervention

E1. Sets priorities and identifies clear and measurable objectives for intervention.

_____

_____

E2. Involves the client in setting goals and choosing intervention and develops a relevant and feasible contract or service agreement.

_____

_____

E3. Understands various perspectives, theories, and models that guide interventions.

_____

_____

E4. Is able to determine the most feasible and effective level of intervention (micro, mezzo, or macro).

_____

_____

E5. Selects specific and relevant interventions matched to the client's situation, needs, available resources, and the agency's purpose.

_____

_____

Category F: Termination and Evaluation

F1. Helps clients evaluate movement toward agreed-upon goals and objectives.

_____

_____

F2. Terminates helping relationship appropriately and constructively.

_____

_____

F3. Seeks out and uses tools and instruments that can measure client progress and evaluate the effectiveness of an intervention.

_____

_____

F4. Seeks out and uses tools and instruments that can measure and evaluate one's own performance and practice.

_____

_____

F5. Is able to examine and critique one's own performance in an objective and non-defensive manner.

_____

_____

Category G: Understanding Social Problems

G1. Identifies and describes the social problems or conditions that the agency addresses.

_____

_____

G2. Identifies and describes the social problems or conditions faced by clients of the agency.

_____

_____

G3. Understands how social problems develop as a result of the interaction between individuals, social systems, and the larger social environment.

_____

_____

G4. Is aware of the major social problems addressing the community.

_____

_____

G5. Utilizes an ecosystems perspective and social systems theory to analyze social problems.

_____

_____

Category H: Social Policy and Social Change

H1. Identifies and analyzes social policies affecting clients of the agency.

_____

_____

H2. Recognizes the positive and negative impacts of social policy on clients.

_____

_____

H3. Understands how social policies develop and are modified over time.

_____

_____

H4. Identifies needed changes in social policy.

_____

_____

H5. Is able to participate in social change or social justice efforts.

_____

_____

Category I: Diversity

I1. Is aware of and sensitive to client issues related to diversity (e.g., culture, ethnicity, gender, age, socioeconomic status, disability, and sexual orientation).

_____

_____

I2. Treats all people with respect regardless of their behavior, characteristics, and background.

_____

_____

I3. Understands the effects of stereotypes, prejudice, discrimination, and oppression on individuals, families, and communities and on the formation of social policy.

_____

_____

I4. Is effective in communicating with persons of differing backgrounds and life experiences.

_____

_____

I5. Is able to individualize procedures for assessment, planning, intervention, and evaluation for diverse clients.

_____

_____

Category J: Communication Skills

J1. Effectively uses nonverbal communication and verbal helping skills (e.g., empathic responding, active listening, mediating, and counseling).

_____

_____

J2. Effectively uses written communication (e.g., correspondence, reports, and records).

_____

_____

J3. Is able to engage and work with nonvoluntary, resistant, or hard-to-reach clients.

_____

_____

J4. Recognizes the underlying meaning and significance of clients' concerns and situation.

_____

_____

J5. Handles questions and disagreements with other staff and agency policies and procedures with understanding, tact, and diplomacy.

_____

_____

Category K: Knowledge and Use of Self

K1. Takes the initiative in developing and implementing learning activities.

_____

_____

K2. Uses supervision for guidance, learning, and professional growth.

_____

_____

K3. Understands how personal values, beliefs, and ethics enhance or interfere with social work practice.

_____

_____

K4. Is aware of own biases and deals with them appropriately.

_____

_____

K5. Recognizes personal changes needed in order to function more effectively as a social worker (e.g., habits, personal style, and level of knowledge).

_____

_____

Additional notes and comments:

_____

_____

_____

_____

_____

_____

SUGGESTED LEARNING ACTIVITIES

- Compare the practicum evaluation instrument used by your school with the evaluation tool used to evaluate the performance of social workers and other professional staff in your agency.

ADDITIONAL SUGGESTIONS AND HINTS

- In Sheafor, Horejsi, and Horejsi (2000), read the sections on "Developing Self-Awareness" and "Worker Performance Evaluation."

SELECTED BIBLIOGRAPHY

Baird, Brian N. *The Internship, Practicum, and Field Placement Handbook.* Upper Saddle River, NJ: Prentice-Hall, 1996.

Collins, Donald, Barbara Thomlison, and Richard Grinnell. *The Social Work Practicum.* Itasca, IL: F. E. Peacock, 1992.

National Association of Social Workers. *Code of Ethics.* Washington, DC: NASW Press, 1997.

Rothman, Juliet. *The Self-Awareness Workbook for Social Workers.* Boston: Allyn and Bacon, 1999.

Sheafor, Bradford, Charles Horejsi, and Gloria Horejsi. *Techniques and Guidelines for Social Work Practice.* 5th ed. Boston: Allyn and Bacon, 2000.

Weinback, Robert. *The Social Worker as Manager.* 2nd ed. Boston: Allyn and Bacon, 1994.

18

MERGING SELF AND PROFESSION

Goals for Learning

- To identify important considerations in selecting social work as a career
- To identify factors important to your selection of a particular type of social work practice and a practice setting
- To become aware of how the practice of social work might affect your physical and mental health, family, friends, and economic situation
- To develop self-awareness as a person and a professional

Your family and friends have probably asked you the following questions: What is social work? Why do you want to be a social worker? Why do you need a degree in social work? Will you be able to get a job and earn a living? These are good questions and you should be able to answer them and be comfortable with your answers.

Each of us is a unique individual with a unique personality and set of abilities and interests. In addition, each profession and occupation has a unique set of demands and required skills. For you to be satisfied and effective as a social worker, there must be a good match between you and the profession.

Selecting a career or occupation is one of the most important decisions you will make. That decision will have far-reaching implications for your basic contentment in life, the level of satisfaction you find in work, and your economic situation. A good match between your choice of occupation and your interests, abilities, and values will bring you personal satisfaction, challenge, and stimulation. A mismatch can give rise to general discontent and stress-related health problems.

The practicum provides an invaluable opportunity to examine and test the match between who you really are, your values, beliefs, temperament, abilities, and skills and the demands, requirements, and rewards of social work practice. This chapter is designed to help you examine, once again, that match.

BACKGROUND INFORMATION

Most social workers feel "called" to the profession of social work because they are committed to helping others and they find that the profession's values are compatible with their own. They want to make a positive contribution to their community and world and they see that the practice of social work is a way of doing that. Some also feel drawn to the profession because events and experiences in their lives have opened their eyes to certain problems and to the needs of other people.

Those preparing for a career in social work must be familiar with the types of jobs that are available and the demands of the work. They must have a high level of self-awareness so they can make good choices in relation to the type of job they seek, practice self-care and stress management, and balance personal and professional responsibilities. Social workers must be aware of their special gifts, their values, and their biases. Such self-awareness is also critical to becoming a professional who is effective in his or her use of self in relating to clients. Social workers must understand how their particular style and manner of interacting is perceived by others, especially clients. Those planning to enter social work must be emotionally healthy, skilled in communication, able to build and maintain relationships, able to manage stress, and willing to continually learn and grow, both personally and professionally.

Choosing a helping profession as your life's work usually means that you care deeply about those you serve. This commitment to others may take a toll on one's personal life unless the social worker learns to find a healthy balance between work and personal life. It is not possible to make a complete separation between one's personal and professional lives. Our work affects our personal lives and our personal lives affect our work. Sheafor, Horejsi, and Horejsi (2000, 15) observe that the social workers' "own beliefs, values, physical and emotional well-being, spirituality, family life, financial situation, friendships, and all other facets of living will both influence and be affected by the day-to-day experiences of social work practice." Knowing this, it is vital to find a proper and workable balance between one's personal life and one's professional life.

Because it is difficult for an organization or an agency to dismiss an employee who is not performing well, organizations are increasingly cautious about who they hire in the first place. Employers are taking great care to screen the applicants so they can be confident that the person they hire can do the work that needs to be done and will "fit" in the organization and its style of operation. For this reason, the student who has performed well in a practicum setting has a distinct advantage if he or she applies for a job with that same agency because he or she will have demonstrated a beginning ability to fit into the organization.

The practicum student should be alert to what his or her practicum agency and other employers are looking for when they screen job applicants for social work positions. Typically, they are especially interested in six qualities:

1. Skills related to the job to be performed (as described in the job description)
2. Character traits and prior experiences that reflect creativity, flexibility, and an enthusiasm for solving problems
3. An ability to work cooperatively with others
4. An ability to work within an organizational structure and an understanding of the need for authority
5. A genuine interest in and an enjoyment of the type of work to be performed
6. Communication skills (both written and verbal)

In general, there is a close relationship between job satisfaction and one's overall satisfaction with self and life. Those who are satisfied with their job tend to have high self-esteem, are able to manage stress, and believe that they have influence and control over the outcome of their work. Other factors also contribute to job satisfaction. Among them are the following:

- *Overall workload*—Most people prefer jobs that are challenging and that keep them busy, but are not overwhelming or exhausting.
- *Variety*—Most people prefer work that provides some variety. Most people do not care for jobs that are highly repetitive.
- *Opportunity*—Most people desire jobs that will provide opportunities for promotion and advancement.
- *Social Interaction*—Most people prefer jobs that allow friendly, pleasant, and informal interactions with coworkers.

Food for Thought

It's comparatively easy to do a hard thing for a short time, but to do even a slightly difficult thing steadily is a serious challenge to commitment. This calls for doggedness, for persistence. . . .

Some people who want to bring about [social] change indulge in grandiose plans. . . . They get carried away by dreams and never actually do anything. . . .

To want to do some generalized good for some unspecified people is usually a waste of time and energy. But if you identify the people to be helped, specify what they need, and prepare yourself to meet that need, then you can get results.

"Do gooders" are dismissed as cranks when they don't develop the skills necessary to bring about improvements. Doing good requires knowing how . . .

Those who work to bring about changes are able to see even in darkest circumstances how improvements are possible if the right kind of effort is made. They can see beyond inconsistencies, human frailty, and fearsome injustice to the goal that beckons them. The constant presence of that goal carries them on and sets them apart from others who do not make a difference. (Armstrong and Wakin 1978, 82–89)

[A barrier to effective social work] is insufficient self-awareness. By this we mean a lack of understanding of your own culture (including ethnic heritage, values, beliefs, expectations, and behavior). We also may have a lack of sensitivity to our own biases. All of us grow up exposed to a variety of beliefs about other groups and interpretations of what is "good" or "right." This is part of what makes us a product of our culture. It is also what often makes us ethnocentric. We may conclude that things are "crazy," "odd," or "different" because they are not what we are used to. Thus, we tend to see life through a set of cultural sunglasses that colors all we experience, personally and professionally. (Kirst-Ashman and Hull 1993, 403)

Self-awareness and critical inquiry go hand in hand. Both encourage contextual awareness—exploring how past and present environments influence what you do, value, and believe and how, in turn, you influence your environments. Critical thinking will help you discover . . . beliefs you have accepted without critical thought which, on reflection, you find problematic.

Critical thinking helps free us from the prisons of unexamined views that limit our vision. It encourages us to examine the perspective within which we reason and the effect of our own cultural experiences in developing them. It can help us identify topics or positions to which we have a strong initial reaction in one direction that prevents critical inquiry. Thinking carefully about problems and possible ways to solve them helps us detect contradictions between what we do and what we say we value. It teaches us to be aware of how our emotions affect our beliefs and actions. (Gambrill 1997, 132–133)

Without work, all life goes rotten, but when work is without soul, life stifles and dies.
—*Albert Camus*

The key to understanding others is to understand oneself.
—*Helen Williams*

Our souls are not hungry for fame, comfort, wealth, or power. Those rewards create almost as many problems as they solve. Our souls are hungry for meaning, for the sense that we have figured out how to live so that our lives matter, so the world will be at least a little bit different for our having passed through it. . . .

If a person lives and dies and no one notices, if the world continues as it was, was that person ever really alive? I am convinced that it is not the fear of death, of our life ending, that haunts our sleep so much as the fear that as far as the world is concerned, we might as well never have lived. (Kussner 1986, 18)

The world would be better off if people tried to become better. And people would be better if they stopped trying to become better off.
—*Peter Maurin*

Many people spend their whole life climbing a ladder—only to discover much too late in life that the ladder was leaning against the wrong wall.
—*Author unknown*

GUIDANCE AND DIRECTION

Learning the practice of social work requires an integration of professional knowledge and ethics with a high level of self-awareness. It is not enough to know "about" people, to have skills, to know theories, or to understand models and techniques.

You as a "person" must merge with the you as a "professional." Remember that all the skills and knowledge in the world will not make you an effective social worker. You also need to bring your personal gifts, strengths, creativity, passion, and commitment to the social work profession.

Who you are as a person is just as important as what you know or can do. View your practicum as an opportunity to grow both personally and professionally, and to blend your unique personality and style with the requirements of your chosen profession.

Continually seek opportunities to enhance your professional growth. For example, read books and journals, attend workshops and in-service training, try out new skills and techniques, think critically about intervention strategies, carefully observe the behavior and practice of workers in your agency, and spend time talking with knowledgeable and skilled practitioners.

Put your thoughts in writing. We suggest keeping a journal during your practicum. Record your ideas and questions about your experiences and observations, list key concepts you are learning, and describe what you are discovering about yourself. Review it often and reflect upon your use of self, your biases, your gifts, and how these affect your work.

Ask for feedback from coworkers, your practicum instructor, and clients. Use this information to better understand who you are, what you have to offer, and what you may need to change in order to become a skilled and effective social worker.

Continue to think about how well your professional and personal lives fit together. Do you have the temperament to be a social worker? Are you able to handle the demands and the stress of the job? What demands of the job make you most uncomfortable? What tasks and activities make you anxious? Do you like to do what social workers do? Can you put your knowledge into practice? What additional knowledge do you need to more effectively enhance your personal skills? Which of the profession's values do you feel most strongly about?

View your practicum as job-related experience. It is relevant preparation for practice and the job market. Do your best and remember that the skills you develop now, combined with favorable evaluations and recommendations from your practicum instructor, can help you obtain employment in the profession.

Observe how workers in your agency deal with challenges such as high caseloads, low salaries, unmotivated and difficult clients, seemingly intractable social problems, funding cuts, and the stress of dealing with deeply emotional and painful situations on a daily basis. Begin now to develop stress management skills and habits that will help you avoid excessive job-related stress or burnout. Learn how to set limits, define personal boundaries, make time for your family and yourself, and maintain a positive outlook on clients and the work you do.

Begin now to develop the habit of monitoring your own personal growth. Ask yourself these questions regularly:

- Am I growing as a person and a professional?
- Do I know myself better than I did last month? Last year?
- Am I satisfied with who I am and what I am doing?
- If I am not satisfied, what can I do about it? What will I do about it?
- How can I continue to grow and change in a positive way?

MERGING SELF AND PROFESSION: A WORKBOOK ACTIVITY

The questions presented below are intended to encourage careful thought about how your choice of social work as a career will affect your "whole being" and your many other roles and responsibilities.

1. What is it about a career in social work that you find most positive and attractive?

   _____

   _____

   _____

   _____

2. What is it about a career in social work that you find most negative or aversive?

   _____

   _____

   _____

   _____

3. Given your abilities, work experiences, and the current job market, what can you expect as a starting salary for the job you are likely to get after graduation?

   _____

   _____

4. Given your current personal and family responsibilities, can you manage on a social worker's salary? Will you be content and at peace with this income?

   _____

   _____

5. Given probable changes in your personal and family life over the next five, ten, and twenty years, will your salary keep up with your income requirements?

   _____

   _____

   _____

   _____

6. What impact, both positive and negative, will your choice of a social work career have on, for example:

a. Your family

_____

_____

b. Your friendships and social activities

_____

_____

c. Your health and level of stress

_____

_____

d. Your personal interests, recreation, and leisure activities

_____

_____

e. Your spiritual and religious practices and participation

_____

_____

f. Your identity and sense of belonging to a culture, ethnic group, or religious group

_____

_____

7. What have you learned about yourself during the practicum that confirms your choice of social work as a profession?

_____

_____

8. Do you hope to work in an agency or program that serves a particular language, ethnic, or religious group? If yes, why is this an important goal for you?

_____

_____

_____

9. After five years of experience and employment as a social worker, what type of work would you like to be doing? After fifteen years? After twenty-five years?

_____

_____

_____

_____

Additional notes and comments:

_____

_____

_____

_____

_____

SUGGESTED LEARNING ACTIVITIES

- If you have doubts or questions about whether social work is a good career for you, arrange to take a battery of occupational interest and aptitude tests that may provide you with additional information and insights.
- Interview experienced social workers in your agency and in other agencies. Ask about their level of job satisfaction, as well as the pros and cons of a career in social work. If they could do it all over, would they select a social work career?
- Consult the publication *Occupational Outlook* for projections concerning the future job market for social workers.
- Speak with social workers who have obtained advanced degrees (MSW, Ph.D., or DSW) and ask them to help you consider the possibility of further education.

ADDITIONAL SUGGESTIONS AND HINTS

- In Sheafor, Horejsi, and Horejsi (2000), read the sections on "Merging Person with Profession" and "Getting a Social Work Job."
- Examine the social work–related job openings advertised in local and regional newspapers, public agency bulletins, and in NASW news. (The NASW Website is: www.socialworkers.org)

SELECTED BIBLIOGRAPHY

Armstrong, Richard, and Edward Wakin. *You Can Still Change the World.* New York: Harper and Row, 1978.

Gambrill, Eileen. *Social Work Practice.* New York: Oxford University Press, 1997.

Gibelman, Margaret. *What Social Workers Do.* Washington, DC: NASW Press, 1995.

Kirst-Ashman, Karen, and Grafton Hull. *Understanding Generalist Practice.* Chicago: Nelson-Hall, 1993.

Kussner, Harold. *When All You Ever Wanted Isn't Enough.* New York: Pocket Books, 1986.

Rothman, Juliet. *The Self-Awareness Workbook for Social Workers.* Boston: Allyn and Bacon, 1999.

Sheafor, Bradford, Charles Horejsi, and Gloria Horejsi. *Techniques and Guidelines for Social Work Practice.* 5th ed. Boston: Allyn and Bacon, 2000.

19

LOOKING AHEAD, LEADERSHIP, AND SOCIAL JUSTICE

As your practicum nears its completion, you have nearly fulfilled all of the requirements necessary to obtain your degree. You are, no doubt, considering some job possibilities and also seriously thinking about the personal ramifications of entering the world of social work. This is a time of transition. What lies ahead for you? What kind of social worker do you hope to become? And, perhaps even more important, what kind of person do you want to become? In this chapter we invite you to reflect on these questions.

As social workers, teachers of social work, and the authors of the book you have been reading, we desire three things for you:

1. That you become an informed, effective, and ethical social worker
2. That you become a leader within your profession and your community—one committed to the pursuit of social and economic justice
3. That you become the person you want to be and live a life filled with meaning and purpose

In this final chapter, we offer some suggestions on how you might achieve these three ends.

BECOMING THE SOCIAL WORKER YOU WANT TO BE

It is both exciting and rather daunting to think about being a social worker. There are many problems to be addressed and many clients to be served. Injustices need to be challenged and a number of programs need to be designed or redesigned. There is so much to be done—but so few resources.

Because you have completed the requirements for a social work degree in a program accredited by the Council on Social Work Education, your teachers have concluded that you are ready to begin the practice of social work. Although you may still feel rather ill prepared to assume the responsibilities of a social worker, your teachers and supervisors believe that you possess the knowledge and basic skills needed to move into a social agency and apply what you have learned. You have been educated in an academic setting, trained in a social agency, and exposed to many social problems and various ways of addressing them. Do not underestimate what you have learned and what you are capable of doing.

Reflect often on the preamble to the *Code of Ethics* (NASW 1997, 1) which states:

> The primary mission of the social work profession is to enhance human well-being and help meet the basic needs of all people, with particular attention to the needs and empowerment of people who are vulnerable, oppressed, and living in poverty. A historic and defining feature of social work is the profession's focus on individual well-being in a social context and the well-being of society.

This statement describes a profession deeply committed, both by its history and current practice, to creating communities and a society that will nurture the well-being of individuals and families and to making sure that all people have access to the basic resources and opportunities necessary to live with dignity. You have entered a profession that is committed to challenging those systems and institutional structures that do not treat people in a fair and humane manner. If we as social workers do not speak out against and seek to correct a social or economic injustice we are, in effect, giving our tacit approval to the current state of affairs.

In your employment as a social worker, we ask that you view the practice of social work as being much more than the tasks and activities listed in your job description or suggested in your agency's mission statement. Work hard at whatever you are hired to do, but also assume the additional responsibility of becoming an advocate for those who are not able to speak for themselves. Social work, at its unique best, is about going beyond one's job description and acting on a commitment to social justice by weaving together the networks of people and resources that can bring about needed changes at the community, state, and national levels.

The preamble statement also reflects the contextual or the person-in-environment perspective that is fundamental to the way social workers view people, assess human problems and concerns, and design interventions. Social workers, whether employed to work at the micro or macro level, must be cognizant of the wider societal context of the lives and problems of their clients and the context of the agencies, programs, and interventions that address these client concerns. For example, a social worker in a counseling role should question why so many of his or her clients need assistance in dealing with issues of childhood abuse, and should respond to this situation by becoming part of those efforts that address the etiology of abuse and neglect with programs of prevention. Conversely, social workers attempting to pass legislation protecting the rights of the poor would be well advised to understand the personal plight of those individuals potentially affected by any social policy changes.

The realities and time pressures associated with employment in an agency that has a particular mission and program set in motion a number of forces that tend to narrow a social worker's range of concerns, interests, and vision. Work hard to resist the effects of these forces. Strive to maintain a wide range of interests, involvements, and professional activities. Seek out new ideas, even when they are not immediately applicable in your everyday work.

As you enter into the work of a particular agency, you may discover that the agency uses an unfamiliar conceptual framework or rationale to guide its practice activities. As you are exposed to new practice frameworks, remember that each one needs to be examined in terms of its potential to enhance practice effectiveness, its appropriateness for use with particular types of clients in particular settings, its research base, its stated or implied assumptions about clients and the process of change, and its compatibility with social work values.

Carefully consider why you might prefer one approach to other possibilities. Most likely, you prefer a particular practice framework because it is the one most compatible with your beliefs about human behavior and human problems, and because it instructs you, the professional, to perform those tasks and activities to which you are especially attracted. While it is natural to pursue your own interests, we ask that you seek to broaden and deepen your understanding of the various perspectives, theories, and models used in social work practice and carefully examine the assumptions underlying each approach. Strive to understand the strengths and limitations of each one. Be open to gaining insights and guidance from several practice frameworks.

Document your work and study the outcomes of your practice, both individually and in concert with other professionals and agencies. Be ready to change your approach if you are not being as effective as you think possible. Needless to say, much of what social workers do and much of what clients experience is difficult to measure, but resist the temptation to use this as an excuse for not making a genuine effort to evaluate your practice. You cannot improve your practice unless you are willing to look at it critically and allow others to offer constructive criticisms.

To the extent possible, build your knowledge base by drawing on findings from empirical and scientific studies, but remember that there are many sources of useful knowledge. Some are empirical, some are not. Balance the positivist view of knowledge building, which rests on the scientific method, with contributions from *practice wisdom* (the collective experiences of practitioners) and also with the insights derived from study of the humanities, religion, and classic and modern literature.

As you attempt to understand and utilize new research findings and theories drawn from the social and behavioral sciences, consider the observation by sociologists that such knowledge is "socially constructed." Our knowledge of a social or psychological phenomena or a particular human problem is shaped and limited by the context in which it was studied, by the language used to describe it, and is very much tied to our culture, history, economics, and politics. Our knowledge is, at best, incomplete and only temporarily true. The awareness that knowledge is a social construction helps us to put data and conclusions in perspective and better realize that the concepts and theories used in practice, no matter how elegant and impressive, are purely human inventions. It is your prerogative and your responsibility to thoughtfully question all findings and claims, regardless of their source.

In a similar vein, recognize that the concept of *client* is a human invention or social construction that has arisen out of our cultural views and presumptions about who is in need of help, who is powerless to help him or herself, and who is qualified to help another person. Always be sensitive to the possibility that agencies, social workers, and other professionals can misuse their power and authority to label a person, family, or group as troubled and in need of certain services or interventions.

Become involved in those professional organizations that can support your work, challenge you intellectually, and remind you that others are also involved in the struggle to create a just society. Remember that you have a voice in the ongoing development and shaping of the profession, and that social work educators need to hear your observations and suggestions as much as clients need your skills. Voice your opinions about directions you believe the profession should take based on your observations and your projections of future needs. Speak up when you see your profession becoming focused too heavily on one aspect of social work to the detriment of its overall mission.

Remain in the world of ideas and commit to lifelong learning. There are numerous approaches you can take to continue learning and growing, which will not only make you more effective, but will also make you a better, more informed, and capable person. We suggest that you follow these guidelines:

- Continue to read professional literature and attend advanced training sessions.
- Join or form a group of professionals that takes seriously its commitment to continuing education and peer supervision.

- Look globally and internationally for possible solutions to nagging and serious social problems.
- Continue to learn from your clients who experience on a daily basis what you may only observe, read about, or imagine.
- Seek to identify the connections between social conditions and either the social problems or the social benefits resulting from them.
- Stay connected to universities and schools of social work through conferences, by offering guest lectures, and by supervising practicum students.
- Talk on a regular basis to those with whom you fundamentally disagree in order to retain an open mind and clarify your own beliefs and values.

Recognize your ability to be a catalyst for change. To be a catalyst means that you bring individuals and groups together, contribute your skills and knowledge, and stimulate positive movement or changes that would not have occurred without your intervention. Remember that you are not alone in your efforts to help others. There are many social workers who will support and encourage you in your efforts. Seek them out, offer your support in return, and find avenues of renewal for yourself, both personally and professionally.

Take care of yourself, see the good in the world as well as the problems, celebrate large and small successes, learn to laugh, and cultivate the sources of your passion and strength. Utilize your family, friends, spiritual beliefs, and core values to guide you, and take pride in your chosen profession.

BECOMING A LEADER AND A SEEKER OF SOCIAL JUSTICE

As a social worker you will encounter many situations of oppression and social and economic injustice. You will also encounter situations in which agency policies, programs, and practices are in need of revision in order to make them more fair and effective. You will want to change these situations but may quickly discover that bringing about needed and meaningful change is a difficult and slow process. In order to bring about change you must be willing and able to assume the role, tasks, and responsibilities of leadership. Desirable changes do not happen by accident. Rather, they are set in motion by individuals who assert themselves, articulate their beliefs, and step forward to take on the hard work of leading.

Although it may be true that a few leaders are the so-called born leaders, most had to learn the skills of leadership much like they learned any other skill. Aspiring leaders must consciously and continually cultivate the development of those qualities, ways of thinking, attitudes, and interpersonal skills that are associated with effective leadership.

Leadership is much more than having good ideas. In fact, effective leaders are not usually highly creative and innovative thinkers. Such individuals tend to become impatient with the slowness of change and frustrated with the hesitations and limitations of those they wish to lead.

Leaders must have a clear vision of what they want to accomplish. Equally important, they must be able to articulate this vision and explain it in words that the followers understand. The vision must be one that can be translated into action steps and programs that are feasible and realistic.

It is the leader's vision that gives him or her the critically important sense of purpose, direction, and self-confidence to make difficult decisions. This sense of purpose must be evident in all that the leader does. Nothing destroys the capacity to lead more quickly than indecisiveness and the unwillingness to take action when action is clearly necessary. It is often said that it is better for a leader to occasionally make a bad decision than to avoid making a critically important decision.

Good leaders lead by example. Followers are inspired and motivated by the resolve, courage, hard work, and sacrifices of their leaders. Leaders must model the behaviors they want to see in others. They should not ask others to do what they are unwilling to do.

Leaders must demonstrate respect and genuine concern for the wishes, values, and abilities of those they lead. They must be willing to curtail some of their own preferences and plans in order to avoid moving too far ahead of the followers. Leaders cannot lead unless there are people who choose to follow them.

Effective leaders must maintain open and honest communication with their followers. This communication must keep followers focused on the goal while at the same time attending to the concerns, fears, and ambivalence they may have about investing their time, energy, and money in working toward this goal.

Good leaders anticipate possible conflicts and disagreements among their followers. They are proactive in taking steps to prevent or resolve these conflicts before they can distract from goal achievement and splinter the followers into competing factions.

Leaders must be skilled in the art of collaboration and building bridges between individuals and organizations. They must reward others for their cooperation and share the credit for success with others, even those with whom they may disagree. Leaders must be willing to compromise when this is a necessary step toward reaching the sought-after goal.

The exercise of leadership always occurs within a context of competing and conflicting forces. Leaders shape, guide, and redirect those forces, so they move in directions that produce the desired effect and move people toward the desired goal. Because leaders must function within environments and situations that are unpredictable and always changing, they must be willing to take necessary risks and cope with ambiguity and uncertainty.

Effective leaders possess a high level of self-awareness. They understand their own strengths and limitations and constantly examine their own motives and behavior. Many leaders destroy their capacity to lead by allowing feelings of self-importance and a need for recognition to dominate their decisions or by becoming arrogant and overly confident because of past successes.

The capacity to lead is often tied to having a positive reputation within one's organization or community, having prior experience with the issue that has drawn people together, and having a well-developed network of personal and professional contacts. For this reason, an individual who changes jobs frequently or moves from community to community may limit his or her potential for becoming a leader.

In addition to the factors mentioned above, the following qualities and characteristics are important to the exercise of effective leadership:

- Capacity to think critically and examine personal decisions and actions
- Capacity to speak and write clearly so they can articulate a vision and purpose in ways people can understand
- Perseverance when faced with difficulties and disappointments
- Ability to delegate responsibility and teach or empower others to perform as well as they can
- Ability to make difficult decisions in situations that are complex and fluid
- Willingness to assume personal responsibility for one's decisions and actions
- Personal flexibility, openness to new ideas, and the ability to work with people with various abilities and with people from diverse backgrounds
- Ability to create a sense of belonging and community among those working toward the same goals
- Ability to make effective use of available time and get things done

Clearly, it is a challenge to be an effective leader in one's agency or one's profession. It is an even more difficult undertaking when the leader's goal is to promote social and economic justice.

At a fundamental level, justice can be defined as fairness in relationships. Although there are several categories or types of justice, matters of social justice and economic justice are of special concern to social workers.

Social justice refers to the basic fairness and moral rightness of the social arrangements and institutional structures that impact the people of a community or society. While closely related to economic justice, social justice focuses more on how society is organized and whether governmental and corporate policies and powerful groups recognize basic human rights and the dignity and worth of all people.

Economic justice (also called distributive justice) can be defined as that dimension of justice having to do with the material or the economic aspects of a community or society. Economic justice denotes the fair apportioning and the distribution of economic resources, opportunities, and burdens. Principles of economic justice relate to fairness in, for example, wages paid for work performed, access to jobs, access to credit, prices charged for essential goods and services, and taxes imposed.

Although people will easily agree on the need for justice, they often disagree about what specific actions, reforms, and laws are truly fair and would, therefore, bring society closer to the ideal of social and economic justice. In other words, there is usually agreement on the goal but often disagreement on the means or methods of reaching it. Some refer to this distinction as the difference between the *concept of justice* and peoples' *conceptions of justice.* The attainment of justice is elusive because different people use different criteria for judging what is fair and just.

Because social and economic injustices are, by definition, embedded in existing institutional arrangements, many political, economic, and cultural forces are at work maintaining the unjust conditions. Those who seek change will encounter many powerful individuals and groups who will want to maintain the status quo. In order to secure real change, a leader working for social justice must be willing to take substantial risks and make significant personal sacrifices.

Goldenberg (1978, 4–13) identifies several mechanisms (presumptions, beliefs, and deliberate actions) used by those in power to rationalize and perpetuate the oppressive and unjust conditions from which they benefit, directly or indirectly. These include:

- *Containment.* Efforts to restrict the opportunities and resources available to others in order to retain power and control over them.
- *Expendability.* A belief that some people and groups are more valuable to society and, therefore, devalued persons can be discarded, displaced, or ignored for the benefit of the society as a whole.
- *Compartmentalization.* Limiting people's exposure to enriching and empowering ideas, roles, and images in order to lessen their discontent. Creating and maintaining conflict and division among those without power in order to prevent them from developing a sense of shared problems, solidarity, and unity.
- *Personal culpability.* A belief system that presumes all of the social and economic problems experienced by people are matters of personal choice and moral character. Thus, because these are individual problems, existing systems and structures need not be changed and those with power are excused from trying to improve social and economic conditions for the people of a society.
- *Individual remediation.* A belief system holding that self-improvement is the only real answer to the existence of social problems. Thus, those who want a better life or who desire political power should first "pull themselves up by their bootstraps." Only after they prove their worth should they expect to participate in the political and economic decisions affecting their lives.

Those who work for justice must be alert to the fact that the belief systems and attitudes that perpetuate social and economic injustice can also be found in the thinking of those who are members of the various helping professions.

Among social workers, one can find a range of attitudes toward and perspectives on the appropriate place of social and political change in social work practice and on how such change is best achieved. Goldenberg (1978, 21–27) describes four of these:

1. The *social technician* identifies with and supports society's dominant values and its institutional structures. A professional with this orientation seeks to help individuals adjust to the existing system and sees little need for changing social systems.

2. The *traditional social reformer* believes that oppressive social systems can be changed over time and works methodically to make those changes. The emphasis is on fact finding as a way of helping those with power to understand the problem and decide that it is desirable and reasonable to make changes. The reformer trusts the tools of negotiation and mediation to build bridges between those with power and those without.

3. The *social interventionist* believes that bringing about needed social change will require conflict, consciousness raising, and change from the bottom up. An individual holding to this orientation assumes that those in power will accept change only when their survival and self-interest depends on it.

4. The *social revolutionary* is basically at odds with and rejects existing social institutions and the usual avenues of seeking change. The revolutionary believes that current systems and institutions are corrupt and cannot be salvaged. This individual is not satisfied with small steps or incremental change and believes that radical and revolutionary approaches are necessary to take power away from those who have it.

A good leader remembers the history of the movement in which he or she is involved, as well as the lessons of the past. We recommend that you reflect in a critical and appreciative manner on the evolution of the social work profession and the many significant contributions of social workers to social justice and the building of a social welfare system. Be aware of the contributions of social work in such areas as Social Security, civil rights, child labor laws, Medicaid, unemployment insurance, minimum wage, the peace movement, and many others. Consider the contributions made by those who developed theories of practice, assumed leadership in the academic preparation of professional social workers, and the countless clients whose lives and stories have provided the motivation and inspiration for such service.

While appreciating the progress made by a profession only a century old, look also to the future and the continuing evolution of the social work profession. Claim your history, be proud of it, and become part of the development of new knowledge, improved skills, and deeply felt values.

We urge you to find ways to build a world that will be a better place because you have challenged injustices and held fast to the vision of a world in which opportunity and possibility are the possessions of all.

BECOMING THE PERSON YOU WANT TO BE

The Russian writer Leo Tolstoy observed that "Everybody thinks of changing humanity; nobody thinks of changing themselves." As social workers involved in the process of helping others make desired changes, we should not forget to look inward, examine our own attitudes and behavior, and seek changes that will make us better human beings.

Many social workers say that social work is not what they do, but it is who they are. They feel that their professional lives are guided by their personal beliefs and values, and they believe that being a social worker allows them to live out the beliefs and values they hold dear and feel passionate about. We like that notion because it indicates a compatible merger between person and the profession (see Chapter 18). However, we ask that you always remember that you are now and will always be more than your profession and your job. If your whole identity is tied up in being a social worker, we suggest that you broaden your horizons and life experiences. Narrowness is not a healthy condition.

Any effort to make changes in how we are living our life must begin with serious reflection on our answer to the question: "Who am I?" This is not a question about the facts of our existence, our accomplishments, or what we list in our resume. Rather, it is a question about the manner of our existence and our basic orientation and attitudes toward life and the people in our life. Who do others— family, friends, and colleagues—say that I am? Do I want to be the person that others experience and perceive me to be?

As you seek to become the person you want to be, remember that we tend to become how we behave. We are, to a considerable degree, creatures of habit and our character is formed by the behaviors we repeatedly choose for ourselves. We often assume that our lives are shaped mostly by the big events and by large-scale societal forces but, in reality, our lives are shaped much more by the dozens or even hundreds of small decisions we make each day in response to the people around us, to the circumstances and situations in which we must live our lives, and to the opportunities and options we encounter.

Because the very ordinary and small choices are so powerful in the shaping of our lives, strive as Gandhi urges to "become the change you desire to see in others." If you desire others to have more compassion and understanding, strive each day to become more compassionate and more understanding of others. If you desire others to be more generous and more involved in bringing about needed change, strive each day to be more generous with your time and money and involve yourself more deeply in social action and social change. If you desire others to be honest and responsible, strive to be honest and responsible in all of your own choices and actions, both the big ones and the small ones.

Humans are said to be mimetic creatures. In other words, much of how we live and how we think we want to live our life is a function of our wanting to imitate or mimic what we see others doing. We seem to have an innate desire to copy the behavior and beliefs of others and try to become like them. As social beings, we fear being different from others and being alone. Thus, in order to change how we live our lives, we need concrete models or examples of the type of person we desire to become. Without such models—real people whom we can imitate—our images and goals for self-change remain vague or too general.

Because of this, we urge you to identify persons, both social workers and non-social workers, who you wish to emulate and who can serve as your models. Consider, for example, those who have made a positive contribution to social welfare thought and action in our own country such as Jane Addams, Dorothea Dix, Bertha Capen Reynolds, Edith Abbott, Wilber Cohen, Dorothy Day, and Whitney Young. And, of course, also consider as possible models the many individuals whose lives have impacted the whole world and whose values and concern for the poor and oppressed closely parallel those of the social work profession; for example: Jesus of Nazareth, Mohandas Gandhi, Elie Wiesel, Martin Luther King, Jr., Cesar Chavez, and Mother Teresa.

Food for Thought

I swore never to be silent whenever and wherever human beings endure suffering and humiliation. We must always take sides. Neutrality helps the oppressor, never the victim. Silence encourages the tormentor, never the tormented.

—*Elie Wiesel*

◆◆◆

Injustice anywhere is a threat to justice everywhere. We are caught in an inescapable network of mutuality, tied in a single garment of destiny. Whatever affects one directly affects all indirectly.

—*Martin Luther King, Jr.*

◆◆◆

We must realize that social injustice and unjust social structures exist only because individuals and groups of individuals deliberately maintain or tolerate them. It is these personal choices, operating through structures, that breed and propagate situations of poverty, oppression, and misery.

—*Pope John Paul II*

◆◆◆

Several decades ago, Mohandas K. Gandhi (my grandfather) warned against what he called the seven social sins that give rise to social injustice and social problems such as poverty, crime, and violence. These are: politics without principle, wealth without work, commerce without morality, pleasure without conscience, education without character, science without humanity, and worship without sacrifice.

—*Arun Gandhi*

◆◆◆

A good leader creates more leaders, not more followers.

—*Author unknown*

◆◆◆

We must be careful to conform our behavior to our beliefs, rather than conforming our beliefs to our behavior.

—*Author unknown*

◆◆◆

Life is a mystery to be lived, not a problem to be solved.

—*Author unknown*

◆◆◆

Service is the rent you pay for room on this earth.

—*Shirley Chisholm*

◆◆◆

The proper measure of social justice in a society is how those without power and influence are treated. We usually treat those having money and power with fairness and respect because we fear the consequences of not doing so or because we hope to get something from them. True justice and genuine compassion is reflected when we treat those who have no power or anything we might want with dignity, fairness, and respect.

—*Charles Horejsi*

When seeking a model or mentor, look for one who has demonstrated a strong commitment to service, which is a core value in social work. Martin Luther King, Jr., reminds us of the greatness that is inherent in service to others:

> Everybody can be great, because anybody can serve. You don't have to have a college degree to serve. You don't have to make your subject and your verb agree. You don't have to know about Plato and Aristotle to serve. . . . You only need a heart full of grace and a soul generated by love.

SELECTED BIBLIOGRAPHY

Goldenberg, Ira. *Oppression and Social Intervention.* Chicago: Nelson-Hall, 1978.

Jansson, Bruce S. *Becoming an Effective Policy Advocate: From Policy Practice to Social Justice.* 2nd ed. Pacific Grove, CA: Brooks/Cole, 1999.

National Association of Social Workers. *Code of Ethics.* Washington, DC: NASW Press, 1997.

Payne, Malcolm. *Modern Social Work Theory.* 2nd ed. Chicago: Lyceum, 1997.

APPENDIX A

SAMPLE AGREEMENT BETWEEN AN AGENCY AND A UNIVERSITY

Practicum Student Name _____

Agency Name _____

Practicum Instructor _____

Faculty Supervisor Name _____

Practicum Coordinator Name _____

The Practicum Coordinator Agrees to:

- Assume responsibility for the overall direction and coordination of the practicum program.
- Screen student applicants and assess their readiness for a practicum.
- Assist students and agencies in the placement process.
- Assign a faculty supervisor to work conjointly with the practicum instructor and student.
- Provide guidelines for evaluating the student.
- Provide orientation and training for agency supervisors.
- Be available to students, practicum instructors, and faculty supervisors to facilitate the resolution of problems that may arise.
- Assign a grade for each student's practicum.
- Assume responsibility for removing a student from a placement should that become necessary.

The Faculty Supervisor Agrees to:

- Assume responsibility for working out a plan for student supervision with the practicum instructor and the student.
- Meet at least twice per semester with the student and practicum instructor together.
- Assume responsibility for end-of-semester evaluations of the students' performance in conjunction with the practicum instructor.
- Assist the student in developing a learning contract to structure the practicum experience.
- Assist the student in applying and integrating theory into practice.
- Assist the student in writing the practicum-related integrative paper.
- Assist in orienting new agency supervisors to the university's curriculum and practicum program.
- Act as a resource person for students in regard to questions, resources, and suggestions for learning opportunities.

The Practicum Instructor Agrees to:

- Provide a minimum of one hour per week of direct supervision to the student
- Orient new students to agency structure and function, student responsibilities, policies and procedures, and commonly used community resources
- Assist the student in developing a learning contract to structure the practicum experience
- Structure assignments to help the student learn a broad range of social work interventions common to generalist social work practice
- Assign duties and responsibilities of increasing difficulty and challenge as appropriate in consultation with the student
- Provide suitable office space and support staff
- Employ the student primarily as a learner who will assume numerous responsibilities of benefit to the agency rather than as someone who will fill the needs of an understaffed agency
- Follow procedures outlined in the university's practicum manual
- Monitor student performance, regularly providing feedback to the student
- Complete a formal evaluation of the student at the end of each semester
- Reimburse the students for out-of-pocket expenses incurred in the same manner as for agency employees
- Refrain from sexual harassment of the student

The Student Agrees to:

- Meet with the agency and faculty supervisors together twice per semester
- Develop and follow a learning agreement in conjunction with both agency and faculty supervisors
- Adhere to the National Association of Social Workers' *Code of Ethics*
- Behave in a professional manner, taking responsibility as an adult learner to understand duties, seek supervision when needed, and carry out assignments
- Be in attendance at the agency at days and times agreed upon by the student and agency supervisor and, if unable to attend, notify the agency supervisor at the start of the work day
- Work 450 hours over two semesters on a volunteer basis (**NOTE:** practicum students may not receive salary, wages, contract fees, or other benefits of an agency employee)
- Abide by agency policies and procedures, including confidentiality
- Provide proof of professional malpractice insurance unless covered by the practicum agency, in which case a written verification of such coverage must be provided to the practicum coordinator
- Prepare for supervisory conferences by adhering to deadlines, completing work, and formulating questions about assignments
- Discuss with the agency or faculty supervisor any areas of disagreement, dissatisfaction, or confusion in respect to any part of the practicum experience
- Bring to the attention of the faculty supervisor any questionable professional practices within the agency
- Complete an evaluation of the practicum experience at the end of the second semester

The agency and the university agree that neither will discriminate against any individual on the basis of age, sex, race, religious belief, national origin, disability, or sexual orientation.

This contract may be terminated by the agency or the university without cause, upon providing thirty days written notice.

SIGNED:

_____	_____	_____	_____
Student	Date	Practicum Instructor	Date
_____	_____	_____	_____
Faculty Supervisor	Date	Practicum Coordinator	Date

APPENDIX **B**

SAMPLE LEARNING AGREEMENT

The following sample learning agreement presents some goals for learning that can be reasonably expected of a typical social work practicum. Spaces are provided for the student to devise his or her own tasks and activities to attain each set of goals, and his or her own criteria for monitoring progress and evaluating performance. This form can be used to structure the practicum experience and maximize learning. Note that some of the goals may need to be modified to fit the requirements of a particular program of social work education and the unique characteristics of a particular practicum setting.

246

STUDENT: _____ DATE: _____ AGENCY: _____ AGENCY SUPERVISOR: _____

INSTRUCTIONS: Student learning goals have been outlined in the left-hand column. Students (in consultation with their practicum instructors) are to select activities that will help them reach these goals. Students are also to describe how their learning and performance will be evaluated. At the end of each semester, students will be evaluated by the practicum instructor on their learning and performance.

Learning Goals	Tasks & Activities to Reach Goals	Monitoring/Evaluation Criteria
1. *Social Work as a Profession* • Develop an understanding of generalist social work practice. • Perform a variety of social work roles (e.g., broker, counselor, networker, case manager, educator, advocate, program planner, facilitator, policy analyst, researcher). • Gain experience at various levels of practice (e.g., micro, mezzo, and macro). • Apply the National Association of Social Workers' *Code of Ethics* in a practice setting. **2.** *Organizational Context of Practice* • Apply organizational analysis techniques to the practicum agency. • Understand the practicum agency's history, mission, purpose, and function. • Understand the practicum agency's structure and funding. • Understand the practicum agency's methods for evaluating its effectiveness. **3.** *Community Context of Practice* • Understand the features of the community that impact clients (e.g., population, unemployment rates, housing costs, attitudes toward diverse populations, or available recreation).		

Learning Goals	Tasks & Activities to Reach Goals	Monitoring/Evaluation Criteria
• Identify both the strengths and problems of the community. • Become aware of the range of community resources available and gaps in services. • Utilize a variety of community resources. 4. *Assessment* • Develop assessment skills for individuals, families, groups, organizations, and communities. • Develop skills in problem and strength identification. • Identify the major social systems involved with the problem or concern being addressed. • Become familiar with the ongoing nature of assessment. 5. *Planning and Intervention* • Acquire skills in goal setting, identifying measurable objectives, and planning interventions. • Select an appropriate level of intervention for individual client/client system needs (micro to macro). • Develop intervention plans matched to client/client system needs, including client in selection of intervention. • Develop intervention skills based on theoretical understanding of client needs and of interventions selected. 6. *Termination and Evaluation* • Develop skills in appropriate termination and empowerment of clients. • Utilize tools and instruments to evaluate client progress.		

Learning Goals	Tasks & Activities to Reach Goals	Monitoring/Evaluation Criteria
• Utilize tools and instruments to evaluate own professional performance. • Utilize tools and instruments to evaluate agency effectiveness. 7. *Understanding Social Problems* • Understand one or more social problems from an ecosystems perspective. • Understand the major social problems addressed by the practicum agency (e.g., etiology, incidence, causal factors, impact, consequences, and prevention). • Understand how social problems develop as a result of the interaction among individuals, social systems, and the larger social environment. • Identify the major social problems facing the community. 8. *Social Policy and Social Change* • Analyze the development of social policies. • Analyze the effectiveness of social policies. • Assess the impact of social policies on clients. • Participate in social policy and social justice efforts. 9. *Diversity* • Recognize the impact of diversity (e.g., culture, gender, age, disability, class, sexual orientation, or religion) on clients. • Understand the impact of oppression, discrimination, prejudice, and stereo-typing on clients.		

Learning Goals	Tasks & Activities to Reach Goals	Monitoring/Evaluation Criteria
• Analyze the practicum agency's ability to effectively and sensitively address the needs of diverse clients/client systems. • Communicate effectively and sensitively with members of diverse groups, individualizing interventions for diverse clients. 10. *Communication Skills* • Communicate clearly and effectively in written form. • Communicate clearly and effectively in verbal form with clients, including non-voluntary, or hard-to-reach clients. • Communicate clearly and effectively in verbal form with coworkers and other professionals. • Demonstrate awareness of underlying client concerns. 11. *Knowledge and Use of Self* • Recognize the impact of own personal issues, biases, values, and attitudes on clients and make needed changes. • Establish effective and purposeful relationships with clients and coworkers. • Seek professional growth by taking initiative in designing and implementing own learning activities. • Utilize professional supervision and training for guidance and learning.		

CREDITS